OPEN ROAD'S BEST OF

Ireland

by Dan McQuillan

Open Road Travel Guides – designed for the amount of time you *really* have for your trip!

Open Road Publishing

Open Road's new travel guides.
Designed to cut to the chase.
You don't need a huge travel encyclopedia – you need a
selective guide to steer you right. If you're going on vacation for a
few weeks or less, get a guide that brings you the *best* of any
destination for the amount of time you *really* have for your trip!

Open Road – the guide you need for the trip you want.

The New Open Road *Best Of* Travel Guides.
Right to the point.
Uncluttered.
Easy.

Open Road Publishing
P.O. Box 284, Cold Spring Harbor, NY 11724
www.openroadguides.com

Front cover photo©ShutterStock.com; page 122 photo©zh1yong
(flickr.com); page 145 photo©dyobmit (flickr.com); page 225
photos©by SteuveFE (from flickr.com); page 227 and back cover
photo©Piotr (flickr.com).

About the Author
Dan McQuillan is the author of Open Road's *Ireland Guide*,
Scotland Guide, and *Dublin Made Easy*.

CONTENTS

Your Passport to the **Perfect Trip!**

6. CONNACHT 97

Highlights: Connemara, Galway, Westport, Aran Islands, Croagh Patrick

7. ULSTER 115

Highlights: Belfast, Dunluce Castle, Giant's Causeway, Donegal

8. IRELAND IN TWO WEEKS 140

9. BEST SLEEPS & EATS 190

INDEX   **250**

Maps

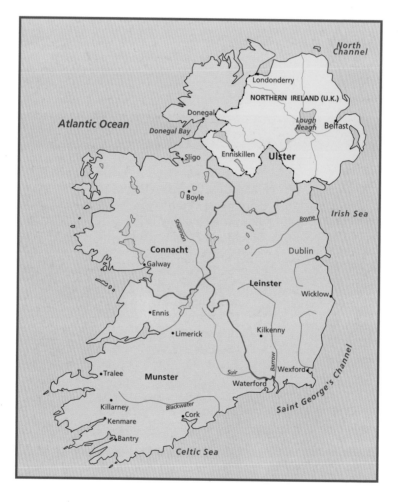

1. INTRODUCTION

I have traveled to many beautiful and exciting parts of the world, but I am always enchanted when I return to Ireland. And you'll be enchanted too. From the Cliffs of Moher to Dublin and Dunluce, from the Book of Kells to the Creevykeel Court Tomb, you'll experience some of the best and most beautiful sights this world has to offer.

On many of your previous travels you have probably sent postcards home to family and friends. Well, Ireland *is* a postcard. Grandeur and simplicity, mirth and meditation are all found in abundance on this beautiful green island. And I'll help you experience the very best Ireland has to offer.

Ireland is a place you must experience. Talk to the locals. Watch the buskers (street performers) ply their trade. Talk to the school children who clamor to have their pictures taken. Relax as your car or bicycle is engulfed by a sea of sheep or cattle headed nowhere in particular and in no hurry.

Ireland is a mystical, magical land where leprechauns and shamrocks, miracles and massacres are woven together as tightly as the knit of an Aran sweater. Come prowl through the ruins of an ancient race. Drink their beer and listen to their tales. Learn of their past and appreciate their future. And maybe even envy their wee green corner of the world.

If this is your first trip to the Emerald Isle, it's a good bet it won't be your last. Ireland's many charms have a way of enticing you to return again and again.

2. OVERVIEW

We're going to lead you to the very best sights Ireland has to offer: the Blarney Stone and the Book of Kells, the Waterford Crystal Factory, the Cliffs of Moher, the Rock of Cashel – these are names of legend. But we'll also take you to amazing off-the-beaten path sights: 5,000-year-old passage graves in Newgrange, the brooding ruins of Dunluce Castle, the ancient remains of a ritual murder victim in the National Museum – and you'll even share a banquet with the lord of a medieval castle!

Ireland is divided into **four provinces**: Leinster, Munster, Connacht, and Ulster. These provinces, along with a chapter for Dublin, are the primary destination chapters in this guide.

Here are the high points of each of the destination chapters:

Dublin
Dublin is Ireland's capital city, and also one of the Emerald Isle's oldest cities. It is rich in wonderful hotels and inns, fine restaurants and fun pubs, and more than a few impressive sights. **Christchurch** and **St. Patrick's Cathedral** are perhaps its most

recognizable buildings.

At St. Patrick's, you'll be awed by the immense beauty of the cathedral. Considered the National Cathedral of the Church of Ireland, St. Patrick's was founded in 1191, and historians believe St. Patrick himself performed baptisms here over 1,500 years ago.

The **Book of Kells** is one of the cultural sights you shouldn't miss in Dublin. This is one of the most celebrated attractions in Ireland: four volumes worth of illustrations of the four Gospels painstakingly drawn by 9th-century monks. The elaborate artwork that graces the pages of the Latin text is truly a sight to behold, and a sight to be sure to see while you're in Dublin.

The **National Gallery of Ireland** is one of the gems in Dublin's tiara. It is an impressive gallery that features some of the finest art on display in western Europe. Matching the National Gallery in excellence is the **National Museum of Ireland**. Sort of Ireland's Smithsonian Institute, this museum is over 100 years old. A fabulous collection of Irish antiquities is highlighted by items in the National Treasury, including the Ardagh Chalice, Cross of Cong, and the Tara Brooch.

While Dublin is a delightful place to visit, it has had its share of dark days throughout history. **Dublin Castle** was the seat of government for the hated English conquerors, and **Kilmainham Jail** is the site of numerous executions and many more incarcerations. The **General Post Office**, fondly known as the GPO, is where Irish patriots defiantly declared Ireland's independence from Britain. In Irish history, it is comparable to Lexington Green. Eventually the revolution that started here resulted in independence for Ireland.

Leinster
Leinster (pronounced *Linster*) is the Irish province that covers Ireland's east coast. Historically, much of northern Leinster was under control of the English, conquerors and occupiers of Ireland. Today, Leinster offers a variety of great sights and attractions not far from Dublin.

A short ride south of Dublin is **Glendalough**, site of an extensive monastic settlement and hermitage dating back to the 6th century. At the west end of the valley, Glenealo stream cascades in a waterfall into the valley, encompassed by heavily forested mountains. Add some exquisite and ancient ruins, and this is a wonderful place to visit.

Not far from Glendalough is fabulous **Powerscourt Gardens**. You've probably seen pictures of Powerscourt Gardens before – they are popular scenes used to depict the beauty of Ireland. The gardens were originally laid out beginning in 1745, and were revised to their present grand design in the mid-1800s. They cascade in a series of terraces down a slope from an ancient mansion house.

The central-western part of Leinster consists of the wide flat plain called **The Curragh**, and is the Kentucky of Ireland. It is here that a number of national horse races are held, as well as the location of a number of stud farms, including the internationally famous **National Stud** in Tully.

An hour's drive north of Dublin you'll find several well-preserved burial mounds dating back five millennia. The most notable is **Newgrange**, where you can tour one of the finest cross-shaped ancient passage graves in existence.

Munster

Munster comprises six counties in the southwestern quarter of the island. Much of Munster is rural, and the scenic views in this province are a match for any in the rest of the country. Breathtaking seascapes, rugged offshore islands, and country roads wending through green fields are typical of the scenery here.

If you know of only one place in Ireland, it is probably the **Blarney Stone**. Many folks are unaware that the Blarney Stone is part of **Blarney Castle**. The famous stone is located atop an ancient keep (castle stronghold) underneath its battlements.

Waterford City is the location of the **Waterford Crystal Factory**, the world-renowned lead crystal manufacturer. The factory has a nice gallery, and their one-hour tour takes you within a few feet of the artisans who blow and cut the glass – much as it has been done for several hundred years at this site.

One of the most impressive ruins in Ireland is the **Rock of Cashel**, found in County Tipperary. You'll want to save plenty of film for one of the most awe-inspiring sites in Ireland.

On the western edge of Ireland, rising dramatically and abruptly from the foaming sea, are the **Cliffs of Moher**. These incredible cliffs feature sheer 700-foot drops to the crashing ocean. They make for an impressive photo opportunity regardless of the weather.

And of course, little **Killarney**, nestled as it is in the heart of some of the prettiest scenery in the country, is a place you simply must see. The natural beauty of the area will leave you in awe.

Connacht

Connacht is located in the western part of Ireland. Much of this province consists of wide-open spaces embellished by beautiful heather enhancements. It also has a couple of energetic seaports in County Galway and County Westport. The **Connemara** district of **County Galway** is rugged and beautiful.

Off the western coast of Ireland, a trip to the **Aran Islands** is a trip into Ireland's past. Winding rock walls, ancient ruins, prehistoric forts, and megalithic tombs greet visitors with stony silence.

Known as Ireland's Holy Mountain, **Croagh Patrick** sits regally on the south side of **Clew Bay** and holds an important position in Irish history and legend. Legend has it that it was from Croagh Patrick that St. Patrick rid Ireland of its snakes. Croagh Patrick is an impressive mountain, and the site of yearly pilgrimages by many Catholic faithful.

Ulster

Ulster is a politically divided province. It consists of nine counties, six of which constitute **Northern Ireland**, which is a part of the United Kingdom. The three remaining counties are part of the Republic of Ireland. Despite this political segregation, scene for scene, vista for vista, Ulster may have the most spectacular scenery on the island. Unfortunately, due to the troubles of recent years, most American and Canadian visitors have chosen not to visit Ulster in general, and Northern Ireland in particular. Even during the most tumultuous times in Northern Ireland, however, visitors to Ulster have encountered very few problems. I have traveled there many times and have not had any difficulties (other than locking my keys in my car).

What is there to see here? For starters, one of the most fascinating ruins on the island is **Dunluce Castle**, on the northern coast of Northern Ireland. It is also one of the most photographed castles

anywhere. It sits majestically atop an outcropping that juts abruptly out of the Atlantic Ocean.

Giant's Causeway is one of the most amazing geologic sites on the Emerald Isle. The Causeway consists of more than 40,000 hexagonal basalt pillars of varying heights. The symmetry is astounding, and well worth a visit. If you are the adventurous type, then perhaps **Carrick-a-Rede** is the place for you - a rope bridge that stretches across an 80-foot span from the mainland to an island.

Finally, **County Donegal** on the northwest coast of Ireland is simply beautiful. Every turn of the road, every hill you top seems to reveal another beautiful lake or seascape. Donegal is one of the three counties in Ulster that is part of the Irish Republic.

3. DUBLIN

Dublin is a wonderful, bustling, friendly city with many superb sights. Some of the finest parks, museums, art galleries and antiquities in all of Europe are found within a compact area, most of them within easy walking distance of one another. These treasures include the **National Museum of Ireland** (Ireland's Smithsonian), the 9th-century illustrated gospels known as the **Book of Kells**, and a fabulous art gallery – the **National Gallery of Ireland** – home to the works of a number of grand masters as well as many of Ireland's own artists.

If cathedrals are of interest to you, then two of the finest in Ireland are **St. Patrick's** and **Christchurch**. If you enjoy city parks, **St. Stephen's Green**, **Merrion Square** or **Phoenix Park** (Europe's largest city park) are first-rate. To add a little spice, try the pedestrianized walkway **Grafton Street**, with its many street performers, or stroll through the many antique shops on **Francis Street**.

ONE GREAT DAY IN DUBLIN

You're in luck: the best sights are within easy walking distance of each other, so you won't waste time traveling. Visit **St. Patrick's Cathedral**. From there, stroll through beautiful St. Stephen's Green, one of Dublin's most beautiful parks, and then spend some time exploring the shops and sights on **Grafton Street**, Dublin's best pedestrian shopping street. Then it's on to the National Gallery of Ireland and Trinity College, to see the fabled **Book of Kells**. Along the way I'll steer you to Dublin's top landmarks.

Morning

To begin your day on a jazzy note, visit Elephant & Castle for breakfast. Located in the trendy Temple Bar district, it is just a hop, skip and jump from your first stop, **St. Patrick's Cathedral**.

St. Patrick's Cathedral was founded in 1191. Historians believe that St. Patrick himself performed baptisms at this site. There are many interesting things to see here – don't miss the "Door of Reconciliation" – a memorial to the courage of a man who wanted a bitter feud to end, and took drastic steps to make it so. The self-guided tour should take you 30 to 45 minutes, depending on how long you linger at the various spots. *Info:* Patrick Street. Tel. (01) 475-4817. Open daily 9am to 6pm. Admission is €4.50 for adults, less for seniors, students, and children; family tickets available.

From St. Patrick's Cathedral, head a few short blocks over to **St. Stephen's Green**, one of Dublin's most beautiful parks. This 22-acre park is a popular place to find some peace and serenity. Spend a few minutes and feed a few ducks and swans, peruse a Braille garden, check out some of its many memorials and statues, or just enjoy the lush greenery.

Directly across from the northwest corner of St. Stephen's Green is your next stopping – or rather your next strolling – point: **Grafton Street**, a pedestrianized street. It is considered *the* place to shop in Dublin. In fact, to see how the "other half" lives, stop into Brown Thomas, which features many designer brands and try on some expensive duds. In addition to the shops and the energy you'll find here, take a moment and enjoy the many buskers – street entertainers – who regularly entertain Grafton Street visitors.

Afternoon

By now, you're probably getting a little hungry, so take a moment and stop at **Bewleys** on Grafton Street, a busy bistro with opportunities for people watching if you dine on the upper mezzanine.

As you complete your visit on Grafton Street, head over to the **National Gallery of Ireland**. Two of the best stops here are the Italian renaissance section and the room devoted to paintings by Jack B. Yeats, brother of Irish author W. B. Yeats (talented family!). *Info:* Merrion Square West. Tel. (01) 661-5133. www.nationalgallery.ie. Open Monday through Saturday 9:30am to 5:30pm (Thursday until 8:30pm), Sunday from noon until 5:30pm. Admission is free.

From the National Gallery, head the short walk over to the **National Museum of Ireland**. There are a number of fascinating displays which take you through the history of Ireland from the Bronze Age to the present. Don't miss the exhibit entitled *Ar Thóir na Saoirse*, which is Gaelic for "The Road to Independence." It is a permanent exhibit that deals with the major personalities and events that took place from 1916 to 1922 as Ireland finally forged her independence. *Info:* Kildare Street. Tel. (01) 677-7444. www.museum.ie/archaeology. Open Tuesday through Saturday 10am to 5pm and Sunday from 2pm to 5pm. Admission is free (except for special exhibits).

After the National Museum, head north to **Trinity College** to see their exhibit of the **Book of Kells**. Written (drawn?) in the 9th century, the Book of Kells features elaborate ornamental drawings of the four

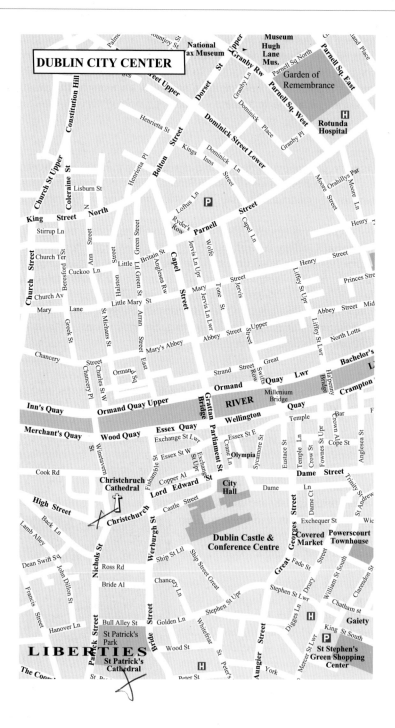

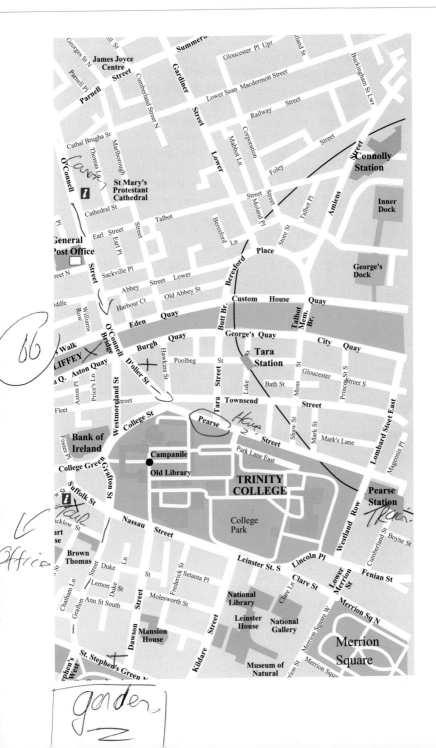

ALTERNATIVE PLAN
Not a museum or art gallery aficionado? If that's the case, rather than spend several hours visiting the National Gallery and National Museum, after you see St. Patrick's Cathedral but before you visit St. Stephen's Green, slip a block or two west of St. Patrick's Cathedral and explore **Francis Street**, Dublin's Antiques Row. Or perhaps you'd prefer a tour of the **Guinness Storehouse**, just a few blocks northwest of St. Patrick's Cathedral.

Gospels. The title pages of each Gospel are particularly elaborate. There are also gorgeous pictures throughout the book depicting many scenes from Christ's life, including his temptation and arrest. *Info:* Trinity College Colonnades. Tel. (01) 677-2941. Generally open daily 9:30am to 5pm; Sunday hours are shorter during the off-season. Admission is €8 for adults, less for seniors, students, and children; family tickets available.

Evening
Finish up your day by hopping a DART train at either the Connolly, Tara or Pearse Street stations and head for Howth and the **Abbey Tavern**, Tel. (01) 839-0307, where you'll enjoy a traditional Irish meal and be treated to traditional Irish music, dancing and merriment.

A FANTASTIC DUBLIN WEEKEND

The **best restaurant in Ireland**, intriguing museums, galleries and unique sights and sounds all combine to create a wonderful weekend in Ireland's capital city.

Friday Evening
Head straight to **Grafton Street** for a fun and memorable evening of mirth and frivolity. Half-way down Grafton Street at the intersection of Grafton and Duke Streets, you'll spot a tourist sign directing you to the **Dublin Literary Pub Crawl**. Local actors take turns entertaining their guests with tales of Ireland's most

noteworthy writers. Four or five pubs are part of the tour, as are the grounds of Trinity College. You'll experience a rollicking good time, full of literary one-liners, a little irreverence, lots of laughs, (a little bawdy at times), and plenty of good, (mostly) clean fun. *Info:* Duke Street. Tel. (01) 670-5602. www.dublinpubcrawl.com. Operating May through September: nightly at 7:30pm, and Sundays at noon. October through April: Sundays at noon, Thursday through Saturday 7:30pm. Admission is €7.50.

Saturday
Start your first full day in Dublin with a stop at **St. Patrick's Cathedral**. St. Patrick's was founded in 1191, but its history goes back much further. St. Patrick himself once performed baptisms on this site, making it the oldest Christian site in Dublin. Originally built outside the Dublin city walls, the location earned St. Patrick's the reputation of being the "church of the people."

Dining Tips

• During your pub crawl, you may have filled up on pub grub or assorted snacks, but if you are still hungry, head for **Pasta Fresca**, just off Grafton Street, for great made-on-the-premises pasta.
• Make reservations at **Restaurant Patrick Guilbaud**, Tel. 01 676-4192, for Saturday night.

ALTERNATIVE PLAN
If Friday night pub crawling isn't your scene (it is enjoyable even if you don't imbibe), then perhaps you'd enjoy seeing what's cooking at the **National Concert Hall**, just southeast of St. Stephen's Green. Most weekends throughout the year you can find a variety of concerts offered there.

In 1492, two of Ireland's most powerful men had been warring. One sought sanctuary in the Chapter House on the grounds of St. Patrick's, and a standoff ensued. Tired of the war, the other chopped a hole in the door. As an act of reconciliation and to show his willingness to lay down arms (figuratively as well as literally, apparently!), he thrust his arm through the hole and grasped the hand of his enemy, ending the war. The door – called the "Door

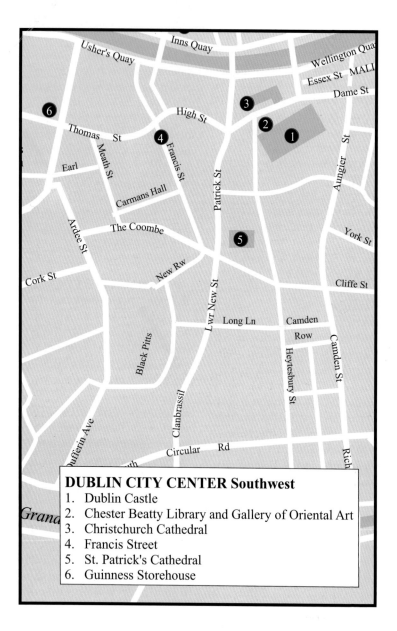

DUBLIN CITY CENTER Southwest
1. Dublin Castle
2. Chester Beatty Library and Gallery of Oriental Art
3. Christchurch Cathedral
4. Francis Street
5. St. Patrick's Cathedral
6. Guinness Storehouse

Dean of St. Patrick's

Jonathan Swift, the author of *Gulliver's Travels*, was Dean of St. Patrick's from 1713 to 1745. His pulpit is still on display in the cathedral, along with sundry items belonging to him. At the west end of the nave you'll find Jonathan's bust. Next to his bust you'll see the pointed epitaph that he penned for himself: "Here he lies, where bitter indignation can no longer lacerate his heart. Go traveler and imitate if you can one who was, to the best of his powers, a defender of Liberty."

of Reconciliation" - is on display in the northeast section of the cathedral. *Info:* Patrick Street. Tel. (01) 475-4817. Open daily 9am to 6pm. Admission is €4.50 for adults, less for seniors, students, and children; family tickets available.

Just west of St. Patrick's Cathedral is **Francis Street** – known as Dublin's *Antiques Row*. Francis Street has become the de-facto antique section of Dublin. Although you'll find antique shops elsewhere in Dublin, nowhere is there the concentration as thick as you'll find here on Francis Street.

Head east until you come to St. Stephen's Green, and you'll find **Grafton Street**, a long pedestrian open-air mall. Grafton Street is a fascinating blend of antique, jewelry, and upscale shops, with a generous mix of *buskers* (street entertainers). Be sure and check out the very upscale department store Brown Thomas (aka *BT*), as well as Weirs Jewelers. Give yourself plenty of time to stroll along the crowded sidewalks and sample a wee bit of this aspect of Irish culture.

At the north end of Grafton Street, don't miss the **Molly Malone Statue**, standing at the corner of Suffolk and Grafton Streets. Molly Malone is a featured character in an old Irish folk song. The bodice on Molly's dress is so scandalously low (even for a statue!) that she has several nicknames: *The Tart with the Cart* and *The Dish with the Fish!*

By now, you're probably getting a little hungry, so I'd suggest a stop at **Café En Seine** on Dawson Street, just one block east of

Grafton Street. This trendy cafe is an art deco, quasi-Parisian restaurant that attracts all kinds of patrons.

After lunch, walk down the street to the **National Gallery of Ireland** – the finest art gallery on the island. Don't miss the room devoted to impressionist Jack Butler Yeats, brother of Irish writer William Butler Yeats. In addition, there is a fine European collection, including works by such notables as **Rembrandt, Degas, El Greco, Goya, Monet, Reynolds, Rubens, Titian, Van Dyck**, and others. *Info:* Merrion Square West. Tel. (01) 661-5133. www.nationalgallery.ie. Open Monday through Saturday 9:30am to 5:30pm (Thursday until 8:30pm), Sunday from noon until 5:30pm. Admission is free.

From the National Gallery head one street east to Kildare Street and the **National Museum of Ireland**. The National Museum of Ireland has a number of fascinating displays which take you through the history of Ireland from the Bronze Age to the present. The *Treasury Exhibition* is worth a visit; it includes the lovely Tara Brooch (8th-century), the Ardagh Chalice (8th-century), and the silver and bronzed Cross of Cong (12th-century), and much more.

An exhibit that will give you a good sense of Ireland's struggle for independence is highlighted by *Ar Thóir na Saoirse*, which is Gaelic for "The Road to Independence." It is a permanent exhibit that deals with the major personalities and events that took place from 1916 to 1922 as Ireland finally forged her independence. *Info:* Kildare Street. Tel. (01) 677-7444. www.museum.ie/archaeology. Open Tuesday through Saturday 10am to 5pm and Sunday from 2pm to 5pm. Admission is free (except for special exhibits).

After finishing your tour of the National Museum, head over to **Trinity College** and one of the highlights of your trip to Dublin: the **Book of Kells**. The ornately illustrated four Gospels were written by the monks of the Kells monastery in County Meath. Written (drawn?) in the 9th century, the Book of Kells is four volumes of elaborate ornamental drawings of the four Gospels. The title pages of each Gospel are particularly elaborate. There

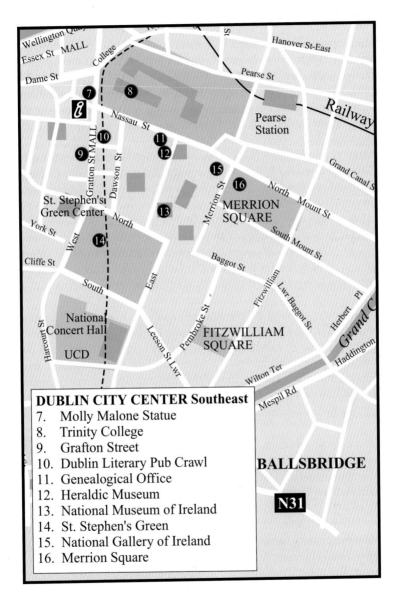

DUBLIN CITY CENTER Southeast
7. Molly Malone Statue
8. Trinity College
9. Grafton Street
10. Dublin Literary Pub Crawl
11. Genealogical Office
12. Heraldic Museum
13. National Museum of Ireland
14. St. Stephen's Green
15. National Gallery of Ireland
16. Merrion Square

are also gorgeous pictures depicting many scenes from Christ's life, including his temptation and arrest.

The Book of Kells is kept in a glass case in a room with muted lighting. Two Gospels are shown at a time, and the pages are turned each day. *Info:* Trinity College Colonnades. Tel. (01) 677-2941. Generally open daily 9:30am to 5pm; Sunday hours are shorter during the off-season. Admission is €8 for adults, less for seniors, students, and children; family tickets available.

After you view the Book of Kells, depart via the lavish **Long Room of the Old Library**. For nearly 200 years, Trinity College has been receiving a copy of every book published in Ireland and England, and many of them are on display here in the Old Library. Included are the first editions of some of Shakespeare's works, as well as copies of the original printing of the *Proclamation of 1916* (Ireland's equivalent of the Declaration of Independence). Watch for a copy of the *Proclamation of 1916* as soon as you enter the Long Hall. (It's usually displayed on your left.)

After being wowed by the Book of Kells and the Long Library, traverse Grafton Street (watch for new buskers!) to **St. Stephen's Green**. There is a children's playground, lots of ducks for the children (and you) to feed, a Victorian bandstand (where free lunch-time concerts are given throughout the summer), and a unique garden designed especially for the blind. The plants are labeled in Braille, and they are also resilient enough to be handled.

Don your sports coat, tie, or dress and head over to Merrion Street and **Restaurant Patrick Guilbaud**, Tel. 01 676-4192, housed in an old Georgian home that has been exquisitely renovated. The food is marvelous. From the roast quail to the poached Connemara lobster, it is as tasteful to the eye as it is to the palate.

Dining Alternative

If you're not in the mood for dressing up or can't get reservations at Patrick Guilbaud, try **Gallagher's Boxty House**, Tel. (01) 677-2762. Gallagher's offers a more casual dining experience, and features traditional Irish meals.

Sunday

You'll start your day off at **Guinness Storehouse**, one of Dublin's top tourist sights. The 60-acre brewery produces four million pints of Guinness beer *per day*. Tours of the brewery itself are no longer conducted, but a fine audiovisual presentation on the history of the brewery is available in the Hop Store. At the close of the presentation, a complimentary sample of Guinness is available to those who wish to sample the dark brew. *Info:* Crane Street. Tel. (01) 453-8364 (information line) or (01) 408-4800 (for reservations for large groups, or to talk to the Hop Store). Open April through August daily from 9:30am until 6pm, September through March daily from 9:30am to 5pm. Admission is €9 for adults, less for seniors, students, and children; family tickets available.

From the Guinness Storehouse, stroll east along the River Liffey for about six blocks until you come to the **Ha'penny Bridge**, and then cross over to the other side of the bridge. Ha'penny (pronounced hay'-penny) Bridge is the only strictly pedestrian bridge in Dublin, and it derives its name from the toll charged to use the bridge in earlier days.

Once on the north side of the bridge, continue your walk another block east to O'Connell Street, and turn left (north). The first thing that dominates your view of O'Connell Street is the **Spire of Dublin,** a 393-foot stainless steel pole. The Irish have a penchant for nicknaming their monuments, and this one is no exception. The Spire of Dublin is often called, among other things, *the Stiffy by the Liffey, the Pointless Point,* and (my favorite) *the Stiletto in the Ghetto.*

Once you've overcome your surprise at the Spire of Dublin, head north on O'Connell Street toward the Spire. Before you arrive at it, on your left you will come to the **General Post Office**, better known as the **GPO**. Its mark on history goes much beyond postal service: it was the flash point of the 1916 Easter Rising, which ended in Ireland gaining her independence from England. Irish rebels proclaimed their message of a new republic from the captured GPO. The ensuing battle destroyed most of the area around O'Connell Street. Some of the GPO's massive stone columns still bear the scars of flying bullets. The words of the proclamation read by the rebel leaders on that fateful Easter morning are inscribed in a green marble plaque in the GPO. *Info:* Tel. (01) 872-8888. Open Monday through Saturday 8am until 8pm, Sundays from 10:30am to 6:30pm.

Inside the GPO is a magnificent statue of **Cuchulainn** (pronounced Koo-hoo'-lin). He was a legendary Irish warrior. He was the leader of the Red Branch Knights, an elite army charged with defending Ulster from her many enemies. Legend says that after a lifetime of warring, Cuchulainn fought in one last ferocious battle. Mortally wounded, he is said to have lashed himself to a stone so that he could face his enemies while remaining on his feet. His foes wouldn't approach his body, the legend says, until a bird landed on the shoulder of the lifeless warrior. The statue depicts his last moments. It is an appropriate tribute to those few warriors who took on the British Empire almost single-handedly and wrested Ireland from her grasp.

Near the GPO, catch a bus for your next stop today. Watch for buses 13, 19 or 134, and hop on for a short ride to the **National Botanic Gardens**. The gardens boast over 20,000 plant species spread over 45 acres. The greenhouses house an astounding variety of exotic plants and trees, such as orchids, banana trees, and palm trees. *Info:* Glasnevin Road. Tel. (01) 837-7596 or (01) 837-4388. Generally open Monday through Saturday from 9am until 6pm, Sundays from 11am to 6pm; slightly shorter hours during the winter. Admission is free.

Catch a bus back into town – watch for any bus labeled *An Lar* (which means City Center). It will deposit you across the street from the GPO. Once there, head north on O'Connell Street until you come to the **Garden of Remembrance**, at the intersection of O'Connell and Pearse Streets. On the fiftieth anniversary of the Easter Rising of 1916, which led to Ireland's independence, the Garden of Remembrance was built to commemorate those who gave their lives that Ireland might be a free nation. (Think of it as the Minuteman statue in Lexington, Massachusetts.) *Info:* Parnell Square. Generally open daily from 9:30am to 7pm, shorter during the winter months. Admission is free.

From the Garden of Remembrance, head over to the **Dublin Writer's Museum**. This museum is one of the most elegant, tasteful and well thought-out museums in Ireland. Be sure to check out the permanent exhibits that feature famed Irish authors such as **Samuel Beckett, Brendan Behan, George Bernard Shaw, Jonathan Swift**, and **Oscar Wilde**. Paintings, photographs, letters, and memorabilia are all part of the various exhibits. *Info:* 18/19 Parnell Square. Tel. (01) 872-2077. Open Monday through Saturday from 10am to 5pm, and Sundays from 11am to 5pm. Open later during the summer. Admission is €6.70 for adults, less for seniors, students, and children; family tickets available.

ALTERNATIVE PLAN

If a writer's museum doesn't float your boat, catch either bus 37, 38 or 39 and head out to Phoenix Park for an enjoyable afternoon of people-watching and the possibility of a polo match or cricket game.

Once you've finished your day's sightseeing, hop on the DART at Pearse, Tara or Connolly Street stations and head out to Howth and the **Abbey Tavern**, Tel. (01) 839-0307. You'll have a good meal and a delightful traditional Irish music show. Before or after dinner, be sure and walk the short distance to the quay and walk along the seashore, enjoying a wonderful sunset over the Irish Sea. Through the years, some of my most stunning sunset photos of Ireland were taken here.

A WONDERFUL WEEK IN DUBLIN

With a week in Dublin, you can spend more time at the sights discussed in previous sections, plus you can take in a lot more, such as **Dublin Castle**, the **GPO**, the vast grounds of **Phoenix Park**, and, further afield, the ancient ruins of **Glendalough**.

RECOMMENDED PLAN: With a week, you'll be able to see Dublin's top sights as well as many of her off-the-beaten-track gems. Start off by taking a couple of days to explore the sights south of the Liffey, then a day poking around the sights on the north side of the Liffey. Then expand your horizons and visit some places in the Dublin area that aren't within easy walking distance. Finally, finish off your time in Dublin with short day trips to several ruins and gardens.

South of the Liffey

Start your exploration of the south side of the Liffey with a visit to the **National Museum of Ireland.** Be sure to take notice of the building itself. There are marble floors, brass railings, intricate crown moldings, and beautiful carved wood doors. You'll learn of Ireland's history from the Bronze Age (2200 BC to 700 BC) to the present. Be sure and stop in at the Treasury Exhibition (the only part of the museum requiring a modest admission fee), which includes the lovely Tara Brooch (8th-century), the Ardagh Chalice (8th-century), and the silver and bronzed Cross of Cong (12th-century), and much more.

One of the highlights of this museum is a replica of the Newgrange passage grave in County Meath. The actual cross-shaped tomb, about an hour north of Dublin, is nearly 5,000 years old and is wonderfully preserved. If you can't make the drive to see the original, be sure to take a look at the replica here. *Info:* Kildare Street. Tel. (01) 677-7444. www.museum.ie/archaeology. Open Tuesday through Saturday 10am to 5pm and Sunday from 2pm to 5pm. Admission is free (except for special exhibits).

From the National Museum, head north on Dawson Street past the National Library, and slip into the **Heraldic Museum.** Co-located with the **Genealogical Office**, the Heraldic Museum has a fine display of coats of arms that extend back many centuries. Stop and find yours! In addition, they'll have maps that list the traditional ancestral homes of thousands of Irish surnames. Perhaps you are one of the 70% of American visitors to Ireland that have at least one progenitor of Irish ancestry. *Info:* 2 Kildare Street, Tel. (01) 603-0311. Generally open Monday through Friday from 10am to 5pm, and Saturday from 10am to 12:30pm. Admission is free.

Don't Miss ...

• **The Book of Kells** – illustrated Gospels over 1,200 years old
• **St. Patrick's Cathedral**
• **St. Stephen's Green** – a bit of quiet in the city
• **Chester Beatty Library** and **Gallery of Oriental Art** – fabulous collection
• **Phoenix Park** – serenity amid the chaos
• **National Museum of Ireland** – Ireland's Smithsonian

Around the corner from the Heraldic Museum is the **National Galley of Ireland**, which has one of the finest collections of art in Ireland. I suppose every major Irish artist – and many not-so-major artists – are represented here. In addition, there is a fine European collection, including works by such notables as **Rembrandt, Degas, El Greco, Goya, Monet, Reynolds, Rubens, Titian, Van Dyck**, and others. One of the museum's most extraordinary aspects is a four-story circular staircase lined with paintings of three centuries worth of notable personalities in Irish history, a kind of wall of fame. For a peek into a poignant past, watch for *The Wounded Poacher*, by Henry Jones Thaddeus (1859–1929). Thaddeus depicts a wounded poacher being attended to by his loving wife in their simple, earthy cabin. The detail in the picture is amazing.

Guided tours are offered on Saturday afternoons at 3pm and Sundays at 2:30pm, 3:15pm, and 4pm. *Info:* Merrion Square West. Tel. (01) 661-5133. www.nationalgallery.ie. Open Monday through Saturday 9:30am to 5:30pm (Thursday until 8:30pm), Sunday from noon until 5:30pm. Admission is free.

Once leaving the gallery, cross the street to **Merrion Square**. Here is a place to get away from the omnipresent Dublin traffic. Built in 1762, it is a lovely assemblage of gardens, shrubs, and trees. Over the years, a number of Ireland's most important and esteemed citizens called the fine Georgian townhouses around Merrion Square home, including **Oscar Wilde's** parents (Number 1), **Daniel O'Connell** (Number 58), **W. B. Yeats** (Numbers 52 and 82) and the **Duke of Wellington** (Number 24 Upper Merrion Street). Many of the homes have plaques identifying their famous inhabitants. Some would say the best restaurant in Ireland is here as well at Number 21, **Restaurant Patrick Guilbaud**.

On Saturdays and Sundays along the sidewalks outside Merrion Square, local artists can be found selling their work. There is something there to fit every taste: landscapes, animals, abstract art, and portraits — you name it, they sell it. There are so many pieces to be seen it feels like an outdoor museum. This is also a great place to chat with the local artists.

Cafe En Seine

When you're hungry, I'd suggest a stop at Café En Seine on Dawson Street, just one block east of Grafton Street. This trendy cafe is an art deco, quasi-Parisian restaurant that attracts all kinds – from the bohemian to the business person, from the avant-garde to the traditionalist.

Cross the street to **St. Stephen's Green**. St. Stephen's Green is a very peaceful, serene city park.

There are a number of memorials in the park that are worthy of your attention. The Romanesque arch over the main entrance at the northwest corner of the park is called the Fusiliers Arch, and t is a memorial to the Dublin Fusiliers who fought and died during the Boer War. There is a memorial dedicated to **W. B. Yeats**. Don't miss the fountain and statue of the Three Fates, a statue given to the Irish by a grateful German government for the relief they provided to the needy at the close of World War II.

There is a children's playground, lots of ducks for the children (and you) to feed, a Victorian bandstand (where free lunchtime concerts are given throughout the summer), and a unique garden designed especially for the blind. The plants are labeled in Braille, and they are also resilient enough to be handled.

Head east from St. Stephen's Green until you come to **St. Patrick's Cathedral**. Founded in 1191, this is thought to be the oldest Christian site in Dublin. Physically, St. Patrick's is impressive. The largest church in Ireland, its west clock tower rises 141 feet above Patrick Street, and the spire atop the tower rises another 101 feet, making the tip of the spire nearly 250 feet above your head. As you might expect, St. Patrick's also boasts a number of stunning stained glass windows. It's hard to believe that Oliver Cromwell showed his contempt for this magnificent structure by demanding that his horses be stabled inside the cathedral. This was a practice he replicated throughout the country at other churches, cathedrals, and town halls. **Jonathan Swift**, the author of *Gulliver's Travels*, was Dean of St. Patrick's from 1713 to 1745. His pulpit is on display in the cathedral, along with a bust of the great man and sundry items belonging to him.

In 1492, two of Ireland's most powerful nobles had been warring. The Earl of Ormond sought sanctuary in the Chapter House, and a standoff ensued. Tired of the war, the Earl of Kildare chopped a hole in the door. As an act of reconciliation, he thrust his arm through the hole and grasped the hand of his enemy, ending the war. The door, called the "Door of Reconciliation," is on display in the northeast section of the cathedral. *Info:* Patrick Street. Tel. (01) 475-4817. Open daily 9am to 6pm. Admission is €4.50 for adults, less for seniors, students, and children; family tickets available.

Christchurch Cathedral was built in 1038 for the Norse King Sitric Silkenbeard. The original wooden structure was replaced with stonework in 1220. In 1831, the cathedral received one final major facelift, and was redone in the Gothic style you see today. This magnificent cathedral includes a self-guided tour through the ancient crypt below the cathedral. You should be able to complete the crypt tour in about 15

Antiques Detour

Francis Street has become the de-facto antique section of Dublin. Although you'll find antique shops elsewhere in Dublin, nowhere is there the concentration as thick as you'll find here on Francis Street, just a block west of St. Patrick's Cathedral.

minutes. On the way out of the crypt, look for the mummified bodies of a cat and rat. Long ago, these enemies apparently participated in a deadly game of "cat and mouse." The rat raced into an organ pipe with the cat hot on his tail. The cat became lodged in the pipe, and both diner and dinner perished. *Info*: Tel. (01) 677-8099. Temple Bar District: Christchurch Place. Generally open daily from 10am until 5pm. Admission is €3 for adults, less for seniors, students, and children; family tickets available. Access to the crypt is included in the admission price.

One of the top sights for Dublin visitors is the **Guinness Storehouse**. Some say that a trip to Dublin would not be complete unless you try their world famous Guinness beer. And there is no better place than the sprawling, 60-acre Guinness Brewery where Dubliners swear the beer tastes better! Tours of the brewery itself are no longer conducted, but a fine audiovisual presentation on the history of the brewery is available in the Hop Store. At the close of the presentation, a complimentary sample of Guinness is available to those who wish to sample the dark brew. Although interesting, this is a very expensive tour for what you get. *Info:* Crane Street. Tel. (01) 453-8364 (information line) or (01) 408-4800 (for reservations for large groups, or to talk to the Hop Store). Open April through August daily from 9:30am until 6pm, September through March daily from 9:30am to 5pm. Admission is €9 for adults, less for seniors, students, and children; family tickets available.

Your next stop will be **Dublin Castle**, the symbol of English rule over Ireland for 600 years, from the early 13th century until the independence of Ireland in 1922. A one-hour guided tour escorts you around the grounds and through the State Apartments, which formerly served as the residences for the English Viceroys. Today the State Apartments are used primarily for ceremonial affairs from time to time.

Several of the rooms are exceptionally exquisite. The most impressive are the Apollo Room (sometimes called the Music Room), the Round Drawing Room, and the Wedgwood Room. The highlight of the Castle is St. Patrick's Hall. This large room (82 feet by 40 feet) is graced with a hand-painted ceiling and beautiful gilded pillars. It is the venue for Irish presidential inaugurations and various state functions. The oldest section of Dublin Castle is the Record Tower (the public is not allowed in), a part of the original structure dating from 1220.

On the grounds of Dublin Castle is the **Royal Chapel**, also known as the **Church of the Holy Trinity**. This charming little church has beautiful oak panels and lovely stained-glass windows. The exterior is embellished with the carved heads of all the kings and queens of England. The Royal Chapel was completed in 1814. It served the Anglican Church for over 125 years, but now serves as a Catholic Church. *Info:* Castle Street. Tel. (01) 679-7831 or (01) 677-7129. Open Monday through Friday 10am to 4:45pm, Saturdays, Sundays and bank holidays from 2pm until 4:45pm. Last admission is 15 minutes before closing. Admission is €4 for adults, less for seniors, students, and children; family tickets available.

Adjacent to Dublin Castle is the **Chester Beatty Library and Gallery of Oriental Art**. This outstanding collection of Oriental art and antiquities contains rare books and manuscripts, miniature paintings, over 270 ancient copies of the Koran, clay tablets from Babylon, and some of the earliest known Biblical papyri in existence. You'll easily be able to spend a fascinating hour or two here, viewing these wonderful antiquities. *Info:* The Clocktower Building behind Dublin Castle. Open Monday through Friday from 10am to 5pm, Saturday from 11am to 5pm and Sunday from 1pm to 5pm. Admission is free.

After visiting the Chester Beatty Library, head for **Trinity College** and the **Book of Kells**, the ornately illustrated four Gospels

 written by the monks of the Kells monastery in County Meath. Written (drawn?) in the 9th century, the Book of Kells is four volumes of elaborate ornamental drawings of the four Gospels. The title pages of each Gospel are particularly elaborate. There are also gorgeous pictures depicting many scenes from Christ's life, including his temptation and arrest.

The Book of Kells is kept in a glass case in a room with muted lighting. Two Gospels are shown at a time, and the pages are turned each day. The pages are calfskin made from 185 calves! As you look at the incredible craftsmanship and stunning artwork of the books, it's hard to imagine that these lovely works were once hidden under a roll of sod to protect them from the ravages of invaders!

After seeing the Book of Kells, you are treated to a fascinating stroll through the lavish **Long Room of the Old Library** on your way out. This impressive room is over 200 feet long and 40 feet wide. For nearly 200 years, Trinity College has been receiving a copy of every book published in Ireland and England, and many of them are on display here in the Old Library.

Included in the holdings of the library are first editions of some of Shakespeare's works, as well as copies of the original printing of the *Proclamation of 1916* (Ireland's equivalent of the Declaration of Independence). Watch for a copy of the *Proclamation of 1916* as soon as you enter the Long Hall. (It's usually displayed on your left.) In addition, there is a wonderful 15th-century harp on display. It is in remarkable condition, from its oak and willow woodwork to its 29 brass strings. *Info:* Trinity College Colonnades. Tel. (01) 677-2941. Generally open daily 9:30am to 5pm; Sunday hours are shorter during the off-season. Admission is €8 for adults, less for seniors, students, and children; family tickets available.

Near Trinity College, at the corner of Suffolk and Grafton Streets watch for the bronze, life-size statue of **Molly Malone**. Often referred to by Dubliners as *The Dish with the Fish!* Molly Malone is a featured character in an old Irish folk song. The song is taught to school children, sung in pubs, and bellowed at rugby, soccer, hurling, and Gaelic football games. The bodice on Molly's dress is so scandalously low (even for a statue!) that she has another name: *The Tart with the Cart.*

Molly stands at the entrance to **Grafton Street**, a long pedestrian open-air mall. Grafton Street is a fascinating blend of antique, jewelry, and upscale shops, with a generous mix of *buskers* (street entertainers), ranging from musicians to magicians, jugglers to Marionette masters, and a host of other talented individuals. Street peddlers also hawk their wares, ranging from silk ties and silver rings to cassettes and macramé. While there, stop into the upscale department store Brown Thomas, which features many designer brands and try on some expensive duds, or swing by Weirs jewelers to see the latest in Irish jewelry.

Half-way down Grafton Street at the intersection of Grafton and Duke Streets, you'll spot a tourist sign directing you to the **Dublin Literary Pub Crawl**. Local actors take turns entertaining, informing, shocking, and delighting their guests with tales of Ireland's most noteworthy writers: Brendan **Behan, James Joyce, W. B. Yeats, Oscar Wilde, Oliver Goldsmith, George Bernard Shaw**, and others. Four or five pubs are part of the tour. Along the way the actors regale you with stories and anecdotes from the lives of these writers.

You'll find out which journalist referred to himself as a "bicycle built for two" (and why) and learn which writer characterized himself as "A good drinker who had trouble with writing." A rollicking good time, full of literary one-liners, a little irreverence, lots of laughs, (a little bawdy at times), and plenty of good, (mostly) clean fun. *Info:* Duke Street. Tel. (01) 670-5602. www.dublinpubcrawl.com. Operating May through September: nightly at 7:30pm, and Sundays at noon. October through April: Sundays at noon, Thursday through Saturday 7:30pm. Admission is €7.50.

North of the Liffey

Start your tour north of the Liffey by stopping into the **General Post Office** – the GPO. The GPO was the flashpoint for the 1916 Easter Rising – the event that set in motion the events that eventually led to Ireland's independence from England. Irish rebel leaders seized the GPO and bravely proclaimed their message of a new republic. The ensuing battle destroyed most of the area around O'Connell Street. Some of the GPO's massive stone columns still bear the scars of flying bullets. The words of the proclamation read by the rebel leaders on that fateful Easter morning is inscribed in a green marble plaque in the GPO. *Info:* Tel. (01) 872-8888. Open Monday through Saturday 8am until 8pm, Sundays from 10:30am to 6:30pm.

A few blocks east of the GPO you'll come to **St. Michan's Church**. Built in 1095, St. Michan's was rebuilt to its current state in 1686. Be sure and notice the beautiful woodwork throughout the chapel, as well as the "stool of repentance," where misbehaving parishioners did public penance. The most unusual aspect of St. Michan's is the partially mummified remains of three 17th-century people in the vaults. The limestone in the ground of the vaults removed moisture from the air, preserving the bodies remarkably well. If the mummified cat and mouse at Christchurch made you queasy, you might want to pass on these fellows. *Info:* Church Street. Tel. (01) 872-4154. Generally open Monday through Friday from 10am to 12:30pm, and from 2pm to 5:30pm, and Saturdays from 10am until 1pm. Only open in the afternoons during the winter. Admission to the vaults is €3 for adults, less for seniors, students, and children; family tickets available.

Swinging back to the northeast, you'll come to the **Dublin Writer's Museum**. This exquisitely restored Georgian home houses the Gorham Library on the first floor. Be sure to take a look at its beautiful ceiling. Don't miss the permanent exhibits in the museum which feature famed Irish authors such as **Samuel Beckett, Brendan Behan, George Bernard Shaw, Jonathan Swift,** and **Oscar Wilde**. Paintings, photographs, letters, and memorabilia are all part of the various exhibits. *Info:* 18/19 Parnell Square. Tel. (01) 872-2077. Open Monday through Saturday from 10am to 5pm, and Sundays from 11am to 5pm. Open later during the

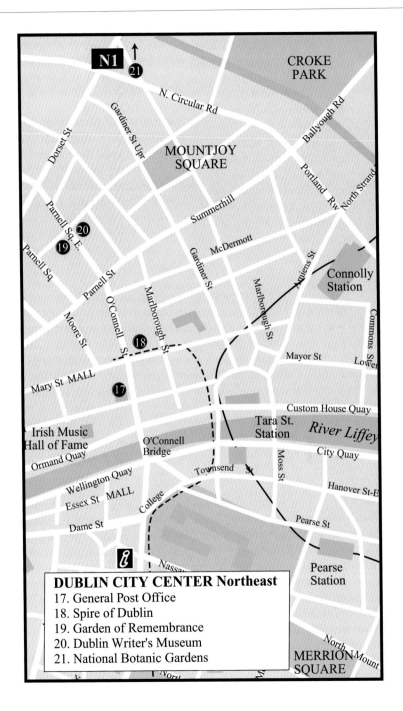

N1

CROKE PARK

N. Circular Rd

Dorset St

Gardiner St Upr

MOUNTJOY SQUARE

Ballyough Rd

Portland Rw

North Strand

Parnell Sq. E.

Summerhill

Parnell Sq

Parnell St

McDermott

Gardiner St

Marlborough St

Aniens St

Connolly Station

Commons Street

Moore St

O'Connell St

Marlborough St

Mayor St

Lower

Mary St MALL

Custom House Quay

Tara St. Station

River Liffey

Irish Music Hall of Fame

Ormand Quay

O'Connell Bridge

Moss St

City Quay

Hanover St-E

Wellington Quay

Townsend St

Essex St MALL

College

Dame St

Pearse St

Pearse Station

Nassau

North Mount

MERRION SQUARE

DUBLIN CITY CENTER Northeast
17. General Post Office
18. Spire of Dublin
19. Garden of Remembrance
20. Dublin Writer's Museum
21. National Botanic Gardens

Lunch & Literature!

If you find yourself getting hungry during your perusal of the sights on the north of the Liffey, stop into **The Winding Stair** at 40 Ormond Quay Lower. This three-story bookstore features tall shelves of new and used books, and a third-story café that overlooks the Liffey.

summer. Admission is €6.70 for adults, less for seniors, students, and children; family tickets available.

Nearby is the **Garden of Remembrance**, a memorial to those who gave their lives for Ireland's independence (like the Minuteman statue in Massachusetts.) This is a very peaceful and contemplative place where visitors can think about Irish patriots who gave their lives for a free Ireland.

The square features an ornamental pond in the form of a crucifix, and the setting is very serene and peaceful. Just beyond the small pond is a statue that looks like children chasing geese and making them fly away. It is in reality a statue of the children of Lir, who were turned into swans by their wicked stepmother (according to legend). *Info:* Parnell Square. Generally open daily from 9:30am to 7pm, shorter during the winter months. Admission is free.

Dublin's Suburbs

There are a number of Dublin sights worth seeing that are not within easy walking distance of the downtown area. It will take you a couple of days to do them justice.

Start by catching bus 13, 19 or 134, for the short ride to the **National Botanic Gardens**. This is a real treat and worth the short bus ride. The gardens boast over 20,000 plant species spread over 45 acres. Over 400 feet of greenhouses offer an astounding variety of exotic plants and trees, such as orchids, banana trees, and palm trees. For a special treat, cross over the wooden bridge into the extraordinary rose gardens. *Info:* Glasnevin Road. Tel. (01) 837-7596 or (01) 837-4388. Generally open Monday through Saturday from 9am until 6pm, Sundays from 11am to 6pm; slightly shorter hours during the winter. Admission is free.

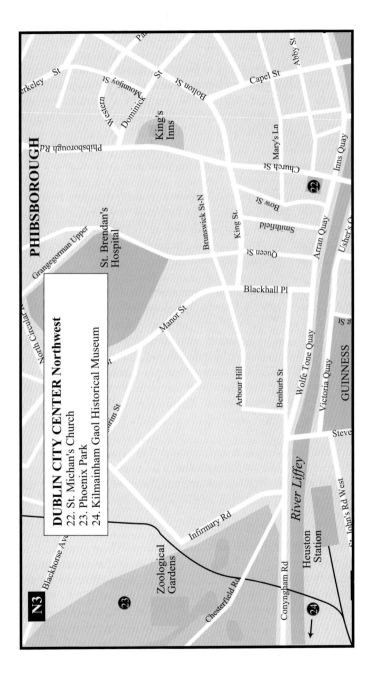

DUBLIN CITY CENTER Northwest

22. St. Michan's Church
23. Phoenix Park
24. Kilmainham Gaol Historical Museum

From the National Botanic Gardens, hop a bus back to the city center (any bus displaying the words *An Lar* – Irish for City Center). Get off near the GPO, and then grab either bus 37, 38 or 39. If you're driving, head to Dublin's west side. A short ride or drive will bring you to **Phoenix Park**. Originally opened to the public over 250 years ago, it is the largest city park in Europe at over 1,700 acres, and it is a delightful place to visit. This beautiful park is not named after the mythological bird that rises from the ashes, but rather from the Irish words *fionn uisce* (clear water), which sounds like Phoenix in English.

On nice days, old men and women in their Sunday best sit on many of the park benches, just enjoying the nice weather and watching the people go by. Families cavort on the grass, visit the zoo, and feed the omnipresent ducks. Lovers walk arm and arm oblivious to the beauty around them.

One of the more popular attractions in Phoenix Park is the **Dublin Zoo**. It has a wide variety of animals, and an area for the children to get "up close and personal" with a number of less exotic creatures like rabbits, chickens, and goats. The famous MGM lion claims the Dublin Zoo as his birthplace. *Info:* Phoenix Park. Tel. (01) 677-1425. Open Monday through Saturday from 9:30am until 5pm and Sunday from 10:30am to 9pm sometimes later (check before you visit). Admission is €9.80 for adults, less for seniors, students, and children; family tickets available.

The **polo grounds** are just beyond the zoo, and practices or matches are fun to watch, whether you understand all the rules or not (I don't). The horses are magnificent, and to see them wheeling and charging is really a treat. The riders aren't bad either.

With a visit to **Kilmainham Gaol Historical Museum**, you'll step into the darker side of Ireland's past. This restored prison gives its guests a peek into the terrible conditions endured by Irish patriots awaiting execution or a one-way ticket to Australia. Among the most infamous acts committed here was the execution of those who penned their names to the Proclamation of the Republic in 1916 (the Irish equivalent of the Declaration of

Independence). You'll chill as you view the Hanging Room and you'll cringe as you walk about the prison yard where executions took place. A short audiovisual presentation is included in the tour, and gives you the highlights of the Irish struggle for independence. *Info*: Inchicore Road. Tel. (01) 677-6801. Open daily generally from 9:30am until 4pm, sometimes later (check before you visit). The last tour begins one hour before closing. Admission is €5 for adults, less for seniors, students, and children; family tickets are available.

If you're a **James Joyce** fan, and don't care for one of the sights suggested for today, you may want to visit the **James Joyce Tower**, but you'll need a car to get there. Located in the Dublin suburb of Dun Laoghaire (pronounced Dun Leary – really!), it's about a 45-minute drive from downtown Dublin. Internationally famed author and Irish son James Joyce lived here for a short time around the turn of the last century. A collection of Joycean artifacts are on display in the James Joyce Tower: his waistcoat,

Howth & Abbey Tavern

At the end of your day's activities, catch the DART train out to Howth. This delightful seaside village will afford you opportunities for strolling along the Irish Sea and within the winding streets of the town. Be sure and bring your camera for stunning shots of sunset over the Irish Sea. Finish off with a visit to the **Abbey Tavern** for an evening of traditional Irish food, music and entertainment.

cigar case, a tie, numerous first editions of his book, a piano and guitar once belonging to him, and his death mask. *Info*: Sandy Cove, Dun Laoghaire. Tel. (01) 280-9265 or (01) 872-2077. Open April through October Monday to Saturday from 10am to 5pm (closed from 1pm to 2pm for lunch) and Sunday from 2pm to 6pm. The rest of the year you need to call for an appointment. Admission fee is €5.50 for adults, less for seniors, students, and children; family tickets are available.

South of Dublin
There are a couple of sights within easy striking distance of Dublin for delightful day trips. For your first day's trip, hop in

Attention Gardeners!

If you enjoyed the floral magnificence of Powerscourt and would like more of the same, head south to Ashford and Mt. Usher Gardens, and then over to Tully and the Japanese Gardens. You'll be treated to even more floral splendor and variety.

your rental car and head south toward the town of Enniskerry and you'll find **Powerscourt Gardens and Waterfall**. Powerscourt Gardens cascade in a series of terraces down the slope from Powerscourt House. The gardens are filled with verdant greenery: sculpted shrubs, trees, and many varieties of flowering plants, set among statues, fountains, and walkways. You could easily spend half a day wandering through the various gardens of Powerscourt.

Three miles south of the gardens is **Powerscourt Waterfall**. The highest waterfall in Ireland, the water cascades more than 400 feet off the edge of Djouce Mountain. It serves as a favorite picnic area for tourists and locals alike. *Info:* Enniskerry. Tel. (01) 204-6000. The gardens are open March through October daily from 9:30am until 5:30pm. Admission is €9 for adults, €7.50 for students and €5 for children under 12 (under 5 free). The waterfall is open all year from 9:30am until 7pm. Admission to the waterfall area is €4.50 for adults, less for seniors, students, and children; family tickets are available.

After enjoying the beauties of Powerscourt, head further south to **Glendalough**. "The glen of the two lakes" – *Glen Da Locha* – is perhaps one of the most serene places in the world. Two lakes grace the valley with their elegance and beauty. Heavily forested mountains encompass the valley. Add to the natural beauty some exquisite and ancient ruins, and this is a wonderful place to visit. The best place to begin your tour of Glendalough is at the visitor's center. Here they have a fine audio-visual presentation on Glendalough and its history.

Near the visitors centre you'll find some of the finest religious ruins in Ireland. Towering above the trees, the well-preserved 100-foot tall **Round Tower** stands as a mute witness of past oppressors and as a sentry against future invaders. Nearby is **St. Kevin's Kitchen**, an 11th-century stone church. And don't miss **St. Kevin's Cross**, (it would be hard to), an 11-foot granite cross 1,300 years old.

Other ruins of interest in Glendalough include **St. Savier's Church** (12th century), **Church of our Lady** (the oldest ruin in the lower valley), and the **Priest's House**, site of burials for priests. On the end of Upper Lake you'll find an old fort (**Caher**) dating from the late Bronze or early Iron age. *Info*: Near Laragh. Tel. (0404) 45325. Generally open 9am to 6pm, with shorter hours during the winter (check before you visit). Admission is €2.90 for adults, less for seniors, students, and children; family tickets are available.

North of Dublin

About a 45-minute drive north of Dublin you'll find **Newgrange,** one of Ireland's most impressive ancient sights. The Newgrange burial mound is an enormous, well-preserved grave dating back to nearly 3,000 BC. During the winter solstice (December 21), rays from the sun glide down the narrow passageway gradually lighting the burial chamber. For those unable to be at Newgrange during the winter solstice, modern technology recreates the effect. Including the roundtrip drive from Dublin, a little time in the Visitors Center and time at Newgrange, you can easily spend five or six hours on this excursion. *Info:* Entrance to the Visitors Center is just south of Slane off the N2. Tel. (041) 988-0300. Open March through November, with hours generally from 9:30am to 5pm, sometimes later (check before you visit). Admission is €5.80 for adults, less for seniors, students, and children; family tickets available.

About six miles north of Drogheda on the N1, watch for the first Dunleer exit north of Drogheda, then follow the signs to Monasterboice. It is not signed particularly well from the N1, but watch for the lonely round tower off the west side of the N1 and make your way over to it.

Monasterboice offers one of the premier exhibits of finely pre-served high crosses in Ireland. It is the monastic settlement of Monasterboice, which takes its name from the Irish *Mainstir Buithe*, which means "St. Buithe's Abbey." The site consists of the ruins of two churches, a round tower, and three high crosses. The 10th-century **Cross of Muiredach**, is a remarkably well preserved High Cross. Almost 17 feet tall, it portrays scenes depicting Adam and Eve, Cain and Abel, Christ as the Judge, and Michael weighing souls. It also contains a depiction of the crucifixion. **Tall Cross** (21 feet high) depicts the sacrifice of Isaac by Abraham, the Vigil at the Tomb, Judas' kiss of betrayal, and the crucifixion. *Info:* There is no charge to visit Monasterboice. Just park your car in the small carpark across the street, and let yourself in the gate.

Now head toward Navan and the **Hill of Tara**. Eight miles south of Navan just off the N3 (watch for the signpost) is the Hill of Tara, one of the most significant historic, religious, secular, and mythi-cal sights in Ireland. It is the ancient site of the coronation of the Celtic kings of Ireland. Atop this legendary hill is a statue of St. Patrick, and a small pillar called the *Lia Fial*, the stone believed to have been used as an ancient coronation stone. Today, little else is on the Hill of Tara except grass-covered mounds and the occa-sional grazing sheep – the new kings of Tara. *Info:* Near Navan. Open May through September generally from 10am to 5pm, sometimes longer. Admission is €2 for adults, less for seniors, students, and children; family tickets are available.

4. LEINSTER

Leinster is a province filled with antiquities and beautiful scenery. If you spend any time at all here (you should), don't miss **Newgrange**, the 5,000-year-old passage grave, or **Glendalough**, the 6th-century monastic settlement south of Dublin. In between, you'll find Ireland's mythic **Hill of Tara**, where Ireland's ancient kings were crowned, and several fine sets of ruins, including Monasterboice, Mellifont Abbey and Jerpoint Abbey.

If it's natural beauty you are most interested in, you'll not be disappointed either. From **Powerscourt Gardens** to the **Vale of Avoca**, to the **Ring of Hook** at Ireland's southeast tip, you'll be enthralled with the beauty and serenity you'll find here.

ONE GREAT DAY IN LEINSTER

Leinster is the easternmost province of Ireland and has some fascinating sites to see. The sites are easily reached by car. Start your day by heading to **Newgrange**, a 5,000-year-old burial mound. From there, visit the **Hill of Tara**, one of the most revered sites in Ireland. Next, a couple of ancient ruins will round out your day: Monasterboice and Mellifont Abbey. This trip assumes you're visiting from Dublin.

About 45 minutes north of Dublin you'll find **Newgrange,** one of Ireland's most impressive ancient sights. The Newgrange burial mound is an enormous, well-preserved grave dating back to nearly 3,000 BC. *Info:* Entrance to the Visitors Center is just south of Slane off the N2. Tel. (041) 988-0300. Open March through November, with hours generally from 9:30am to 5pm, sometimes later (check before you visit). Admission is €5.80 for adults, less for seniors, students, and children; family tickets available.

After your time at Newgrange, drive six miles north of Drogheda on the N1 and watch for the first Dunleer exit north of Drogheda, then follow the signs to **Monasterboice**. This site offers some of the premier exhibits of finely preserved high crosses in Ireland.

 St. Buithe founded a monastery on this site during the 5th century. The site consists of the ruins of two churches, a round tower, and three high crosses. *Info:* There is no charge to visit Monasterboice. Just park your car in the small carpark across the street, and let yourself in the gate.

About eight miles south of Navan on the N3 you'll find the **Hill of Tara**. The Hill of Tara is one of the most significant historic, religious, secular, and mythical sights in Ireland. It is the ancient site of the coronation of the Celtic kings of Ireland. Atop this legendary hill is a statue of St. Patrick, and a small pillar called

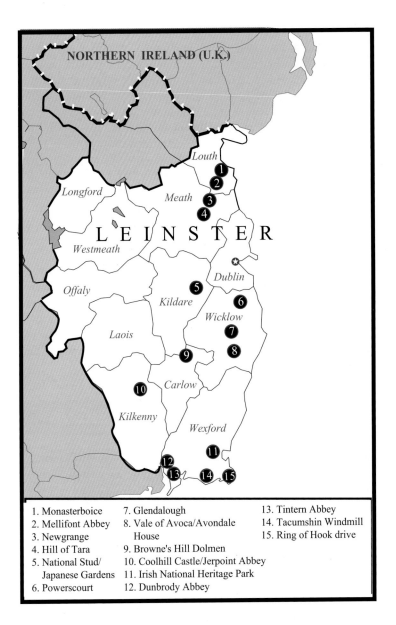

NORTHERN IRELAND (U.K.)

Longford

Louth

Meath

1
2
3
4

LEINSTER

Westmeath

Dublin

Offaly

Kildare

5

6

Wicklow

7

Laois

9

8

10

Carlow

Kilkenny

Wexford

11

12
13

14

15

1. Monasterboice
2. Mellifont Abbey
3. Newgrange
4. Hill of Tara
5. National Stud/
   Japanese Gardens
6. Powerscourt

7. Glendalough
8. Vale of Avoca/Avondale
   House
9. Browne's Hill Dolmen
10. Coolhill Castle/Jerpoint Abbey
11. Irish National Heritage Park
12. Dunbrody Abbey

13. Tintern Abbey
14. Tacumshin Windmill
15. Ring of Hook drive

Lunch Break

As you journey either to or from northern Leinster, watch for **An Sos Café** in the little town of **Castlebellingham**. This local eatery serves great food and atmosphere!

the *Lia Fial*, the stone believed to have been the ancient coronation stone for the High Kings of Ireland. Today, little else is on the Hill of Tara except grass-covered mounds and the occasional grazing sheep – the new kings of Tara. *Info:* Near Navan. Open May through September from 10am to 5pm, sometimes longer. Admission is €2 for adults, less for seniors, students, and children; family tickets are available.

To cap your day, stop in at **Mellifont Abbey**, near Tullyallen (three miles northwest of Drogheda just off the R168). Founded in 1142 by St. Malachy O'Morgair, only bits and pieces of the original buildings are still available to see, but the remains are enough to tell you it was an extensive site in its day. In fact, its Irish name *An Mhainistir Mhor*, means "The Big Monastery." Portions of the cloister still exist, along with parts of a chapter house built in the 12th century. *Info*: near Tullyallen. Tel. (041) 982-6459. Open from May through October daily from 10am to 6pm. Admission is €1.90 for adults, less for seniors, students, and children; family tickets are available.

A FANTASTIC LEINSTER WEEKEND

A fabulous evening of **traditional Irish entertainment**, ancient burial mounds and **intriguing ruins and gardens** await you on this great Leinster weekend.

Friday Evening

Head for the small town of **Howth**, northeast of Dublin, and the **Abbey Tavern**. Here you'll find a pretty good meal and a delightful traditional Irish music show. Before or after dinner, be sure and walk the short distance to the quay and walk along the seashore, enjoying a wonderful sunset over the Irish Sea. Through the years, some of my most stunning sunset photos of Ireland were taken here.

Saturday

About a 45-minute drive north of Dublin you'll find **Newgrange,** one of Ireland's most impressive ancient sights. The Newgrange burial mound is an enormous, well-preserved grave dating back to nearly 3,000 BC. During the winter solstice (December 21), rays from the sun glide down the narrow passageway gradually lighting the burial chamber. For those unable to be at Newgrange during the winter solstice, modern technology recreates the effect. Including the roundtrip drive from Dublin, a little time in the Visitors Center and time at Newgrange, you could easily spend five or six hours on this excursion. *Info:* Entrance to the Visitors Center is just south of Slane off the N2. Open March through November, with hours generally from 9:30am to 5pm, sometimes later (check before you visit). Admission is €5.80 for adults, less for seniors, students, and children; family tickets available.

Relatively close to Newgrange are two other sights you should definitely spend a few minutes perusing: the Hill of Tara and Monasterboice. About six miles north of Drogheda on the N1, watch for the first Dunleer exit north of Drogheda, then follow the signs to **Monasterboice.** It is not signed particularly well from the N1, but watch for the lonely round tower off the west side of the N1 and make your way over to it. This site offers one of the premier exhibits of finely preserved high crosses in Ireland. It is the monastic settlement of Monasterboice, which takes its name from the Irish *Mainstir Buithe,* which means "St. Buithe's Abbey."

St. Buithe founded a monastery on this site during the 5th century. The site consists of the ruins of two churches, a round tower, and three high crosses. Two of the high crosses at Monasterboice are among the best examples of high crosses in the world. One of them, the **Cross of Muiredach,** is remarkably well preserved. An inscription at the base of the cross says, "A prayer for Muiredach by whom this cross was made." This 10th-century High Cross stands almost 17 feet tall, and has scenes depicting

Adam and Eve, Cain and Abel, Christ as the Judge, and Michael weighing souls. It also contains a depiction of the crucifixion. **Tall Cross** (21 feet high) depicts the sacrifice of Isaac by Abraham, the Vigil at the Tomb, Judas' kiss of betrayal, and the crucifixion. One other cross, the **North Cross**, only partially survived the years. Scholars speculate that these crosses served more than an artistic outlet for some sculptor; they believe the crosses were used by monks to teach their non-reading followers about the scriptures. *Info:* There is no charge to visit Monasterboice. Just park your car in the small carpark across the street, and let yourself in the gate.

After examining Monasterboice, head toward Navan and the **Hill of Tara**. Eight miles south of Navan just off the N3 (watch for the signpost) is the Hill of Tara, one of the most significant historic, religious, secular, and mythical sights in Ireland. It is the ancient site of the coronation of the Celtic kings of Ireland. Atop this legendary hill is a statue of St. Patrick, and a small pillar called the *Lia Fial*, the stone believed to have been used as an ancient coronation stone. Legend has it that when the High King of Ireland (called the *Ard Ri*) was crowned at this sight, if the coronation was acceptable to the pagan gods, the Lia Fial roared mightily.

Today, little else is on the Hill of Tara except grass-covered mounds and the occasional grazing sheep – the new kings of Tara. *Info:* Near Navan. Open May through September generally from 10am to 5pm, sometimes longer. Admission is €2 for adults, less for seniors, students, and children; family tickets are available.

Sunday
For your Sunday festivities, head south of Dublin on the R117. Near Enniskerry you'll find **Powerscourt Gardens and Water-**

fall. If heaven is half as majestic as Powerscourt Gardens, I'll die a happy man! The gardens cascade in a series of terraces down a slope from the main house.

The gardens are filled with verdant greenery: sculpted shrubs, trees, and many varieties of flowering plants, set among statues, fountains, and walkways. From the top of the terraces, the views sweep across the breathtaking Dargle Valley, culminating in outstanding views of Great Sugar Loaf Mountain and Kippure Mountain. You could easily spend half a day wandering through the various gardens of Powerscourt.

Three miles south of the gardens is **Powerscourt Waterfall**. The highest waterfall in Ireland, the water cascades more than 400 feet off the edge of Djouce Mountain. It serves as a favorite picnic area for tourists and locals alike. *Info:* Enniskerry. Tel. (01) 204-6000. The gardens are open March through October daily from 9:30am until 5:30pm. Admission is €9 for adults, less for seniors, students, and children; family tickets are available. The waterfall is open all year from 9:30am until 7pm. Admission to the waterfall area is €4.50 for adults, less for seniors, students, and children; family tickets available.

From Powerscourt, head south on the R755 to the small town of Laragh where your next stop is **Glendalough – "The glen of the two lakes."** *Glen Da Locha* is perhaps one of the most serene places in the world. In the 6th century, **St. Kevin** sought refuge from the world, and founded a hermitage here. It is easy to see why. Two beautiful lakes and a number of 12th century ruins add up to a memorable visit. Be sure and spend a little time enjoying the perfectly preserved round tower and St. Kevin's Church.

Before you scout out the ruins or the scenery, start at the visitor's center and enjoy the fine audio-visual presentation on Glendalough and its history. *Info:* Near Laragh. Tel. (0404) 45325. Visitors Center open mid-March through May daily with hours generally from 9:30am to 6pm, sometimes later (check before you visit). Admission is €2.90 for adults, less for seniors, students, and children; family tickets available.

Depending on your inclination, Glendalough can take an hour or a half day. If you wish to explore all the ruins and stroll along the shores of the lakes, it will take you the better part of four hours.

Shopping Tip

Stop for a few minutes at Avoca Handweavers, reportedly the oldest handweaving mill in Ireland. Their handweaving looms produce a colorful assortment of woven garments. Visitors can purchase items that catch their eye in a small shop, as well as snag a cup of coffee and a snack before continuing your trip. *Info:* Tel. (0402) 35105. Avoca. Open Monday through Friday from 9:30am to 5:30pm, and Saturday and Sunday from 10am to 6pm.

If you just wish to see the most accessible ruins (the round tower, St Kevin's Kitchen, etc.), then your tour will take about an hour.

If you take four hours to see Glendalough, that will pretty well finish off your weekend in Leinster. If, however, you moved through it quickly, you'll have a few hours left to scope out the countryside. If that is the case, continue south on the R755 to the **Vale of Avoca**, a lush green valley immortalized by **Thomas Moore**. It was in this wooded valley, about a mile and a half north of Avoca at the point where the Avonbeg and Avonmore rivers mingle their waters and change their name to the Avoca River, that he penned the poem *The Meeting of the Waters*. Splendid nature trails wend through the heavy woods and provide a nice diversion. If you're fortunate to be here in early spring, the verdant green of the valley is punctuated with the snow-white cherry blossoms of wild cherry trees.

A WONDERFUL WEEK IN LEINSTER

A week in Leinster will provide you plenty of time to prowl at length through fascinating ruins and breathtaking gardens, like **Jerpoint Abbey, Powerscourt, Newgrange** and **Glendalough.** You'll have time for such great excursions as the **Irish National Heritage Park** and enjoy a seaside jaunt along the **Ring of Hook Drive,** where you'll see even more castles, cathedrals and ruins, in addition to the marvelous coastal beauty of this province.

RECOMMENDED PLAN: We'll work from north to south during this week in Leinster. Take two days in north Leinster and two days in central Leinster scouting out Glendalough and Powerscourt Gardens. You'll spend two days in southwest Leinster exploring sites such as Kilkenny and Coolhill castles and Jerpoint Abbey. For your remaining day, we'll explore the sights in southeast Leinster, seeing Dunbrody and Tintern abbeys, and enjoying a seaside drive and a lighthouse.

North Leinster

Start your tour of Leinster in Ballymascanlon (just north of Dundalk off the N1 and on the R173). In this small hamlet, behind the hotel of the same name, is the **Proleek Dolmen.** A *dolmen* is a simple megalithic tomb that has three or more stones that serve as pillars or pedestals for a large stone (called a capstone) that is placed on top of them. Sometimes these capstones weigh up to 100 tons. The capstone for the 5,000-year-old Proleek Dolmen *only* weighs about 50 tons!

About 20 miles south of Ballymascanlon, and just south of Slane on the N2 are the burial mounds of **Newgrange** and **Knowth**. The Newgrange mound is a well-preserved grave dating back to nearly 3,000 BC. During the winter solstice (December 21), rays from the sun glide down the narrow passageway gradually lighting the burial chamber. For those unable to be at Newgrange during the winter solstice, modern technology recreates the effect.

Don't Miss ...

- **Newgrange** – a 5,000-year-old burial mound
- **Powerscourt Gardens and Waterfall** – beautiful gardens, exquisite views
- **Hill of Tara** – mystical center of Ireland
- **Glendalough** – the ruins of a 6th-century monastic settlement
- **Jerpoint Abbey** – 12th-century Cistercian abbey
- **Ring of Hook** – a beautiful drive by the sea

The burial mound at Knowth is also impressive, though it doesn't have the dramatic winter solstice effect Newgrange offers. Both

Knowth and Newgrange offer splendid examples of ancient artistic/ritualistic craftsmanship, as the tombs are all graced with wonderful stone carvings. These are impressive reminders of ancient man's devotion to his god or gods. These were the burial sites of the ancient kings of Ireland, and are well worth a visit. *Info:* Entrance to the Visitors Center is just south of Slane off the N2. Tel. (041) 988-0300. Open March through November, with hours generally from 9:30am to 5:pm, sometimes later (check before you visit). Admission is €5.80 for adults, less for seniors, students, and children; family tickets available.

After you've completed your exploration of Newgrange and Knowth, watch for the first Dunleer exit north of Drogheda, then follow the signs to **Monasterboice**. It is not signed particularly well from the N1, but watch for the forlorn round tower off the west side of the N1 and make your way over to it. This site offers one of the premier exhibits of finely preserved high crosses in Ireland. It is the monastic settlement of Monasterboice, which takes its name from the Irish *Mainstir Buithe*, which means "St. Buithe's Abbey." St. Buithe founded a monastery on this site during the 5th century.

Two of the high crosses at Monasterboice are among the best examples of high crosses in the world. One of them, the **Cross of Muiredach**, is remarkably well preserved. This 10th-century High Cross stands almost 17 feet tall, and has scenes depicting Adam and Eve, Cain and Abel, Christ as the Judge, and Michael weighing souls. It also contains a depiction of the crucifixion. **Tall Cross** (21 feet high) depicts the sacrifice of Isaac by Abraham, the Vigil at the Tomb, Judas' kiss of betrayal, and the crucifixion. One other cross, the **North Cross**, only partially survived the years.

The forlorn round tower that keeps a silent vigil over Monasterboice is nearly 110 feet tall, even without its peaked cap, which was lost many centuries ago. There is also a six-foot tall granite sundial enclosed with a railing that is interesting to see. *Info:* There is no charge to visit Monasterboice. Just park your car in the small carpark across the street, and let yourself in the gate.

Your next stop should be **Mellifont Abbey**, near Tullyallen (three miles northwest of Drogheda just off the R168). Mellifont Abbey was founded in 1142 by St. Malachy O'Morgair. Only bits and pieces of the original buildings are still available to see, but the remains are enough to tell you it was an extensive site in its day. In fact, its Irish name *An Mhainistir Mhor*, means "The Big Monastery." Portions of the cloister still exist, along with parts of a chapter house built in the 12th century. *Info:* near Tullyallen. Tel. (041) 982-6459. Open from May through October daily from 10am to 6pm. Admission is €1.90 for adults, less for seniors, students, and children; family tickets are available.

After visiting Mellifont Abbey, head toward Navan and the **Hill of Tara**. Eight miles south of Navan just off the N3 (watch for the signpost) is the Hill of Tara, one of the most significant historic, religious, secular, and mythical sights in Ireland. It is the ancient site of the coronation of the Celtic kings of Ireland. Atop this legendary hill is a statue of St. Patrick, and a small pillar called the *Lia Fial*, the stone believed to have been used as an ancient coronation stone. Legend has it that when the High King of Ireland (called the *Ard Ri*) was crowned at this sight, if the coronation was acceptable to the pagan gods, the Lia Fial roared mightily. The pagan Celtic kings would probably roll over in their graves if they knew the statue of this zealous Christian missionary had been erected on the hill of their ancient coronations.

Today, little else is on the Hill of Tara except grass-covered mounds and the occasional grazing sheep – the new kings of Tara. *Info:* Near Navan. Open May through September generally from 10am to 5pm, sometimes longer. Admission is €2 for adults, less for seniors, students, and children; family tickets are available.

Next we'll fan out to the west of Dublin into County Kildare. Take the N2 south to the M50 (the ring road around Dublin), then further south to the N7 – watch for signs to Naas and Kildare. In Tully you'll find the **National Stud and Iron Horse Museum**. This is where breeding stallions are kept. Located with the National Stud is the Iron Horse Museum, a museum that traces equestrian history from the Bronze Age to the present. Be sure and see the skeleton of Arkle, the most famous (and winningest) Irish racehorse. Visitors to the National Stud have fairly free access to the fine horses that are stabled here. *Info:* Tully (near Kildare). Tel. (045) 521617. Open daily from 9:30am until 6pm. Admission for a combined ticket for the National Stud, Iron Horse Museum and the Japanese Gardens is €7 for adults, less for seniors, students and children. A family ticket is also available.

While in Tully be sure and stop in to see the **Japanese Gardens**. Early in the 20th century, Lord Wavertree commissioned famous Japanese landscape designer Tassa Eida to design and lay out these gardens. The results of his work are exquisite. The design symbolizes man's passage through mortality and into eternity. *Info:* Tully (near Kildare). Tel. (045) 521617. Open daily from 9:30am until 6pm. Admission for a combined ticket for the National Stud, Iron Horse Museum and the Japanese Gardens is €5 for adults, less for seniors, students and children. A family ticket is also available.

Central Leinster

Continue your journey by heading south of Dublin on the R117. Near Enniskerry you'll find **Powerscourt Gardens and Water-fall**. You've probably seen pictures of Powerscourt Gardens before – they are popular scenes used to depict the beauty of Ireland. The gardens cascade in a series of terraces down a slope from the main house. Powerscourt House was completed in 1740 for Sir Richard Wingfield, the first viscount of Powerscourt. The gardens are filled with sculpted shrubs, trees, and many varieties of flowering plants, set among statues, fountains, and walkways. Breathtaking views are a bonus. You could easily spend half a day wandering through the various gardens of Powerscourt.

Three miles south of the gardens is **Powerscourt Waterfall**. The highest waterfall in Ireland, the water cascades more than 400 feet off the edge of Djouce Mountain. It serves as a favorite picnic area for tourists and locals alike. *Info:* Enniskerry. Tel. (01) 204-6000. The gardens are open March through October daily from 9:30am until 5:30pm. Admission is €9 for adults, less for seniors, students, and children; family tickets are available. The waterfall is open all year from 9:30am until 7pm. Admission to the waterfall area is €4.50 for adults, less for seniors, students, and children; family tickets available.

Your next stop is due south down the R755 to **Glendalough** – "The glen of the two lakes." *Glen Da Locha* is perhaps one of the most serene places in the world. In the 6th century, **St. Kevin** sought refuge from the world, and founded a hermitage here. It is easy to see why. This beautiful valley is home to two lovely lakes and many ruins. The woods around Glendalough are laced with walking paths to enjoy.

The best place to begin your tour of Glendalough is at the **visitor's center**. Here they have a fine audio-visual presentation on Glendalough and its history. It will give you a feel of the area and the specific sites you want to see. Some of the more interesting ruins in Glendalough include the 6th-century *Teampaill na Skellig* (Church of the Rock), and Reefert Church. Some of the "newer" ruins include the Round Tower, St. Kevin's Kitchen and the Cathedral. All are in superb condition considering they were built in the 11th and 12th centuries. *Info:* Near Laragh. Tel. (0404) 45325. Visitors Center open mid-March through May daily from with hours generally from 9:30am to 6pm, sometimes later (check before you visit). Admission is €2.90 for adults, less for seniors, students, and children; family tickets available.

Depending on your inclination, Glendalough can take an hour or a half day (although you are shorting yourself if you take less than two hours!). If you wish to explore all the ruins and stroll along the shores of the lakes, it will take you the better part of four hours. If you just wish to see the most accessible ruins (the round tower, St. Kevin's Kitchen, etc.), then your tour will take about an hour.

Head south again on the R755 and you'll come to the **Vale of Avoca**, a lush green valley immortalized by **Thomas Moore**. It was in this wooded valley, about a mile and a half north of Avoca at the point where the Avonbeg and Avonmore rivers mingle their waters and change their name to the Avoca River, that he penned the poem *The Meeting of the Waters*. Splendid nature trails wend through the heavy woods and provide a nice diversion. If you're fortunate to be here in early spring, the beautiful green of the valley is punctuated with the snow-white cherry blossoms of wild cherry trees.

In the market for sweaters, scarves, and other hand-woven gifts? Stop in **Avoca Handweavers**, reportedly the oldest handweaving mill in Ireland. You'll learn that some of their weavers are second- and third-generation weavers. Their handweaving looms produce a colorful assortment of woven garments. Visitors can purchase items that catch their eye in a small shop, as well as snag a cup of coffee and a snack before continuing your trip. *Info:* Tel. (0402) 35105. Avoca. Open Monday through Friday from 9:30am to 5:30pm, and Saturday and Sunday from 10am to 6pm.

Just south of Rathdrum on the R755 you'll find Avondale Forest Park, the setting for **Avondale House**, birthplace and former residence of **Charles Stewart Parnell** (1846-1891). Charles was a gifted and eloquent Parliamentary speaker and untiring advocate for the cause of home rule for Ireland. Parnell's home has been meticulously restored and is a pleasure to visit. The guided tour lasts about an hour. *Info:* Tel. (0404) 46111. Open March to October daily from 11am to 6pm. Admission is €4.50 for adults, less for seniors, students and children. A family ticket is also available.

Your next stop is the **Browne's Hill Dolmen**. About two miles east of Carlow on the R725 is the largest *dolmen* in Ireland. (A dolmen is a prehistoric tomb or monument, which consists of a large flat rock resting on a series of upright smaller stones.) Located in Browne's Hill, the large rock on top was once elevated by a number of smaller stones underneath. Its weight (102 tons!), the weather, and the elements have all combined to cause one end of the capstone to drop to the ground. *Info:* In a field on the Carlow-Wexford road just outside Carlow. Admission is free.

Southwest Leinster
As you head further south in Leinster, you'll come to Kilkenny. The best sights in Kilkenny are **St. Canice's Cathedral** and **Kilkenny Castle** - be sure you don't miss them.

As you approach **Kilkenny Castle**, you'll be impressed with the lovely manicured grounds. Inside the castle, a one-hour guided tour includes visits to a number of the castle's rooms. Many of the furnishings you'll see are original to the castle. My favorite room is the library, which has a number of books that have been here for hundreds of years!

By far the most impressive room in the castle is the remarkable Long Gallery, a long hall with 60-foot ceilings. Its walls are decked out with the portraits of the Butler family - 500 years' worth! *Info:* The Parade, Kilkenny. Tel. (056) 21450. Open daily with hours generally from 9:30am to 5pm, with longer summertime hours (check before you visit). Admission is €4.50 for adults, less for seniors, students, and children; family tickets are available.

Not far from Kilkenny Castle is **St. Canice's Cathedral**, an impressive gray granite house of worship. Modeled after many of the English churches of the period (13th century), St. Canice's stands firm and straight despite the efforts of a number of plunderers, including Cromwell's forces. *Info:* Corner of Dean and Parliament Streets, Kilkenny. Tel. (046) 64971. Open

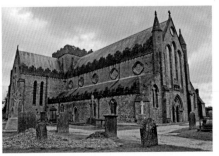

Best Out-of-the Way Castle Ruin

On the road between Kilkenny and Thomastown (the R700), watch for the signs directing you to Graiguenamanagh Abbey. Turn there, and watch for a weathered signpost directing you to **Coolhill Castle**. After several twists and turns on a very narrow single-lane road, you'll come to a grand castle. This fascinating ruin standing as a forlorn sentinel in the middle of a farmer's field is a mere shadow of its former self. But there is enough of its ancient round structure left to help you imagine what a magnificent place it must have been at one time – someone's pride and joy. Long since abandoned, the castle now stands guard over rolling fields, grazing sheep, and landscape that appears to be stitched together by a giant hand.

Monday through Saturday with hours generally from 9:30am to 6pm, and Sunday from 2pm to 6pm, although winter hours are more abbreviated (check before you visit). Admission is €2.

Southeast of Kilkenny and two miles south of Thomastown on the N9 you'll find **Jerpoint Abbey**, considered one of the finest monastic ruins in Ireland. The ruin is large - it is nearly the exact length and width of a football field. There are a series of interesting sculptures in the cloister, probably likenesses of some of the monks who served at Jerpoint Abbey. There are several interesting tombs in the church, including one of Bishop Felix O'Dulaney, whose effigy depicts a snake biting the crosier (a hooked staff, like a shepherd's crooked stick) held by the good bishop.

The small visitor's center provides a history of the monastery. The monastery is a wonderful subject for photographers - amateur as well as professional. It is impressive, and is well worth the small admission fee. *Info:* Near Thomastown. Tel. (056) 24623. Open March through November daily generally from 9:30am to 6pm, although winter hours are more abbreviated (check before you visit). Admission is €2.90 for adults, less for seniors, students, and children; family tickets are available.

Southeast Leinster

At the northern edge of Wexford you'll find the small village of Ferrycarrig, and the **Irish National Heritage Park**. This fun and educational park traces Ireland's heritage from the Stone Age through the conquest of the Anglo-Normans. Thirty acres are filled with a myriad of life-size structures - dwellings, forts, a monastery, Norman castle, etc., to give you an idea of how the ancient Irish lived, worked, and were buried. Actors in period dress answer questions and share their skills at weaving, pole lathing, and pottery through frequent demonstrations. In about two hours you'll get a good overview of about 4,000 years of Irish history. *Info*: Ferrycarrig. Tel. (053) 20733. Open March to November from 10am to 7pm (last admittance at 5pm). Admission is €7.50 for adults, less for seniors, students, and children; family tickets are available.

Pricey But Worth It!

You might consider saving your pennies to stay at one of Ireland's best hotels: **Mount Juliet**, near Thomastown. Even if you don't stay, drive through the grounds and dream of what it would be like to stay there!

Follow the signposts from Wexford toward the beautiful fishing village of Kilmore Quay (the N25 to the R739), where you'll find thatched-roof cottages and pleasant villagers. Along the way, watch for the signposts directing you to Tacumshin; follow those signs to Tacumshin, and you'll be treated to a picturesque sight - the **Tacumshin Windmill**. This old thatched windmill, reminiscent of those Holland is famous for, was built in 1846 and used until 1936. *Info*: Stop into the small store that is in front of the windmill, and the proprietor will unlock the door so you can go inside and view the inner workings of the windmill.

The word for **Kilmore Quay** is picturesque. It is a radiant little village with thatched roofs and whitewashed cottages. Sitting on a small peninsula on the Celtic Sea, the sea views are fabulous, the air is fresh, and the local villagers are warm and cheerful.

The **Ring of Hook Drive** is as peaceful a drive through the Irish countryside as you are likely to take. From Wellington Bridge, take the R733 toward Fethard-on-the-Sea. From there, follow the signs for the Ring of Hook lighthouse and the Celtic Sea. It's a great place to take plenty of pictures.

The Ring of Hook ends at **Duncannon**, just across the harbor from Waterford. At the edge of town you'll find Duncannon Fort. For many years Duncannon was a site of military importance, particularly as protection against marauding ships of (take your choice) Vikings, Anglo-Normans, Irish rebels, the Spanish Armada, Napoleon's navy, etc. *Info*: Duncannon. Tel. (051) 389454, (051) 389188. Open daily June through September from 10am to 5:30pm. Admission is €4 for adults, less for seniors, students, and children; family tickets are available.

Between Arthurstown and Wellington Bridge you'll find the ruins of **Tintern Abbey.** A plaque on the site says, "Founded in 1200 by William Earl Marshall. This abbey was called 'Tintern de Voto' after Tintern Abbey in Wales, from where its monks came." The abbey is largely intact, and has recently undergone extensive renovation. The remains consist of a vaulted chapel, nave, tower, and chancel. *Info*: Open mid-June through late September daily from 9:30am to 6:30pm. Admission is €2.10 for adults, less for seniors, students, and children; family tickets are available.

Little **Ballyhack** sits at the mouth of Waterford Harbor on the R733. Very popular with artists and photographers, this stereotypical Irish fishing village offers plenty to paint, sketch, or photograph: fishing boats, old **Ballyhack Castle**, and the assorted local residents, full of character. Ballyhack Castle originally belonged to the Knights Templar; today its ivy-covered and weathered rock walls keep watch over the harbor. A €5 car ferry will take you across the harbor to another picturesque Irish fishing village in County Waterford: **Passage East**, which competes with Ballyhack for its share of photographers and artists. It's a nice competition - everybody wins.

Three miles north of Ballyhack on the R733 are the imposing ruins of **Dunbrody Abbey** and **Dunbrody Castle.** The Abbey was built in the late 12th century, and the castle (adjacent to the Abbey) is of similar vintage. The ruins are set back from the main road about 150 yards, and on sunny days especially, it makes for marvelous pictures. Sitting next to the peacefully flowing Barrow River, the Abbey must have been a wonderfully serene setting for its former inhabitants to do whatever it was they did at the Abbey.

Stop in at the small visitor's center across the street from the ruins. It encompasses a museum, tearoom, and gift shop. *Info*: near Campile. Tel. (051) 88603. Visitor center open May through September Monday through Friday from 10am to 6pm, Saturday and Sunday 10am to 8pm. Admission is €2 for adults, less for seniors, students, and children; family tickets are available.

Two Weeks in Leinster & Dublin
If you have two weeks to spend in the eastern portion of Ireland, I'd suggest beginning in Dublin. Do not rent a car for the period of time you are seeing Dublin City sights – save yourself the aggravation of trying to drive in Dublin and the cost of your rental car. Now put together the one week in Dublin plan from chapter 3, and the one-week plan for Leinster above, and you're all set!

5. MUNSTER

By far, the most famous sights you'll find in Munster are **Blarney Castle** and **Blarney Stone**, and they are a must if you come to this part of Ireland. However, they are not all Munster has to offer. Close behind Blarney in the hearts and minds of tourists is little **Killarney**, a gem set in the mountains of southwest Munster. While in Killarney, you'll definitely want to reserve a day to tour the scenic and majestic **Dingle Peninsula**, jutting out into the Atlantic Ocean. And just a little further north you'll find the steepest cliffs in Europe – the breathtaking **Cliffs of Moher**.

In the middle of Munster, you'll find such rich treasures as the spectacular ruins of the **Rock of Cashel** and the 12th-century **Cahir Castle**. If your tastes are more for culture and elegance, then don't miss the refined and beautiful **Waterford Crystal Factory** in Waterford.

ONE GREAT DAY IN MUNSTER

Munster is the largest of Ireland's provinces, and has the most to see. I will provide several one-day and weekend recommendations in this chapter so you can perfectly target what you'd like to do. This first one-day itinerary takes you to one of Ireland's most popular tourist destinations: **Killarney**.

Start your tour of Killarney at **Ross Castle**. Ross Castle is about one and a half miles from the town center. As you head out of town towards Muckross House, watch for the signpost directing you to Ross Castle. Turn right and continue a mile or so until you reach the castle. Ross Castle sits along the shores of Lough Leanne, and is one of the finest examples of 14th-century castles in Ireland. A 40-minute tour takes you into the rooms that have been restored to their former (austere) beauty. While none of the furnishings is original to the castle, the own-ers have tried very hard to furnish the castle in period furnishings. *Info*: Ross Road. Tel. (064) 35851. Open daily generally from 10am to 6pm, closing a little ear-lier in early spring and winter (check before

visiting). Admission is €5.30 for adults, less for seniors, students, and children; family tickets are available.

From Ross Castle, get on the N71 and head for **Muckross House and Gardens**. This beautiful Victorian mansion was built for a Member of the British Parliament over 150 years ago. As impres-sive as the house is, I feel the gardens and estate are the real selling points for this attraction. In the courtyard in front of the house you'll find a number of jaunting car drivers anxious to show you

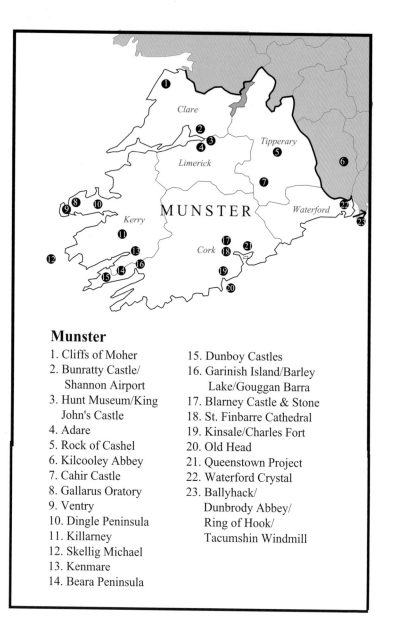

Munster

1. Cliffs of Moher
2. Bunratty Castle/
   Shannon Airport
3. Hunt Museum/King
   John's Castle
4. Adare
5. Rock of Cashel
6. Kilcooley Abbey
7. Cahir Castle
8. Gallarus Oratory
9. Ventry
10. Dingle Peninsula
11. Killarney
12. Skellig Michael
13. Kenmare
14. Beara Peninsula

15. Dunboy Castles
16. Garinish Island/Barley
    Lake/Gouggan Barra
17. Blarney Castle & Stone
18. St. Finbarre Cathedral
19. Kinsale/Charles Fort
20. Old Head
21. Queenstown Project
22. Waterford Crystal
23. Ballyhack/
    Dunbrody Abbey/
    Ring of Hook/
    Tacumshin Windmill

the beauties of the Muckross estate during a leisurely horse-drawn carriage ride.

Also located on the Muckross House estate is the **Muckross Traditional Farms**. These three working farms display a representation of the lifestyles of the rural Kerry folk before the advent of electricity. In addition to actors in period dress performing a bevy of old crafts and chores, there are ducks, chickens, and a variety of other farm animals. *Info*: N71, Killarney. Tel. (064) 3 1440. Open daily with hours generally from 9am to 6pm, sometimes later during the summer (check before you visit). Admission for adults is €5.75 for either sight, or a combined ticket is €8.65 for adults, less for seniors, students, and children; family tickets are available.

From Muckross, head southwest on the N71 on a portion of the **Ring of Kerry**. Shortly after you leave Muckross House, you'll see a sign for **Torc Waterfall** and a small parking area. A few minutes' walk from your car brings you to a splendid waterfall.

ALTERNATIVE PLAN
If hiking up to the Torc Waterfall isn't your cup o' tea, watch for signs directing you to **Kenmare**, a very picturesque town. Walk among the multicolored shops, pubs and restaurants to get a flavor of this corner of southwest Ireland. Stop by **Black Abbey Crafts** on Main Street for an enchanting and surprising collection of crafts, or pop into **Quill's** for that bit of Irish fashion you've been wanting.

Back on the Ring of Kerry, within a few minutes you will come to **Ladies' View**, an area of wonderful views back toward Killarney. During the latter part of the nineteenth century, Queen Victoria was a frequent visitor to the Killarney area. This spot on the Ring of Kerry was a point where her Ladies in Waiting often stopped to stretch their legs and see the views on their trips into the countryside.

A few miles further along the Ring of Kerry you'll come to signs directing you to **Staigue Fort**, an impressive (and largely intact) circle fort dating from the Iron Age. Archaeologists estimate its age at roughly 2,500 years old. The fort is a massive circular structure whose walls are 13 feet thick at the base and nearly seven feet thick at the top. *Info*: Castlecove off the N70. Open year-round. Admission is €1 donation in an honor box (you're on your honor to contribute!).

After your visit to Killarney and the areas round about it, stop in at **The Bricín Restaurant** on High Street in Killarney. This marvelous restaurant oozes class and elegance, and is a most pleasant place to relax, dine, and review your day's activities.

ANOTHER GREAT DAY IN MUNSTER

This day trip takes you to several of Ireland's best-known ruins: **Blarney Castle** and the **Rock of Cashel,** with a few fun stops in between.

Five miles north of Cork City is the town of Blarney and its famous stone. **Blarney Stone** is located atop an ancient castle keep underneath its battlements. To kiss the stone – which legend says grants the kisser the gift of *blarney* (flattery) – you'll traverse 120-ish steps up a spiral staircase. *Info*: Blarney. Tel. (021) 438-5252. Open Monday through Friday, with hours generally from 9am to 6:30pm, sometimes later (check before you visit). They are also open year round on Sunday from 9:30am to 5:30pm. Admission is €8 for adults, less for seniors, students, and children; family tickets are available. (Children under 8 are free).

From Blarney, head northeast on the N8 to the market town of Cahir (pronounced "Care") and the 12th-century **Cahir Castle.** You can readily see how its picturesque setting and imposing presence must have been awe-inspiring in its day. The castle is well worth an hour of so of your time to stop and explore. *Info*: Cahir Town. Tel. (052) 41011. Open daily with hours generally from 9:30am to 5:30pm, although hours vary slightly throughout the year (check before you visit). Admission is €2.90 for adults, less for seniors, students, and children; family tickets are available.

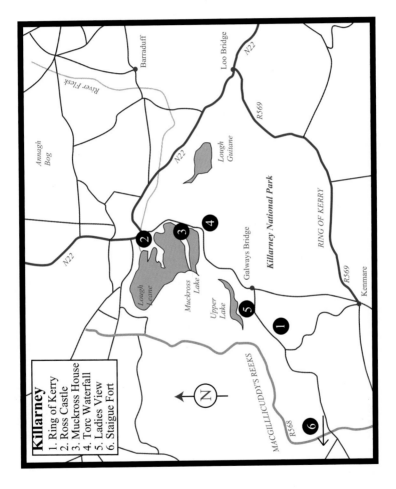

Killarney
1. Ring of Kerry
2. Ross Castle
3. Muckross House
4. Torc Waterfall
5. Ladies View
6. Staigue Fort

From Cahir, continue on the N8 and it's a short ride to the **Rock of Cashel**. These ruins are amazingly well preserved, and the visitors' center at the foot of the Rock of Cashel is informative. Incredible views of the surrounding Tipperary plains await visitors to the site. *Info*: Cahir. Tel. (062) 61437. Open daily with hours generally from 9:30am to 5:30pm, although they close a little later in the summer and a little earlier in the winter (check before you visit). Admission is €5.30 for adults, less for seniors, students, and children; family tickets are available.

If you've worked up an appetite with your sightseeing, stop in at **Legends Restaurant** at the foot of the Rock of Cashel. Most of the tables have stunning views of the ruins, and the food's good too!

From Cashel, take the N8 northeast for about 25 minutes toward Urlingford. Once there, take the R689 south to **Kilcooley Abbey**. A sister abbey to Jerpoint Abbey near Thomastown, these ruins offer an intriguing sight to be prowled through. The abbey is a treasure-trove of sculptural prizes. *Info*: near Urlingford.

A FINAL GREAT DAY IN MUNSTER!

Your final one-day itinerary in Munster starts out in the southeastern town of Waterford, and its world-renowned **Waterford Crystal Factory**. While you're in this part of Ireland, I'd suggest two jaunts from Waterford: a gorgeous **seaside drive** along the southeastern tip of Ireland, and a visit to a **lighthouse and several ancient ruins**.

Your final one-day itinerary in Munster starts out in the south-eastern town of Waterford, and its world-renowned **Waterford Crystal Factory**. The factory includes an extensive showroom
and an hour-long tour that will  change the way you look at lead crystal for the rest of your life. You'll easily spend several hours here. *Info*: Cork Road, Waterford. Tel. (051) 875788. Open daily with hours generally from 8:30am to 5pm. Admission is a little steep (but well worth it) at €9 for adults, less for seniors, students, and children; family tickets are available.

Sharing the harbor with Waterford are two photographers' havens: the tiny, photogenic villages of **Passage East** and **Ballyhack**. A short ferry ride will set you back €5 to cross the harbor between the towns. Just a few miles north of Ballyhack on the R733 are the imposing ruins of **Dunbrody Abbey** and **Dunbrody Castle**. The Abbey was built in the late 12th century, and the castle (adjacent to the Abbey) is of similar vintage. Stop in at the small visitor's center across the street from the ruins. *Info*: near Campile. Tel. (051) 88603. Visitor center open May through September Monday through Friday from 10am to 6pm, Saturday and Sunday 10am to 8pm. Admission is €2 for adults, less for seniors, students, and children; family tickets are available.

From Dunbrody, backtrack toward Ballyhack. At Arthurstown, head south toward Fethard-on-the-Sea. From here you are well on your way toward the **Ring of Hook Drive**. In a country of inspiring sights, this is undoubtedly as peaceful a drive through the Irish countryside as you are likely to take. Follow the signs for the Ring of Hook lighthouse and the Celtic Sea. It's a great place to take plenty of pictures, especially of the lighthouse at the edge of the crashing sea.

After you've enjoyed the lighthouse, head north to the R733, then east to the R736 and south on the R756. Slow down as you pass through the beautiful fishing village of Kilmore Quay, where you'll find thatched-roof cottages and pleasant villagers. Nearby, watch for signposts directing you to Tacumshin; follow those signs and you'll be treated to a picturesque sight — the **Tacumshin Windmill**. This old thatched windmill, reminiscent of those Holland is famous for, was built in 1846 and used until 1936. *Info:* Stop into the small store that is in front of the windmill, and the proprietor will unlock the door so you can go inside and view the inner workings of the windmill.

A FANTASTIC MUNSTER WEEKEND

A fabulous evening of **medieval dining**, and visits to some of the **highest cliffs in Europe**, a famous stone, picturesque ruins and a seaside drive highlight this marvelous weekend trip.

Friday Evening
You're in for a treat on this evening as you dine at the medieval banquet at **Bunratty Castle**, located on the N18 west of Limerick. Period costumes, traditional Irish songs, harp music, and lots of fun are in store for you. This may end up being one of the favorite memories of your Irish vacation. *Info:* Bunratty Castle, N18 near

Limerick. Tel. (061) 360788. The banquet is held twice nightly throughout the year, at 5:30pm and 8:45pm. The late banquet usually fills up first. Prices for the banquet are €52 for all. Children 5 and under dine free.

Saturday

Get started early and head straight for the dramatic **Cliffs of Moher**, which run along the coast for about five miles. One route is to take the N18 west through Ennis, then head northwest on the N85 to Ennistymon. From there, follow the R478 to the Cliffs of Moher. These sea cliffs have awed, intrigued, and astounded visitors and locals alike for centuries with their 700-foot drops to the sea. Superlatives escape me to adequately describe the breathtaking views that await you at these wonders of nature.

You simply must experience them for yourself. The Irish name for the cliffs is *Aillte an Mhothair*, which means "Cliffs of Ruin." *Info:* Visitors Center is open daily from 9:30am until 5:30pm (9am to 8pm during the summer). Admission is free, although the carpark costs €5.

Head southeast from the Cliffs of Moher toward Limerick, then southeast on the N24 towards Cahir (pronounced "Care") and **Cahir Castle,** one of the most recognized castles in the world since it has been used as a setting for several medieval movies (including *Excalibur*). Built in 1142, the castle sits on a rocky outcropping of the River Suir. You can readily see how its picturesque setting and imposing presence must have been awe-inspiring in its day. Strong walls and turrets, a protective moat, and trained archers would have made this an impregnable fortress indeed. The castle features a massive square keep, spacious internal courtyards, and a wonderful "Great Hall." The castle is well worth an hour of so of your time to stop and explore. *Info:* Cahir Town. Tel. (052) 41011. Open daily with hours generally from 9:30am to 5:30pm, although hours vary slightly throughout the year (check before you visit). Admission is €2.90 for adults, less for seniors, students, and children; family tickets are available.

While in Cahir, if you are a fan of antiques from the 17th through 20th centuries, stop by **Fleury Antiques** in the main town square. It is sort of like visiting an exquisite museum where you can take pieces home if you are willing to pay the price. *Info*: The Square, Cahir. Tel. (052) 41226.

From Cahir, it's a short ride northeast on the N8 to the **Rock of Cashel**. Save plenty of film for one of the most awe-inspiring sites in Ireland. The setting for this chapel/round tower/cathedral is on a mound towering some 200 feet above the surrounding plains. The ruins are amazingly well preserved, and the visitors' center at the foot of the Rock of Cashel is informative. Whether you experience bright sunshine, a dull day or a bit of rain while at the Rock of Cashel, it is still well worth the visit. I find that the lowering clouds give the ruins a bit of a mysterious and brooding quality. So regardless of the weather, visit this important and awe-filled site. Incredible views of the surrounding Tipperary plains await visitors to the site. *Info*: Cahir. Tel. (062) 61437. Open daily with hours generally from 9:30am to 5:30pm, although they close a little later in the summer and a little earlier in the winter (check before you visit). Admission is €5.30 for adults, less for seniors, students, and children; family tickets are available.

Backtrack a bit through Cahir on the N8. At Fermoy, take the N72 east to Mallow, then south on the N20 to your next stop: **Blarney Castle** and **Blarney Stone**. Before my first visit to Ireland, I had no idea the Blarney *Stone* was part of Blarney *Castle*. The famous

stone is located atop the ancient keep underneath its battlements. To kiss the stone – which legend says grants the kisser the gift of *blarney* (flattery) – you lay on your back and slide down and under the battlements. One hundred and twenty-ish steps up a spiral staircase will precede your kiss of the Blarney Stone. Stop and spend some time on the grounds in the various gardens and walks – they may well be as memorable as your kiss of the Blarney Stone. *Info*: Blarney. Tel. (021) 438-5252. Open Monday through Friday, with hours generally from 9am to 6:30pm, sometimes later (check before you visit). They are also open year round on Sunday from 9:30am to 5:30pm. Admission is €8 for adults, less for seniors, students, and children; family tickets are available. (Children under 8 are free).

Lodging Tip

Stop in at **Claragh B&B** just outside of Blarney for a delightful Irish hostess and a comfortable B&B (Tel. (021) 488-6308, Waterloo Road).

Sunday

Your next stop is Waterford and its world-renowned **Waterford Crystal Factory**. To get there from Blarney, take the N24 south toward Cork, then hop on the N25 to Waterford City. You have probably come to associate the name *Waterford* with excellence, quality, and exquisite beauty. Now you have the opportunity to see first-hand how they earned this reputation for quality. The crystal factory includes an extensive showroom and an hour-long tour that will change the way you look at lead crystal for the rest of your life. Several years ago, Waterford Crystal was commissioned to create the trophy for the Super Bowl winners; a replica of the trophy is on display, and it is incredible. You'll easily spend several hours here. *Info*: Cork Road, Waterford. Tel. (051) 875788. Open daily with hours generally from 8:30am to 5pm. Admission is a little steep (but well worth it) at €9 for adults, less for seniors, students, and children; family tickets are available.

While you're in this part of Ireland, I'd suggest two jaunts from Waterford: a seaside drive along the southeastern tip of Ireland, and a visit to a lighthouse and several ancient ruins.

Sharing the harbor with Waterford are two photographers' havens: the tiny, photogenic villages of **Passage East** and **Ballyhack**. A short ferry ride will set you back €5 to cross the harbor between the towns. Just a few miles north of Ballyhack on the R733 are the imposing ruins of **Dunbrody Abbey** and **Dunbrody Castle**. The Abbey was built in the late 12th century, and the castle (adjacent to the Abbey) is of similar vintage. Stop in at the small visitor's center across the street from the ruins. *Info*: near Campile. Tel. (051) 88603. Visitor center open May through September Monday through Friday from 10am to 6pm, Saturday and Sunday 10am to 8pm. Admission is €2 for adults, less for seniors, students, and children; family tickets are available.

From Dunbrody, backtrack toward Ballyhack. At Arthurstown, head south toward Fethard-on-the-Sea. From here you are well on your way toward The **Ring of Hook Drive.** In a country of inspiring sights, this is undoubtedly as peaceful a drive through the Irish countryside as you are likely to take. Follow the signs for the **Ring of Hook lighthouse** and the Celtic Sea. It's a great place to take plenty of pictures, especially of the lighthouse at the edge of the crashing sea.

After you've enjoyed the lighthouse, head north to the R733, then east to the R736 and south on the R756. Slow down as you pass through the beautiful fishing village of Kilmore Quay, where you'll find thatched-roof cottages and pleasant villagers. Nearby, watch for signposts directing you to Tacumshin; follow those signs and you'll be treated to a picturesque sight — the **Tacumshin Windmill.** This old thatched windmill, reminiscent of those Holland is famous for, was built in 1846 and used until 1936. *Info*: Stop into the small store that is in front of the windmill, and the proprietor will unlock the door so you can go inside and view the inner workings of the windmill.

ANOTHER FANTASTIC MUNSTER WEEKEND

Not to be outdone by the previous Munster weekend, this trip will provide a lovely peninsular drive around the **Dingle Peninsula**, ancient ruins and some of Ireland's best scenery.

Friday Evening

Begin your weekend with dinner in the **Earl of Thomond Room** at **Dromoland Castle** (on the N18 between Limerick and Ennis). High ceilings, rich dark wood, gorgeous crystal chandeliers, crisp starched linen tablecloths, gleaming china, and an Irish harpist, singer or fiddler all contribute to an elegant and opulent dining experience. As you dine, the watchful eyes of the former Lords and Ladies of the castle gaze down at you from larger-than-life-size portraits spread around the room.

Once you have finished dining, walk among the park-like grounds of Dromoland Castle, then turn in for the night in your room at this 15th-century hotel.

Saturday

Today we'll explore the beauties of the **Dingle Peninsula**. This lovely isthmus into the Atlantic merely offers some of the most exquisite landscapes on the Emerald Isle. Be sure and have plenty of film, because you'll want to use it. Whether a bright sunny day or a day cloaked in mist and mystery, visiting this awesome peninsula is a great way to spend a day or a whole weekend.

From Limerick, take the N21 southwest towards Killarney. Along the way, slow down in the village of Adare and admire its simple beauty. Several ruins along the roadside enhance your trip.

As you approach Castleisland, take the N23 toward Killarney. At Farranfore, watch for signs to the Dingle Peninsula and Castlemaine – you'll now be on the R561. There are numerous interesting villages to stop in, countless landscapes and seascapes to photograph, and a lot of beauty to take in, so you'll want to set aside

"Gaeltacht" Advice

A word to the wise: in the *Gaeltacht* (Irish-speaking) areas of Ireland like the Dingle Peninsula, many signs, including those on the doors of rest rooms, may only be marked in Irish. If you guess, you'll probably guess wrong: *Mná* is for women, and *Fir* is for men. Take heed, lest you experience more of Ireland than you intend!

plenty of time. A full day will allow you the time to see this stunning area without feeling rushed.

Your first stop during your tour of the Dingle Peninsula is little **Dingle** itself - signposted in Irish as *An Daingean* (O'Cush's Fortress). Dingle is located on the southern coast of the Dingle Peninsula on the N86. The shops are inviting, so take a few minutes to stroll about. Be sure and visit the **Cearolann Craft Village**, where you can purchase silver, leather, knitted goods, and many other Irish crafts. For €8 you can also ride out into the harbor to see a popular local tourist attraction – Fungi, the Dingle Dolphin.

Between Ballyferriter and Ballydavid, watch for signposts directing you to **Gallarus Oratory**, and there you'll find an incredibly well-preserved church – one of the earliest in Irish history. The mortar-free masonry has been watertight for over 1,000 years. The inside of the church is about 10 feet by 15 feet. *Info*: Ballydavid. Tel. (66) 915-5333. Open daily.

Connor Pass is a thrilling and beautiful mountainous drive. Be sure and stop at the carpark at the apex of the pass and check out the views. Whether you're looking toward Tralee or back toward Dingle, the views are incredible.

Sunday

Start your Sunday morning in Killarney at **Ross Castle**. A 40-minute tour takes you into the rooms that have been restored to their former (austere) beauty. While none of the furnishings is original to the castle, the owners have tried very hard to furnish the castle in period furnishings. *Info*: Ross Road. Tel. (064) 35851. Open daily generally from 10am to 6pm, closing a little earlier in early spring and winter (check before visiting). Admission is €5.30 for adults, less for seniors, students, and children; family tickets are available.

From Ross Castle, get on the N71 and head for **Muckross House and Gardens**. This beautiful Victorian mansion was built for a Member of the British Parliament over 150 years ago. As impressive as the house is, the gardens and estate are the real selling points here. In the courtyard in front of the house you'll find a number of jaunting car drivers anxious to show you the beauties of the Muckross estate during a leisurely horse-drawn carriage ride.

Also located on the Muckross House estate is the **Muckross Traditional Farms**. These three working farms display a representation of the lifestyles of the rural Kerry folk before the advent of electricity. In addition to actors in period dress performing a bevy of old crafts and chores, there are ducks, chickens, and a variety of other farm animals. *Info*: N71, Killarney. Tel. (064) 3 1440. Open daily with hours generally from 9am to 6pm, sometimes

later during the summer (check before you visit). Admission for adults is €5.75 for either sight, or a combined ticket is €8.65 for adults, less for seniors, students, and children; family tickets are available.

From Muckross, head southwest on the N71 on a portion of the **Ring of Kerry**. Shortly after you leave Muckross House, you'll see a sign for **Torc Waterfall** and a small parking area. A few minutes' walk from your car brings you to a splendid waterfall. The water that comes crashing over the 60-foot cliff comes there innocently enough from a small lake called the **Devil's Punchbowl**. Admire the waterfall, then take the path that ascends higher up the mountain. About 15 minutes higher up the mountain and you are treated to stunning panoramic views of the Lakes of Killarney.

Take a shopping break, if you're so inclined, in **Kenmare** (watch for signs directing you to Kenmare), one of Ireland's more picturesque towns. Walk among the multi-colored shops, pubs and restaurants to get a flavor of this corner of southwest Ireland. Stop by **Black Abbey Crafts** on Main Street for an enchanting and surprising collection of crafts, or pop into **Quill's** for that bit of Irish fashion you've been wanting.

Back on the Ring of Kerry, within a few minutes you will come to **Ladies' View**, an area of wonderful views back toward Killarney. During the latter part of the nineteenth century, Queen Victoria was a frequent visitor to the Killarney area. This spot on the Ring of Kerry was a point where her Ladies in Waiting often stopped to stretch their legs and see the views on their trips into the countryside.

A few miles further along the Ring of Kerry and you'll come to signs directing you to **Staigue Fort**, an impressive (and largely intact) circle fort dating from the Iron Age. Archaeologists estimate its age at roughly 2,500 years old. The fort is a massive circular structure whose walls are 13 feet thick at the base and nearly seven feet thick at the top. *Info*: Castlecove off the N70. Open year-round. Admission is €1 donation in an honor box (you're on your honor to contribute!).

Hungry? Stop in at **The Bricín Restaurant** on High Street in Killarney. This marvelous restaurant oozes class and elegance.

A WONDERFUL WEEK IN MUNSTER

A week in Munster will allow you to see some of Ireland's top tourist destinations, from Blarney Stone to the Waterford Crystal Factory, with the Rock of Cashel and other beautiful sights and shopping in between.

RECOMMENDED PLAN: We'll start in northwest Munster and spend a day viewing the tallest sea cliffs in Europe, several castles and the wonderful museum in Limerick. Your next day will be spent exploring the scenic Dingle Peninsula. From there, you'll spend a couple of days exploring Killarney, Blarney and Cashel. You'll end your week with several days in southeast Munster seeing castles, ruins and plenty of seascapes.

Northwest Munster

Let's start your week in Munster by heading up to the **Cliffs of Moher**. One route is to take the N18 west through Ennis, then head northwest on the N85 to Ennistymon. From there, follow the R478 to the Cliffs of Moher. These sea cliffs have awed, intrigued, and astounded visitors and locals alike for centuries with their 700-foot drops to the sea. Superlatives escape me to adequately describe the breathtaking views that await you at these wonders of nature. You simply must experience them for yourself. The Irish name for the cliffs is *Aillte an Mhothair*, which means "Cliffs of Ruin."

Stop at the visitors' center, where you'll learn a little of the history of the area, and they will give you information on the best cliff-side walks available. Take time for them - they will provide some of your favorite memories of the Emerald Isle. If you'll walk beyond O'Brien's Tower (a small gift shop at the edge of the Cliffs), you'll see some additional beautiful views. If the weather cooperates, you can see the Aran Islands. *Info*: Visitors Center is open daily

Don't Miss ...

- **Cliffs of Moher** – 700 reasons to see these cliffs
- **Dingle Peninsula** – beautiful sights
- **Blarney Stone** – you have to see it!
- **Rock of Cashel** – picturesque ruin
- **Kilkenny Castle** – well-preserved ancient castle
- **Waterford Crystal Factory** – you'll never look at lead crystal the same

from 9:30am until 5:30pm (9am to 8pm during the summer). Admission is free, although the carpark costs €5.

Head back toward Limerick on the N18. Along the way, stop in at **Bunratty Folk Park**. Adjacent to Bunratty Castle is the Bunratty Folk Park. The Folk Park is a wonderful recreation of 19th-century Ireland complete with artisans replicating the various vocations of that time period: candle makers, blacksmiths, millers, basket weavers, etc. It's a lot of fun and very informative. *Info*: on the N18. Tel. (061) 361511. Generally open 9:30am to 6:30pm, shorter during the winter. Admission is €9.50 for adults, less for seniors, students, and children; family tickets are available.

As you enter Limerick from the N18, one of the most prominent sights you'll see is the 13th-century **King John's Castle** on the Shannon River. Head for it, and enjoy the short but informative slide show about the history of Limerick. Following that is a short tour of the castle. There's not much to go into, mostly just the outside walls remain. *Info*: corner of Castle Street and The Parade, Limerick. Tel. (061) 411201. Open daily with hours generally from 9:30am to 5:30pm, though they close earlier in the winter (check before you visit). Admission is €7.50 for adults, less for seniors, students, and children; family tickets are available.

From St. John's, head south a few blocks on Nicholas Street and turn right on Patrick Street. A block or so on your left is the **Hunt Museum Collection**. The most impressive exhibit here is that of Celtic and medieval treasures. Be sure to check out the silver coin they have on display there - legend has it that this little piece of silver was one of

Bunratty Banquet Fun!

Create some lasting memories by **dining medieval-style at Bunratty Castle**. Period costumes, traditional Irish songs, harp music, and lots of fun are in store. You'll be greeted in the main reception hall by the Lord of the castle, and all guests are served honey mead – a fruity wine – or a non-alcoholic fruit drink if you prefer. Then off to the banquet hall where you'll be serenaded by lovely Irish lads and lasses while you dine, sans silverware except for a knife, on a meal similar to what the original Lord of the castle would have eaten. *Info*: Prices for the banquet are €52 for all. Children 5 and under dine free.

30 used as payment for betraying a certain Jewish carpenter/ preacher about 2,000 years ago. *Info*: Patrick Street. Tel. (061) 312833. Open Monday through Saturday from 10am to 5pm, Sunday from 2pm to 5pm. Admission is €6.50 for adults, less for seniors, students, and children; family tickets are available.

Dingle Peninsula

From Limerick, take the N21 southwest towards Killarney. Along the way, slow down in the village of Adare and admire its simple beauty. Several ruins along the roadside enhance your trip.

As you approach Castleisland, take the N23 toward Killarney. At Farranfore, watch for signs to the **Dingle Peninsula** and **Castlemaine** – you'll now be on the R561. The drive around the peninsula is a mere 100 miles. But don't think you can drive it in two hours. The roads, especially along the coastline, are exceptionally narrow and winding. And with numerous interesting villages to stop in, countless landscapes and seascapes to photograph, and a lot of beauty to take in, you'll want to set aside plenty of time. A full day will allow you the time to see this stunning area without feeling rushed.

Your first stop during your tour of the Dingle Peninsula is little **Dingle** itself – signposted in Irish as *An Daingean* (O'Cush's Fortress). Dingle is located on the southern coast of the Dingle Peninsula on the N86. The shops are inviting, so take a few minutes to stroll about. Be sure and visit the **Cearolann Craft Village**, where you can purchase silver, leather, knitted goods, and many other Irish crafts. For €8 you can also ride out into the harbor to see a popular local tourist attraction – Fungi, the Dingle Dolphin.

As you head further out on the Dingle Peninsula, you'll come to **Ventry**, whose fine sandy beaches are the main attraction. **Slea Head** has the honor of being the westernmost edge of Europe. Staggering views of the Atlantic Ocean, with the Blasket Islands in the foreground, await those who stop to gaze, gape, and click their shutters.

Between Ballyferriter and Ballydavid, watch for signposts directing you to **Gallarus Oratory**, and there you'll find an incredibly well-preserved church - one of the earliest in Irish history. The mortar-free masonry has been watertight for over 1,000 years. The inside of the church is about 10 feet by 15 feet. *Info*: Ballydavid. Tel. (66) 915-5333. Open daily.

Connor Pass is a thrilling and beautiful mountainous drive. Be sure and stop at the carpark at the apex of the pass and check out the views. Whether you're looking toward Tralee or back toward Dingle, the views are incredible. Wrap up your Dingle drive by heading into Killarney. Stop in at **Bricín Restaurant** for a nice meal and bed down at **Earls Court**.

Killarney, Blarney & Cashel

This plan can be called "Rings, Stones and Rocks." Your next stop is Killarney. Work your way east to the N22 and head south. Your first stop in Killarney should be **Ross Castle**. Ross Castle sits along the shores of Lough Leanne, and is one of the finest examples of 14th-century castles in Ireland. It was built in the early 15th-century by the O'Donoghue Clan. By the mid-1970s, the castle was a crumbling, ivy-covered hulk. A small exhibition centre shows photographs of the castle prior to its restoration in the mid-1970s. A 40-minute tour takes you into the rooms that have been restored to their former (austere) beauty. While none of the furnishings is original to the castle, the owners have tried very hard to furnish the castle in period furnishings.

The tour is well worth the time and the cost of admission. *Info*: Ross Road. Tel. (064) 35851. Open daily generally from 10am to 6pm, closing a little earlier in early spring and winter (check before visiting). Admission is €5.30 for adults, less for seniors, students, and children; family tickets are available.

From Ross Castle, get on the N71 and head for **Muckross House and Gardens**. This beautiful Victorian mansion was built for a Member of the British Parliament over 150 years ago. As impressive as the house is, I feel the gardens and estate are the real selling points for this attraction. In the courtyard in front of the house you'll find a number of jaunting car drivers anxious to show you the beauties of the Muckross estate during a leisurely horse-drawn carriage ride.

Also located on the Muckross House estate is the **Muckross Traditional Farms**. These three working farms display a representation of the lifestyles of the rural Kerry folk before the advent of electricity. In addition to actors in period dress performing a bevy of old crafts and chores, there are ducks, chickens, and a variety of other farm animals. *Info*: N71, Killarney. Tel. (064) 3 1440. Open daily with hours generally from 9am to 6pm, sometimes later during the summer (check before you visit). Admission for adults is €5.75 for either sight, or a combined ticket is €8.65 for adults, less for seniors, students, and children; family tickets are available.

From Muckross, head southwest on the N71 on a portion of the **Ring of Kerry**. Shortly after you leave Muckross House, you'll see a sign for **Torc Waterfall** and a small parking area. A few minutes' walk from your car brings you to a splendid waterfall. The water that comes crashing over the 60-foot cliff comes there innocently enough from a small lake called the Devil's Punchbowl. Admire the waterfall, then take the path that ascends higher up the mountain. About 15 minutes higher up the mountain and you are treated to stunning panoramic views of the Lakes of Killarney.

You have to bring back some gifts for yourself and your loved ones, right? Walk among the multi-colored shops, pubs and restaurants in **Kenmare** get a flavor of this corner of southwest Ireland. Stop by **Black Abbey Crafts** on Main Street for an enchanting and surprising collection of crafts, or pop into **Quill's** for some Irish fashion.

Back on the Ring of Kerry, within a few minutes you will come to **Ladies' View**, an area of wonderful views back toward Killarney. During the latter part of the nineteenth century, Queen Victoria was a frequent visitor to the Killarney area. This spot on the Ring of Kerry was a point where her Ladies in Waiting often stopped to stretch their legs and see the views on their trips into the countryside.

A few miles further along the Ring of Kerry and you'll come to signs directing you to **Staigue Fort**, an impressive (and largely intact) circle fort dating from the Iron Age. Archaeologists estimate its age at roughly 2,500 years old. The fort is a massive circular structure whose walls are 13 feet thick at the base and nearly seven feet thick at the top. The undulating walls are of varying height owing to erosion, gravity, and theft, but they are about 17 feet at their highest points and 11 feet at their lowest. *Info*: Castlecove off the N70. Open year-round. Admission is €1 donation in an honor box.

If the weather has been calm, you might consider spending a day on **Skellig Michael**, a remote island near Waterville on the Ring of Kerry. Skellig Michael has the ruins of a 9th-century monastic settlement perched on its craggy ridges. More than 650 stone steps hewn out of the mountain lead to the settlement. When you arrive, you'll marvel at the ruins – six old beehive huts, stone walls, two oratories, two churches and various and sundry remains. *Info*: tour boats leave from Ballinskelligs, Cahirciveen, Derrynane Pier, Valentia Island, and Waterville. Several local boat operators will take you out, including Michael O'Sullivan, Tel. (066) 947-4676, Dermot Walsh, Tel. (066) 947-6115, Des Lavelle, Tel. (066) 947-6124, Declan Freehan, Tel. (066) 947-9182 and Joe Roddy, Tel. (066) 947-4268. Be sure to call ahead at least a day for your reservations and to get departure times and locations.

Head back toward Killarney, and at Sneem take the N70 for Kenmare. Walk among the multi-colored shops, pubs and restaurants to get a flavor of this corner of southwest Ireland. Stop by **Black Abbey Crafts** on Main Street for an enchanting and surprising collection of crafts, or pop into **Quill's** for that bit of Irish fashion you've been wanting.

Kenmare is the entrance to the **Beara Peninsula**. From Kenmare, head west on the N70. A drive around the Beara Peninsula is as lovely as the Ring of Kerry, but without the tour buses. Along the way, you'll be greeted by stunning seascapes and spectacular vistas. The area around Eyries offers some especially memorable seascapes.

About a mile before you get to Castletownbere on the Eyeries Road watch for the signpost pointing you to **Dunboy Castles**. The first is an old manor house that must have once been quite an exquisite place in its day. A few hundred yards beyond that you'll find the ruins of a 15th-century O'Sullivan castle. Today, it is a series of grass-covered mounds and arches that beg to be explored and photographed. *Info*: Entrance to the manor house and castle ruins are via an honor box at a gate. Admission is €5 per car (or €1 per person or €1 per cyclist).

As you approach Glengariff, watch for signs to **Garinish Island**. On the island, you'll find formal Italian gardens and other plant life there. The warm Gulf Stream provides the necessary warmth for a number of varieties of sub-tropical plants to flourish. *Info*: Open daily March through September with hours generally from 9:30am to 4:30pm, sometimes later (check before you visit). Sundays are from noon to 5pm. Admission is €5 for adults, less for seniors, students, and children; family tickets are available. A ferry in the harbor will take you across the harbor to the island for €7.50 per person.

From Glengariff, follow the N71 to Bantry and on to Ardgroom. You're headed for Kinsale, but rather than take the inland route, I'd suggest the more picturesque route. From Ardgroom, just continue on the N71 toward Kinsale.

Kinsale is a delightful fishing village that begs to be explored. The town is a tidy affair of narrow winding streets, brightly painted Georgian

Stunning Views!

About one mile north of Glengariff on the road to Kenmare, watch for the signpost directing you to **Barley Lake**. You'll climb a narrow road up, up, up for about three miles. At the top the road ends. From there, just follow the mountain path to an **overlook** for Barley Lake, a high-mountain glacial lake. You'll get a stunning view over the Glengariff Valley.

homes, quays, sea breezes, and intriguing ruins. For hundreds of years Kinsale was an important seaport, until the size and draft of ships overcame the ability to use the harbor in the 18th century. Today, Kinsale offers tourists a clean, picturesque harbor town noted for deep-sea fishing trips and fine seafood restaurants. There always seems to be lots of things going on in Kinsale for you to busy yourself with.

For lunch, stop at one of the best seafood restaurants in Ireland: **Fishy Fishy Café** in Kinsale.

While in Kinsale, check out nearby **Charles Fort**. This hilltop fort is nearly 400 years old, and covers approximately 12 acres. Guided tours are offered during the summer months. *Info*: near Summer Cove. Tel. (021) 477-2684. Open mid-March through October daily with hours generally from 10am to 5pm, sometimes later (check before you visit). Open during the winter on Saturday and Sunday only. Admission is €3.50 for adults, less for seniors, students, and children; family tickets are available.

Southwest from Kinsale on the R604 you'll find **Old Head**. An ancient castle once belonging to the de Courcy family sits atop Old Head outside of Kinsale. The views from here are splendid, and the site is quietly romantic. Farther out on the end of the peninsula is the **Old Head lighthouse.**

From Kinsale, head northeast on the R611 to Cobh (pronounced "Cove"), a harbor town southeast of Cork. This small town lived in the memories of a generation of Irish immigrants, for it was from tiny Cobh that hundreds of thousands of starving Irish left farms, families, and certain death during the Great Potato Famine that lasted from 1845 through 1847. Most of them were headed for America and a fresh start. Their last views of Ireland may well have been the majestic steeples of the neo-Gothic St. Colman's Cathedral sitting regally on the hill above Cobh.

While in Cobh, be sure and stop in to see the **Queenstown Project**. This maritime museum primarily chronicles the experience Irish immigrants had as they bid the Emerald Isle farewell over the past several hundred years. Also, two exceptional exhibits focus on the sea disasters associated with the *Lusitania* and the *Titanic*, both of which touched the town and lives of the residents of Cobh. *Info*: Cobh railway station. Tel. (021) 481-3591. Open daily from 10am to 6pm. Admission is €5 for adults, less for seniors, students, and children; family tickets are available.

After your exploration of Cobh, follow the signs for Cork. Your first stop once there should be **St. Finbarre Cathedral.** Over 1,300 years ago, **St. Finbarre** established a monastery on this site. St. Finbarre's is especially striking at night, when it is well lit and glows brightly for all to see. As you enter St. Finbarre's, look heavenward, and your gaze will be met with angels and the glorified Lord. The interior of St. Finbarre's is a treasure-trove of masterful mosaics, stunning stained-glass windows, and incredible carvings. *Info*: Bishop Street. Open daily from 10am to 5pm. Admission is €2.

Five miles north of Cork City is the town of Blarney and its famous stone. The **Blarney Stone** is located atop an ancient castle keep underneath its battlements. Cormac McCarthy, Lord of Blarney Castle, was a renowned negotiator and flatterer. On one occasion, an exasperated Queen Elizabeth I declared of McCarthy's honeyed words and crafty negotiations: "This is nothing but Blarney - what he says, he never means!" Today, it is said that kissing the Blarney Stone grants the smoocher that same gift of flattery that Cormac possessed. Before your intimate moment with the stone, you'll traverse 120-ish steps up a spiral staircase.

Almost lost in the excitement of kissing the Blarney Stone is Blarney Castle itself. A massive square keep, it stands now as a mere shell of the impressive structure it must have been in its younger days. Its history, like so many other castles in Ireland, is pock-marked with sieges, attacks, and burnings. Cromwell visited here, as did William of Orange after the Battle of the Boyne. (Hint: they didn't come for afternoon tea!) The grounds and gardens are also often overlooked but well worth a visit. *Info*: Blarney. Tel. (021) 438-5252. Open Monday through Friday, with hours generally from 9am to 6:30pm, sometimes later (check before you visit). They are also open year round on Sunday from 9:30am to 5:30pm. Admission is €8 for adults, less for seniors, students, and children; family tickets are available. (Children under 8 are free).

If you want to overnight in the area, one of the most pleasant B&Bs in Ireland is right outside of Blarney: **Claragh B&B**, Tel. (021) 488-6308, Waterloo Road. The B&B is pleasant, but your hostess (Cecelia Keily) is the best! See *Best Sleeps & Eats* chapter for more details.

From Blarney, head northeast on the N8 to the market town of Cahir (pronounced "Care") and **Cahir Castle,** one of the most recognized castles in the world since it has been used as a setting for several medieval movies (including *Excalibur*). Built in 1142, the castle sits on a rocky outcropping of the River Suir. It's a picturesque setting and an imposing presence.

You can stroll inside the castle and along its battlements in relative safety. I say relative safety, because you'll experience first-hand several architectural schemes that helped make the castle safe for its former inhabitants, but that may trip you up if you are not careful. Watch for the staggered heights of the stairs - while merely inconvenient today, they served to make it difficult for enemies to traverse the stairs quickly. And keep your head down as you enter low doorways that helped impede rapid advancement of enemy troops through the castle. The castle is well worth an hour of so of your time to stop and explore. *Info:* Cahir Town. Tel. (052) 41011. Open daily with hours generally from 9:30am to 5:30pm, although hours vary slightly throughout the year (check before you visit). Admission is €2.90 for adults, less for seniors, students, and children; family tickets are available.

Take a breather from medieval sites and review a few items from the 17th through 20th centuries: check out **Fleury Antiques** in the main town square. It is sort of like visiting an exquisite museum where you can take pieces home (if you are willing to pay the price). *Info:* The Square, Cahir. Tel. (052) 41226.

From Cahir, continue on the N8 and it's a short ride to the **Rock of Cashel**. Save plenty of film for one of the most awe-inspiring sites in Ireland. Whether you experience bright sunshine, a dull day or a bit of rain while at the Rock of Cashel, it is still well worth the visit. Personally, I find that the lowering clouds give the ruins a bit of a mysterious and brooding quality. So regardless of the weather, visit this important and awe-filled site.

The Rock of Cashel (also called St. Patrick's Rock) long held a position of prominence in the history of Ireland. It was used for

the coronation of Munster kings from 370 until 1100. The great Brian Boru was crowned here. In the 12th century, Bishop Cormac MacCarthy began construction on Cormac's Chapel. It can still be seen, and is a fine example of the Romanesque architecture used. *Info:* Cahir. Tel. (062) 61437. Open daily with hours generally from 9:30am to 5:30pm, although they close a little later in the summer and a little earlier in the winter (check before you visit). Admission is €5.30 for adults, less for seniors, students, and children; family tickets are available.

If you've worked up an appetite with your sightseeing, stop in at **Legends Restaurant** at the foot of the Rock of Cashel. Most of the tables have stunning views of the ruins.

From Cashel, take the N8 northeast for about 25 minutes toward Urlingford. Once there, take the R689 south to **Kilcooley Abbey**. A sister abbey to Jerpoint Abbey near Thomastown, these ruins offer an intriguing sight to be prowled through. The abbey is a treasure-trove of sculptural prizes. *Info*: near Urlingford.

Southeast Munster/Leinster excursion

Backtrack to the N8, then to the R693 toward Kilkenny. Even though Kilkenny is in **Leinster**, since you're so close, let's slip into Leinster and see the best sights in and around Kilkenny: **St. Canice's Cathedral, Kilkenny Castle** and **Jerpoint Abbey**.

After seeing the impressive stonework of **Kilkenny Castle**, the next thing you will see will be the richly landscaped grounds. They are immaculate with hardly a blade of grass or mum out of place. When you've had your fill of the grounds, venture into the castle. A one-hour guided tour includes visits to a number of the castle's rooms, including the drawing and dining rooms, the library, and some of the bedrooms, which are imposing: each has ample numbers of antiques, tremendous tapestries, and plenty of paintings. Many of the furnishings you'll see are original to the castle, and the library has a number of books that have been here for hundreds of years!

By far the most impressive room in the castle is the remarkable Long Gallery, a cavernous room 45 meters long and 9 meters wide, with a ceiling about 60 feet high. Its walls are decked out with the portraits of the Butler family - 500 years' worth! In addition, splendid 17th-century tapestries grace several of the walls. Look closely at those tapestries - they are linen, silk, and wool, and took 65 Parisian artisans three months to weave them! *Info:* The Parade, Kilkenny. Tel. (056) 21450. Open daily with hours generally from 9:30am to 5pm, with longer summertime hours (check before you visit). Admission is €4.50 for adults, less for seniors, students, and children; family tickets are available.

Not far from Kilkenny Castle is **St. Canice's Cathedral**, an impressive gray granite house of worship. Modeled after many of the English churches of the period (13th century), St. Canice's stands firm and straight despite the efforts of a number of plunderers, including Cromwell's forces. *Info:* Corner of Dean and Parliament Streets, Kilkenny. Tel. (046) 64971. Open Monday through Saturday with hours generally from 9:30am to 6pm, and Sunday from 2pm to 6pm, although winter hours are more abbreviated (check before you visit). Admission is €2.

Southeast of Kilkenny and two miles south of Thomastown on the N9 you'll find **Jerpoint Abbey**, considered one of the finest monastic ruins in Ireland. The ruin is large - it is nearly the exact length and width of a football field. There are a series of interesting sculptures in the cloister. Judging from the flowing robes on many of them, they may represent some of the monks who served at Jerpoint Abbey. There are several interesting tombs in the church, including one of Bishop Felix O'Dulaney. Bishop O'Dulaney's effigy is interesting: it depicts a snake biting the crosier (a hooked staff, like a shepherd's crooked stick) held by the good bishop.

The small **visitor's center** provides a history of the monastery. The monastery is a wonderful subject for photographers – amateur as well as professional. It is impressive, and is well worth the small admission fee. *Info:* Near Thomastown. Tel. (056) 24623. Open March through November daily generally from 9:30am to 6pm, although winter hours are more abbreviated (check before you visit). Admission is €2.90 for adults, less for seniors, students, and children; family tickets are available.

Back on the N9, continue on toward Waterford. The best sight in Waterford is the **Waterford Crystal Factory**. You have probably come to associate the name *Waterford* with excellence, quality, and exquisite beauty. The factory has a nice gallery, and their one-hour tour takes you within a few feet of the master artisans who blow the glass - much as it has been done for several hundred years at this site.

If you go to the Waterford Crystal Factory in hopes of purchasing "seconds" — less than perfect vases, goblets, etc., — forget it. Waterford has one definition of quality, and that is unqualified perfection. Any item that does not meet their exacting specifications is broken, melted down and the glass reused. While on the tour, you will doubtless have the opportunity to hear the nerve-chilling sound of crystal shattering as imperfect specimens are destroyed. You'll easily spend several hours here. *Info:* Cork Road, Waterford. Tel. (051) 875788. Open daily with hours generally from 8:30am to 5pm.

Little **Ballyhack** sits at the mouth of Waterford Harbor on the R733. This stereotypical Irish fishing village offers plenty to paint, sketch, or photograph: fishing boats, old **Ballyhack Castle**, and the assorted local residents, full of character. Ballyhack Castle was originally part of the preceptory (a religious house) of the Knights Templar; today its ivy-covered and weathered rock walls keep watch over the harbor.

6. CONNACHT

Connacht is wild and diverse, offering windswept plains and wooded hills throughout its width and breadth. The **Aran Islands**, lying off the western cost of Ireland, offer a peek into Ireland's most ancient past, including 4,000-year-old **Dun Aengus Fort**. And **Galway** is one of the most pleasant shopping towns in Ireland, filled with great stores, seaside walks and friendly people.

One of the most picturesque sights you'll see in Ireland will be **Kylemore Abbey**, resting majestically along a lake in the middle of the wilderness. For sheer inspiration, don't miss **Croagh Patrick**, near the resort town of **Westport**. Rising abruptly from the bay, views from its heights are a treat.

ONE GREAT DAY IN CONNACHT

Connacht is Ireland's westernmost province. Wild beauties combine with great cities and marvelous ruins. If you have only one day in Connacht, you should spend it in **Galway** and the surrounding areas.

Galway is one of the busiest and most enjoyable of Ireland's cities. Eyre Square is the ideal place to begin your exploration of Galway City. It's often busy with tourists and business people. The gardens in the park are a memorial to John F. Kennedy.

From Eyre Square, head down William Street and turn right on Abbeygate Street, then left on Market Street. Look for the **Lynch Memorial Window**, a black marble skull and cross-bones memorializing the actions of one James Lynch Fitzstephen. As mayor of Galway at the time, James Lynch Fitzstephen had the unimaginable task of sentencing his own son to death for murdering a visitor to the city. When no one could be found to carry out the sentence, Mayor Lynch did the unhappy job himself. From these unfortunate circumstances arose the term "lynch law."

Cong's Movie Fame!

If you take a short drive north of Galway on the N84, you'll come to the small town of **Cong**. In 1951, Cong gained international recognition and interest when it served as the primary setting for the John Ford movie *The Quiet Man*, starring John Wayne, Maureen O'Hara and Barry Fitzgerald. It has not changed much over the ensuing years.

Back out on William Street, which has now changed its name to **Shop Street**, you'll be on a pedestrianized walkway like Grafton Street in Dublin. You'll find some wonderful shops, entertaining pubs, and delicious diners along with the people-watching opportunities. Dip into **Kenny's Books** and peek at thousands of Irish books, old and new. If you've not yet

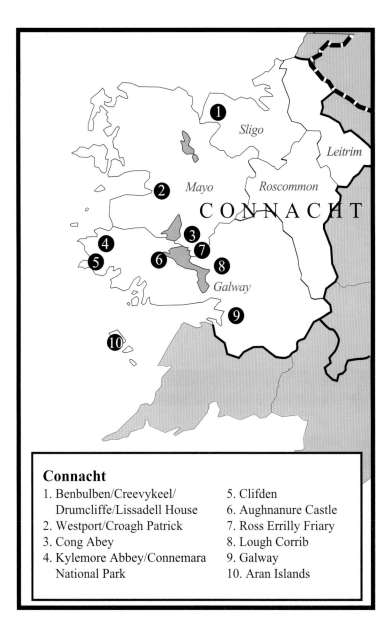

Connacht
1. Benbulben/Creevykeel/
   Drumcliffe/Lissadell House
2. Westport/Croagh Patrick
3. Cong Abey
4. Kylemore Abbey/Connemara
   National Park
5. Clifden
6. Aughnanure Castle
7. Ross Errilly Friary
8. Lough Corrib
9. Galway
10. Aran Islands

Stay in a Castle!

If you want an exquisite (albeit expensive) lodging experience, arrange your schedule to spend the night at **Ashford Castle** on the edge of Cong (www.ashford.ie, Tel. (094) 954-6003, US toll free 800/346-1001).

purchased a Claddagh ring, try **Fallers**, one of the best jewelers in Ireland.

While you're in Cong, check out the ruins of the 12th-century **Cong Abbey.** Take the time to look at some of the gravestones. There are some old and interesting ones here – many of which unfortunately serve as flagstones for the paths and are badly worn.

From Cong, head out on the R345 and turn west on the N59. Soon you'll come to **Kylemore Abbey.** You've probably seen pictures of it before – it is one of the most photographed abbeys in Ireland. Unfortunately, very little of the Abbey itself is open to the public – only one or two rooms in addition to the entry hall. *Info*: Near Letterfrack. Tel. (095) 41113. Open daily with hours generally from 10am to 4pm, until 6pm spring and summer (check before you visit).

Several hundred yards from the Abbey, around the shores of the lake, is a lovely little Gothic Chapel that's worth walking to and looking at: it reminds me of a dollhouse.

ANOTHER GREAT DAY IN CONNACHT

Spend your one day in Connacht on the **Aran Islands**, specifically **Inishmore**, if you want to soak up ancient Ireland. The island is approximately five miles long and two miles wide.

Winding rock walls, an-
cient ruins, prehistoric
forts, and megalithic
tombs greet visitors in
stony silence. You can
walk the rocky roads, rent
bicycles in **Kilronan**, or
take one of the many minibuses or jaunting cars that
are available.

While on Inishmore, be
sure and visit **Dun
Aengus.** This 4,000-year-
old stone-walled fort ends
dramatically and abruptly
at the edge of a precipi-
tous 300-foot drop to the
ocean. Archaeologists
don't know why it was
built or from whom the
people were protecting themselves. Massive walls, some 20-feet
tall and 18-feet wide, encircle the fort. The fort is located about
four miles from Kilronan, so it is a little far to walk. Ride a bicycle
or catch a ride on one of the local minibuses. *Info*: Open daily
during the summer from 10am to 6pm, and during the winter
from 11:30am to 3:30pm. Admission is €2 for adults, less for
seniors, students, and children; family tickets are available.

Near Dun Aengus, you'll come across the impressive ruins of
The Seven Churches. These ancient houses of worship conjure
up myriad thoughts about who – and how – these ancients
worshipped. *Info*: Admission is free.

Closer to Kilronan you'll find **Black Fort**, an ancient fort estimated to have been built around 3,000 BC. As with many of the
other ruins on the Aran Islands, Black Fort has also stymied the
best efforts of archaeologists trying to determine its purpose.
Admission is free. *Info*: The ferry is the least expensive means of
getting to the Aran Islands: €20 round trip for adults, €10 for

children. The ferry takes 90 minutes from Galway, and 30 minutes from Inverin. Following are the ferry companies that ply the waters to the Aran Islands:

• **Doolin Ferries**, Tel. (091) 567283
• **Island Ferries**, Tel. (091) 568903
• **Inis Mor Ferries**, Tel. (091) 566535

You can catch a ferry to the Aran Islands in Galway, Inverin or Rossaveal.

A FANTASTIC CONNACHT WEEKEND

Take **wild and beautiful scenery**, throw in a few ruins and season with an Irish resort town and you have a recipe for a great Connacht weekend.

Friday Evening
Plan to spend your evening dining and lodging at **Ashford Castle** (see "Stay in a Castle," page 100). This 13th-century Norman castle has been renovated to a five-star luxury hotel – the Normans never had it so good! Dine in the Connaught Room, an intimate restaurant overlooking the grounds of the estate. Follow that up with a walk on those grounds, and then retire in exquisite luxury. *Info*: www.ashford.ie, Tel. (094) 954-6003, US toll free 800/346-1001.

Saturday
Since you're in the neighborhood, check out the nearby 12th-century **Cong Abbey**. As you walk through the abbey, take the time to look at some of the gravestones. There are some old and interesting ones here – many of which unfortunately serve as flagstones for the paths and are badly worn.

From the Abbey, head north on the R345/R334 to the N84, then north to **Westport**. Westport is at the head of Clew Bay, an island-studded estuary on this western edge of Ireland. Irish and tourists alike head for Westport to savor her shops, and there are many to be visited. Check out **James Murtagh Jewelers** on Bridge Street for Celtic jewelry, or slip into **Matt Molloy's Pub** for a Guinness or two.

From Westport, take the R335 to Murmisk and the Croagh Patrick Information Center. **Croagh Patrick** is that rather abrupt 2,500-foot peak on the south side of the road overlooking Clew Bay.

Walks up the peak – short or extensive – can be planned at the information center. Even a short walk provides sensational views of island-studded Clew Bay.

Continue on the R335 to the N59, and head west to **Kylemore Abbey.** You've probably seen pictures of it before – it is one of the most photographed abbeys in Ireland. Unfortunately, very little of the Abbey itself is open to the public – only one or two rooms in addition to the entry hall. *Info*: Near Letterfrack. Tel. (095) 41113. Open daily with hours generally from 10am to 4pm, until 6pm spring and summer (check before you visit).

Several hundred yards from the Abbey, around the shores of the lake, is a lovely little Gothic Chapel that's worth walking to and looking at: it reminds me of a dollhouse.

Sunday
Begin with a circular tour of the Connemara countryside by driving west on the N59 to **Clifden**. Then either continue north on the N59 and circle back to Recess, or you can go south on the R341 and see that section of Connemara. Either way is beautiful. After your sightseeing, take the R340 for a scenic seaside to **Galway**.

A Lodge with a View!

Spend the night in Recess at **Ballynahinch Castle Hotel**, the former getaway for a wealthy maharajah (Tel. (095) 31006). This castle hotel offers beautiful views of either the mountains or the lake.

Once in Galway, start at Eyre Square, then head down William Street and turn right on Abbeygate Street, then left on Market Street. Look for the **Lynch Memorial Window**, a black marble skull and cross-bones memorializing the actions of one James Lynch Fitzstephen. As mayor of Galway at the time, James Lynch Fitzstephen had the unimaginable task of sentencing his own son to death for murdering a visitor to the city. When no one could be found to carry out the sentence, Mayor Lynch did the unhappy job himself. From these unfortunate circumstances arose the term "lynch law."

Back out on **Shop Street**, you'll be on a pedestrianized walkway. Much like Grafton Street in Dublin, you'll find some wonderful shops, entertaining pubs, and delicious diners along with the people-watching opportunities. Dip into **Kenny's Books** for a peek at thousands of Irish books, old and new. If you've not yet purchased a Claddagh ring, try **Fallers**, renowned throughout the country as one of the best jewelers in the land.

A WONDERFUL WEEK IN CONNACHT

With a week in this province, you'll have plenty of time to explore, take scenic drives in Connemara, visit the Aran Islands, see some more majestic ruins, and get in some great shopping at your leisure!

RECOMMENDED PLAN: A trip into Ireland's past on one of the Aran Islands is a good way to start your Connacht week. Follow that by seeing Galway's sights, exploring the rugged Connemara beauty, seeing Kylemore Abbey and a few ruins, and visiting a holy mountain will make your week complete.

Aran Islands — Inishmore

So much of what you see in Ireland is a trip into the past. Now take a day and travel even further back by visiting the **Aran Island of**

Inishmore. The island is approximately five miles long and two miles wide. Winding rock walls, ancient ruins, prehistoric forts, and megalithic tombs greet visitors in stony silence. You can walk the rocky roads, rent bicycles in Kilronan, or take one of the many minibuses or jaunting cars that are available.

Don't Miss ...

- **The Aran Islands** – a trip into the past
- **Galway City** – a pleasant shopping city
- **Croagh Patrick** – Ireland's Holy Mountain

While on Inishmore, be sure and visit **Dun Aengus.** This semicircular stone-walled fort ends dramatically and abruptly at the edge of a precipitous 300-foot drop to the ocean. Archaeologists estimate the age of Dun Aengus as 4000 years old, but why it was built and who they were protecting themselves against is still a mystery. Massive walls, some 20 feet tall and 18 feet wide, encircle the fort. The structure is 150 feet across, so you can imagine the kind of effort it must have taken to erect this fortress. It is dizzying at best to walk to the edge of the fort and look over at the crashing sea below. The fort is located about four miles from Kilronan, so it is a little far to walk. Ride a bicycle or catch a ride on one of the minibuses. *Info*: Open daily during the summer from 10am to 6pm, and during the winter from 11:30am to 3:30pm. Admission is €2 for adults, less for seniors, students, and children; family tickets are available.

Near Dun Aengus, you'll come across the impressive ruins of **The Seven Churches** (watch for the signposts with their Gaelic name: *Na Seacht dTeampaill*). These ancient houses of worship – some extending back to the 8th century — conjure up myriad thoughts about who - and how – these ancients worshipped. You'll notice that only two of the churches remain more or less intact – the rest are in ruins. *Info*: Admission is free.

Closer to Kilronan you'll find **Black Fort** (*Dun Duchatair* in Gaelic), an ancient fort estimated to have been built around 3,000 BC. Like Dun Aengus, massive 20-foot walls indicated a desire for privacy at some distant past! As with many of the other ruins on the Aran Islands, Black Fort has also stymied the best efforts of archaeologists trying to determine its purpose. *Info*: Admission is free.

Island-Hopping in the Aran Islands

Inishmore is the Aran island that receives the most visitors. But there are two other Aran islands: Inishmaan and Inisheer.

Inishmaan is the next largest island of the Aran Island chain. Its population of 300-year-round souls brave the wind and the weather to earn a living on the island. As with Inishmore, there are a number of ancient ruins worth poking around in. One of the finest is **Dun Conchubhuir**, a brother stone fort to Dun Aengus on Inishmor – and why not? Conchubhuir (Conor) was Aengus' brother. Massive, stony and circular like Dun Aengus, Dun Conchubhuir also features the remains of beehive hut foundations from centuries ago. *Info*: Open daily during the summer from 10am to 6pm, and during the winter from 11:30am to 3:30pm. Admission is €2 for adults, less for seniors, students, and children.

Finally, **Inisheer** is the smallest of the Arans at barely two miles square. The most visited sight on this island is the mysterious graveyard and ruins of **St. Kevin's Church**. If you've been paying attention to this book, you might wonder is this St. Kevin also is the St. Kevin who founded Glendalough south of Dublin. Not so, according to historians. They feel he was a contemporary of that St. Kevin, and some have even suggested that the two were brothers. Whether they were or not is immaterial. I just know that St. Kevin of Glendalough sure picked a lot prettier and more peaceful site for his worship! Inisheer's St. Kevin's Church is the venue for a special Mass held each year on June 14 in memory of St. Kevin, the patron saint of Inisheer.

Info: The ferry is the least-expensive means of getting to the Aran Islands: €20 round trip for adults, half that for children. The ferry takes 90 minutes from Galway, and 30 minutes from Inverin. Following are the three main ferry companies that ply the waters to the Aran Islands:

- **Doolin Ferries**, Tel. (091) 567283
- **Island Ferries**, Tel. (091) 568903
- **Inis Mor Ferries**, Tel. (091) 566535

Aer Arann flies to the Aran Islands from Inverin. The flight takes all of six minutes. A shuttle bus will take you from the Tourist Office in Galway to the airport one hour before flights depart, which are hourly during the summer months, less often during other times of the year. Return flights occur several times throughout the day. Flying with Aer Arann or some of the other local air charter companies costs €44 per adult, less for children. Tel. (091) 593034, www.aerarann.ie.

Galway City & Connemara

Eyre Square is the ideal place to begin your exploration of Galway City. Eyre Square is the traditional town square that serves as Galway's center point. It's often busy with tourists and business people. It's not a large park, but it is a pleasant one. The gardens in the park are a memorial to John F. Kennedy. The late American president visited Galway on his trip to Ireland less than six months before his assassination in 1963.

There are several interesting items in Eyre Park. My favorite is a whimsical statue of **Padraic O'Conaire,** honoring one of Ireland's great Irish-language poets and a Gaelic story-teller of some reknown.

From Eyre Square, head down William Street and turn right on Abbeygate Street, then left on Market Street. Look for the **Lynch Memorial Window,** a black marble skull and cross-bones memorializing the actions of one James Lynch Fitzstephen. It's by the graveyard at St. Nicholas' church. Look up – it's about eight feet off the ground. As mayor of Galway at the time, James Lynch Fitzstephen had the unenviable task of sentencing his own son to death for murdering a Spanish visitor to the city. When no one could be found to carry out the sentence, Mayor Lynch did the unhappy job himself. From these unfortunate circumstances arose the term "lynch law." The marker reads, "This memorial of the stern and unbending justice of the chief magistrate of this City, James Lynch Fitzstephen, elected mayor AD 1493, who condemned and executed his own guilty son, Walter, on this spot." The records indicate that after the tragedy, Mayor Lynch retired from politics and went into seclusion the remainder of his life.

Back out on **Shop Street**, you'll be on a pedestrianized walkway like Grafton Street in Dublin. You'll find some wonderful shops, entertaining pubs, and delicious diners along with the people-watching opportunities. There is a dizzying number of jewelry, clothing, and other stores, not to mention a number of excellent dining establishments to catch your eye and take your money! Dip into Kenny's Books a peek at thousands of Irish books, old and new. If you've not yet purchased a Claddagh ring, try Fallers, one of the best jewelers in Ireland.

Just below Claddagh Bridge, at the south end of Shop Street, you'll find **Spanish Arch**. In former years it served as one of the town gates. Watch for a squat, gray rock structure with two archways — this is Spanish Arch. Built in 1584, this was the point where Spanish ships unloaded their precious cargoes of brandy, wine, and other liquors in days gone by. To get to Spanish Arch, go south from Eyre Square about three blocks along Merchant Street.

Next to the Spanish Arch you'll find the neat-and-tidy **Galway City Museum**. Inside you'll find a treasure trove of memorabilia of days-gone-by in Galway: old photographs, medieval stonework featuring local coats-of-arm, engravings, city maps, etc. There are several exhibits featuring fishing implements, as fishing was and is an important part of Galway's past and future. It is a pleasant jaunt down Galway's memory lane. *Info:* Open daily 10am to 1pm, and 2pm to 5pm. Tel. (091) 567641. Admission is €1.30 for adults, less for children.

Before you leave Galway, stop in at the tourist office near Eyre Square and arrange for a cruise of **Lough Corrib**. Several companies ply the waters of this large lake north of Galway. This splendid lake in the west of Ireland is large – over 30 miles long – and narrow, at some points only about a half-mile wide. Tradition holds that it possesses one island for every day of the year: 365. The lake is reached from several points, but you can receive a tour of parts of the lake in the small village of Oughterard. Cruises are offered that last between one hour and one day. *Info*: One of the better-known companies is **Corrib Cruises**, Tel. (092) 46029.

Stroll Along the Beach

In the **Salthill** area west of Galway, **boardwalks** along the beach make for a pleasant place to stroll and enjoy the fresh sea breezes. If you are staying in Galway, there are a number of fine B&Bs within just a few steps of these boardwalks. (See *Best Sleeps* section for Connacht.)

Head out of Galway on the N84. About a mile north of Headford on the R334, stand the ruins of 14th-century **Ross Errilly Friary**. The Friary is wonderfully preserved, and absolutely invites exploration. As you wander through the ruins, you'll find the cloister where the monks meditated, the church where they prayed, and other areas for the more mundane aspects of monkish life. The monks were chased off seven times by unfriendly visitors, including once by the legendary Oliver Cromwell himself. The Franciscans kept returning to the friary until it was abandoned in 1753.

Be sure and check out the wonderful tombstones scattered throughout the church and its grounds. Some are quite old. On a recent visit to Ireland, two of my teenage children claimed this was one of their favorite ruins of all those we visited (and we visited many). *Info*: Follow the signs from the center square of Headford.

Back on the N84, soon you'll come to the small town of **Cong**. In 1951, Cong gained international recognition and interest when it served as the primary setting for the John Ford movie *The Quiet Man*, starring John Wayne, Maureen O'Hara and Barry Fitzgerald. It has not changed much over the ensuing years.

While you're in Cong, check out the ruins of **Cong Abbey**, an abbey of the Augustinian order dating from the early 12th century. One of the wealthy and influential benefactors of the abbey commissioned the **Cross of Cong**, a beautiful work of religious art. It stood proudly at Cong Abbey for centuries, but has since been moved to the National Museum in Dublin, as it is considered one of Ireland's religious masterpieces. As you walk through the abbey, take the time to look at some of the gravestones. There are some old and interesting ones here – many of which unfortunately serve as flagstones for the paths and are badly worn.

From Cong, take the R345 to the N59, and head west to **Kylemore Abbey**. You've probably seen pictures of it before – it is one of the most photographed abbeys in Ireland. Nestling snugly along the shores of Kylemore Lake, it was originally built in 1868 as a residence for a wealthy Member of Parliament in the late 1800's. During world War I, Belgian nuns fleeing the approaching German armies came to Kylemore and founded a Benedictine Abbey. The abbey now serves as a secondary school for girls. Unfortunately, very little of the Abbey itself is open to the public – only one or two rooms in addition to the entry hall.

Several hundred yards from the Abbey, around the shores of the lake, is a lovely little **neo-Gothic Chapel** that's worth walking to and looking at: it reminds me of a dollhouse. Take the time to stroll down to the chapel and enjoy its pleasant setting along the beautiful shores of the lake.

For a superb Connemara lodging experience, spend the night at **Lough Inagh Lodge**. Once a hunting lodge, it is now a comfortable and memorable hotel full of antiques, turf fires and warm welcomes. Or try **Rosleague Manor**, an elegant Georgian manor, between Clifden and Westport. (See *Best Sleeps* for Connacht.)

Near Letterfrack, watch for signs directing you to the **Connemara National Park & Visitor Center**. This is the starting point for a number of walking trails through Connemara State Park. Walking trails are short or long, depending on your pleasure. There are those who will tell you that the only true way to appreciate the beauty of Connemara is to get out and walk its hills and vales. As you travel along in Connemara National Park, you'll note the **Twelve Bens** (also called the Twelve Pins), twelve peaks of Connemara. The highest is Benbaun at 2,355 feet in elevation. These mountains are largely devoid of vegetation, except tundra-height plants and low-lying heather. The Twelve Bens are often shrouded in clouds, giving a brooding feeling as they stand guard over the rugged Connemara beauty. *Info*: near Letterfrack. Tel. (095) 41054. Open daily, generally from 10am to 5:30pm, slightly longer during the summer months. Admission is €2.75 for adults, less for children and seniors.

Continue your sightseeing with a circular tour of the Connemara countryside by driving west on the N59 to **Clifden**. The steeples of the local Catholic and Protestant churches lift skyward above the town, and beyond them are even higher *natural* steeples – the Twelve Bens – that rise majestically in the distance. Interesting shops on Main Street in Clifden include **O'Hehir's Woolen Shop**, Market Street, **Lavelle Art Gallery**, and **Clifden Art Gallery**.

Sandwiches 'R Us!

Watch for **Destry's Restaurant** in Clifden, a great sandwich shop.

From Clifden, head east on the N59 until you come to Oughterard. Look for signposts in Oughterard pointing you to **Aughnanure**

Castle, the former stronghold of the vaunted Irish warriors named O'Flaherty. Members of the O'Flaherty clan were frequent visitors to Galway City during the 15th and 16th centuries. But welcome visitors they were not. In fact, the west gate to Galway City once held the inscription: "From the fury of the O'Flahertys, good Lord deliver us." Their castle is a six-story tower house with several squat round towers. It was recently restored and is now open to the public. *Info*: near Oughterard. Tel. (091) 552214. Open from the end of March through October 31 daily from 9:30am to 6pm. Admission is €2.75 for adults, less for seniors, students, and children; family tickets are available.

Westport & Beyond

From the castle, go west on the N59 to Maam Cross, north to Maam, then west a mile or two on the N59 to the R335 to Louisburgh. Resting offshore at the mouth of Clew Bay is the 4,000-acre **Clare Island**. By far its most famous occupant over the centuries was **Grace O'Malley**, the "Uncrowned Queen of the West." She was recognized as a gutsy pirate full of daring and bravado, and more than one ballad has been sung to her feats. The ruins of her home, **Carrigahooley Castle** as well as **Clare Island Abbey**, where Grace was buried, are found on the island. *Info*: Clare Island. Ferries leave from Roonagh Pier, near Louisburgh.

Continue on the R335 to Murmisk and the Croagh Patrick Information Center. **Croagh Patrick** is that rather abrupt 2,500-foot peak on the south side of the road overlooking Clew Bay. Croagh Patrick is known as Ireland's "Holy Mountain." It is the legendary peak where tradition holds that St. Patrick rid Ireland of snakes. Whether you believe the legend or not (by the way, there are no snakes in Ireland), Croagh Patrick is an impressive mountain, and the site of yearly pilgrimages by many Catholic faithful.

There is a **good hiking path** up Croagh Patrick The well-worn path ascends to the top of the mountain with many places to stop and rest along the way. The last Sunday of July is the traditional time of the pilgrimage, when up to 25,000 worshipers, many of them barefoot, make the two-hour trek to the top. But you can do it any time of the year, and the views from the top are nothing short of stunning.

Back on the R335 heading west and you'll come to the resort town of **Westport**. Westport is at the head of Clew Bay, an island-studded estuary on this western edge of Ireland. Irish and tourists alike head for Westport to savor her shops, and there are many to be visited. Check out **James Murtagh Jewelers** on Bridge Street for Celtic jewelry, or slip into **Matt Molloy's Pub** for a Guinness or two.

Beyond Westport, take the N5 east to the N4, then north toward Sligo. Just south of Sligo on the N4, watch for signs directing you to the 17th-century **Parke Castle**. The drive, along the lovely

shores of Lough Gill, is particularly pleasant. The castle sits along the shoreline of the lake, and is particularly impressive at night, when it is basked in bright halogen lights. *Info*: Near Sligo. Tel. (071) 916-4149. Open mid-March through October daily from 10am to 6pm, Admission is €2.75 for adults, less for seniors, students, and children; family tickets are available.

From Parke's Castle, take the R286 back toward Sligo. In Sligo, catch the N15 north. Five miles north of Sligo on the N15 you'll find the ruins of the monastic settlement of **Drumcliffe**. Its Irish name, *Droim Chliabh,* means "Back of the Baskets." Originally the site of a monastery founded in 574 by St. Columba, the settlement lasted until the early 16th century. The only remaining artifacts are a series of gravestones, the remains of a round tower, and an elaborately carved high cross. The high cross and the round tower sit right next to the road. The high cross was placed here about the year 1000, and is deeply carved with a number of figures. Can you identify the scriptural stories depicted there?

Perhaps the most interesting aspect of your visit here is the grave of revered Irish writer W. B. Yeats in the nearby Protestant graveyard. His simple epitaph reads:

Cast a cold eye
On life, on death.
Horseman, pass by!

Just beyond Drumcliffe, watch for signs directing you to **Lissadell House**. Once inside the mansion, you'll be awed by the lovely architecture and plentiful *objets d'art*. You'll enjoy the half-hour tour that spins the history of Lissadell House for you, complete with the tales of some of her most intriguing owners. *Info*: Drumcliffe, off the N15. Tel. (071) 916-3150. Open daily mid-March through September from 10:30am to 6pm. Admission is €6 for adults, less for seniors, students, and children; family tickets are available.

Between Sligo and Bundoran is the large, flat-topped mount called by some "Table Mountain." Deep ravines ring the edges of

the steep slopes of **Benbulben**. Next to Croagh Patrick, Benbulben is perhaps the next most recognizable mountain in Ireland.

Continuing north on the N15, watch for signs directing you to **Creevykeel Court Tomb**. It is one of the finest examples of a classic court tomb in existence today in Ireland. Archaeologists estimate it has been here since 3,000 BC. Upright stones mark the circular ritual court, and lead to a burial chamber. *Info*: On the N15 between Cliffony and Castlegal.

7. ULSTER

This northernmost province of Ireland is politically divided
– half the province is in the Republic of Ireland and the other
half is in **Northern Ireland**. If you are looking for rich
scenery and majestic sights, Ulster may be the place for you.
Stunning seascapes adorn this wild province, along with
ancient stone forts like **Grianan of Ailigh** and picturesque
castles like **Dunluce** and **Donegal**. Nature is at her finest
here, offering such oddities as **Giant's Causeway**, a collection of 40,000 hexagonal basalt pillars of varying sizes. If
you have the nerve, venture across the rope bridge of
Carrick-a-Rede, spanning a distance of 60 feet across an 80
foot drop to the turquoise green ocean below.

Elegance is also available in Ulster at **Belleek Pottery**, and
several museums vie for your attention in **Derry** and **Belfast**.

ONE GREAT DAY IN ULSTER

The best of Ulster is largely scenery and wild beauty, with a few ruins thrown in for good measure. With one day, focus on the town of Donegal and the impressive ruins of and views from Grianan of Ailigh

Start your day in Ulster by heading for **Donegal**, on the west coast of Ireland. Donegal is a pleasant town with a number of fine shops, including **McGinty's Sweater Shop** and **Magee's Tweed Shop**. Take a few moments to walk the town square. Stop in at **Donegal Castle**, in the center of town just off the square. Tours of the castle yield wonderful views of ornate Persian rugs, splendid

French tapestries and information panels telling the history of the castle. *Info*: Donegal, Tirchonaill Street. Tel. (073) 22405. Open mid-March through October daily from 10am to 6pm. Admission is €3.70 for adults, less for seniors, students, and children; family tickets are available.

Take the N56 west out of Donegal for about 30 miles, and you'll soon come to the fishing village of **Killybegs** on the R263. Continue west from Killybegs on the R263 to get to the **Slieve League Mountains**. The cliffs of Slieve League Mountains are the highest in Ireland, sloping nearly 2,000 feet into the ocean. Several cliff walks are available in the area.

Take the R263 to Glencolmbkille, then take the road to Ardara, then the N56 to the N15 towards Letterkenny. From Letterkenny, head north on the N13 and watch for signposts directing you to the **Grianan of Ailigh**. Follow the signs for about two miles up a winding lane to the top of an 800-foot hill and you're at Grianan

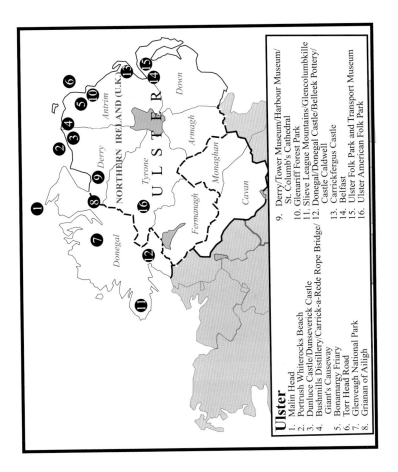

Ulster

1. Malin Head
2. Portrush Whiterocks Beach
3. Dunluce Castle/Dunseverick Castle
4. Bushmills Distillery/Carrick-a-Rede Rope Bridge/
   Giant's Causeway
5. Bonamargy Friary
6. Torr Head Road
7. Glenveagh National Park
8. Grianan of Ailigh
9. Derry/Tower Museum/Harbour Museum/
   St. Columb's Cathedral
10. Glenariff Forest Park
11. Slieve League Mountains/Glencolumbkille
12. Donegal/Donegal Castle/Belleek Pottery/
    Castle Caldwell
13. Carrickfergus Castle
14. Belfast
15. Ulster Folk Park and Transport Museum
16. Ulster American Folk Park

Food & Lodging Tips

Don't pass up the restaurant at the **Kee's Hotel**, Tel. (074) 913-1018, in Stranorlar, on the road between Donegal and Letterkenny. The setting is marvelous, the food delicious. For lodging, stay at **The Arches Country House**, Tel. (074) 972-2029), just outside of Donegal town.

of Ailigh – a 3,000-year-old stone ring fort. The structure you see today was restored about 100 years ago. Impressive views greet you from the top.

A FANTASTIC ULSTER WEEKEND

We'll begin your Ulster weekend in **Donegal**, then move on to **Killybegs, Glenveagh National Park,** and **Derry**. We'll spend some time enjoying the magnificent scenery (including the tallest mountains in Ireland), ancient ring forts, peaceful fishing villages, and stunning views.

Friday Night
Spend your first Ulster weekend evening in "Downtown" Donegal. Catch a bite to eat at **The Weaver's Loft**, above Magee's Tweed Shop. Spend a few minutes walking around the town square, popping into shops or just window shopping.

Head northwest out of Donegal on the N15 to Lough Eske and your lodging spot for the evening: **The Arches Country House** (see *Best Sleeps & Eats* chapter).

Saturday
For our first sight, we'll slip briefly into Northern Ireland. Head south on the N15 through Donegal and on toward Ballyshannon.

At Ballyshannon, take the N3 into Belleek for an elegant treat at **Belleek Pottery**. Belleek china is that creamy-looking china you'll see in gift shops throughout Ireland. Half-hour tours of the factory are available during the week. There is a museum and also a lovely display area/shop where you can marvel at the elegance of Belleek pottery, and of course you can purchase some of their goods if you wish. *Info:* Belleek. Tel. (028) 6865-9300. Open Monday through Friday with hours generally from 9am to 6pm, sometimes later (check before you visit). Saturdays they open an hour later. Sundays they are generally open from 2pm to 6pm. During the winter, they are not open on Saturdays or Sundays. Admission is £4 or €6 for adults, less for seniors, students, and children; family tickets are available.

Your next stop will be back in **Donegal,** with its tourist shops, including **McGinty's Sweater Shop** and **Magee's Tweed Shop**. Take a few moments to walk the town square. Stop in at **Donegal Castle**, in the center of town just off the square. Tours of the castle yield wonderful views of ornate Persian rugs, splendid French tapestries and information panels tell the history of the castle. *Info*: Donegal, Tirchonaill Street. Tel. (073) 22405. Open mid-March through October daily from 10am to 6pm. Admission is €3.70 for adults, less for seniors, students, and children; family tickets are available.

Take the N56 west out of Donegal for about 30 miles, and you'll soon come to the **fishing village of Killybegs** on the R263. Con-

tinue west from Killybegs on the R263 to get to the **Slieve League Mountains**. The cliffs of Slieve League Mountains are the highest in Ireland, sloping nearly 2,000 feet into the ocean. Several **cliff walks** are available in the area. One of them, "One Man's Pass,"  feels not unlike a high-wire act, and is not for the faint of heart or people suffering from fear of heights.

Take the R263 towards Glencolumbkille, then take the road to Ardara, then the N56 to the N15 towards Letterkenny. From Letterkenny, head northwest on the N56 to Termon, then on the R255 toward Dunlewy. Near Churchill, you'll find **Glenveagh National Park.** Glenveagh Lough is simply gorgeous, as is Glenveagh Castle, and it boasts a set of castle gardens that are exquisite. You cannot drive through the park, but walking paths are available. A 45-minute tour of the castle is also interesting. *Info*: Near Churchill. Tel. (074) 37090. Open mid-March through early November daily from 10am to 6:30pm. Admission to the park is €2.50 for adults, less for seniors, students, and children; family tickets are available. Admission to the castle is the same.

Sunday

From Letterkenny, head north on the N13 and watch for sign-posts directing you to the **Grianan of Ailigh,** Follow it for about two miles up a winding lane to the top of an 800-foot hill and you're at Grianan of Ailigh – an impressive stone ring fort. Archaeologists speculate that the fort dates from the Iron Age, making it approximately 3,000 years old! It is a circular structure with three terraced rings one inside the other. On the inside a series of stone walks bring you to the top of the 17-foot tall walls. Their base is a *mere* 13 feet. The structure you see today was restored from a somewhat disheveled state about 100 years ago. Sweeping views greet you from the top.

From the Grianan of Ailigh, follow the N13 toward Londonderry. As you near Londonderry, watch for the R238, and/or signs directing you toward Buncrana. Proceed through Buncrana following the signs for Malin, beyond which is **Malin Head,** the northernmost point of the Emerald Isle. The views, especially those along the southern shoreline, are breathtaking, and it's hard to beat the incredible sunsets from this particular vantage point. If the weather cooperates, you'll be able to see the Scottish island of **Islay,** on the northeast horizon.

Next, set your sights for the Northern Ireland city of **Derry** (also called Londonderry). To begin your tour of the city, you should climb up on the **City Walls** and take a stroll. It should take you no more than an hour to complete the mile-long circuit, but it will provide you with a bird's-eye view of the city and its major sights. Historical markers along the walk help you learn a little of the history of this fair city.

At the northwestern corner of the city walls, you'll find the **Tower Museum**. Effective (and interesting) high-tech presentations march you through the highlights of Derry's history. There are also a number of ancient artifacts, including a dugout boat that was found in the area that has been carbon dated to approximately 520 AD! *Info*: O'Doherty's Tower. Tel. (071) 372411. Open daily from 10am to 1pm, and 2pm to 4:30pm. Admission is free.

In the southeastern corner of the walled city you'll find one of the more popular sites in Derry: **St. Columb's Cathedral**. Built in the early 17th century, inside this Protestant cathedral you'll find exquisite stone and wood carvings. Beautiful stained glass windows, dark wood and tall open-beamed ceilings make for an interesting visit. *Info*: Open April to October Monday through Saturday from 9am to 5pm, and 9am to 4pm Monday through Saturday from November through March. Admission is £1.

Just outside of the city walls at the north end of the city, you'll find the **Harbour Museum**. This small museum has a number of exhibits that feature Derry's maritime history. One of the more interesting exhibits is a memorial to American sailors who perished in WWII. *Info*: Harbor Square. Tel. (071) 37731. Open Monday through Friday from 10am to 1pm and from 2pm to 4:30pm. Admission is free.

ONE GREAT DAY IN NORTHERN IRELAND

If you have only one day to spend in Northern Ireland, take a sea-side drive and see **Giant's Causeway, Carrick-a-Rede Rope Bridge** and **Dunluce Castle**, the top three sights to see in Northern Ireland.

No Euros Here!

Northern Ireland has not joined the Euro currency zone, so the **British pound sterling** is still in use here.

Head for Cushendun, north of Larne. Look for signposts directing you to **Torr Head Road**. This ribbon-like road snakes around the northeastern tip of Northern Ireland, a scarce twelve miles from Scotland at its closest point. It is a very narrow road, but well-maintained. On a clear day the views are stunning, and you might enjoy pulling off the road and listening to the surf crashing against the rocks below you.

Torr Head Road ends about two miles southeast of **Bonamargy Friary** near Ballycastle. Built in the 16th century, it is largely intact and will provide an interesting few minutes of wandering. *Info:* south of Ballycastle on the A2. Admission free.

From Ballycastle, watch for signs directing you to the B15 and **Carrick-a-Rede Rope Bridge**. The rope bridge is suspended 80 feet above the ocean across a chasm 60 feet wide. Now, neither of those may seem high, until you are in the middle of this swaying rope bridge. Access is via

a pleasant half-mile walk up a slight incline. *Info:* near Ballintoy. Tel. (028) 2076-9839 Open daily from March through October with hours generally from 9:30am to 5pm, later during the summer (check before you visit). Admission is £2.50 for adults, less for seniors, students, and children; family tickets are available.

Continuing west on the B15, watch for signs directing you to **Giant's Causeway**, near Bushmills. Giant's Causeway consists of a group of 40,000 symmetric hexagonal stone columns formed millions of years ago by rapidly cooling molten lava. Stop first at the Visitors Center. You can either walk or ride an inexpensive shuttle to the stones. *Info*: on the B146 just off the A2 between Ballintoy and Bushmills. Tel. (028) 7073-1855. Open daily with hours generally from 10am to 5pm, later during the summer (check before you visit). Admission is £2 for adults, less for seniors, students, and children; family tickets are available.

A Great Old B&B

While in this part of Northern Ireland, for a lodging treat spend the night at Whitepark House in Ballintoy, Tel. (028) 2073-1482, a lovely B&B over 250 years old.

Further west along the coast road between Portrush and Bushmills, you come to **Dunluce Castle**. Dunluce is perched atop a natural basalt tower that rises abruptly out of the ocean. Surrounded on three sides by the ocean, and on the fourth by a gorge, Dunluce Castle was once considered an impregnable fortress. *Info*: Near Portrush. Tel. (028) 2073-1938 Open daily with hours generally Monday through Saturday 10am to 6pm and Sunday 2pm to 6pm, later during the summer and earlier during the winter (check before you visit). Admission is £1.50 for adults, less for seniors, students, and children; family tickets are available.

A FANTASTIC WEEKEND IN NORTHERN IRELAND

A **fine museum**, several **intriguing castles**, a miracle of nature and splendid seascapes greet you on this wonderful Northern Ireland weekend. I've got you eating at **Belfast's top restaurant**, but most of the time should be spent outside the city in Northern Ireland's glorious countryside.

Friday Evening

For a dining treat, try **Restaurant Michael Deane** in Belfast. Heralded as the best restaurant in Northern Ireland, perhaps on the entire Emerald Isle, it is a treat. Spend the night at the **Templeton Hotel** on the northern outskirts of Belfast.

Saturday
To start your day off right, take the A2 from Belfast toward Bangor. Just after you go through the town of Hollywood (still on the A2), watch for the signpost directing you to the **Ulster Folk Park and Transport Museum**. The Ulster Folk and Transport Museum features cottages, chapels, schoolhouses, and farms all brought from their original sites and transported here from all over Ulster. The Transport Museum provides a look at the history of transportation in Ulster. You can easily spend three or four hours here. *Info*: Bangor. Tel. (028) 9042-8428. Open daily with hours generally from 10am to 5pm, later during the summer and earlier in the winter (check before you visit). Admission is £5.50 for adults to either the Folk Park or the Transport Museum, £7 for a combined ticket for adults, less for seniors, students, and children; family tickets are available.

Head north of Belfast on the A2 for **Carrickfergus Castle**. This 12ᵗʰ-century castle has an impressive five-story keep, which

 includes a Cavalry Regimental Museum, with several fine examples of ancient weaponry. The views from the top of the keep are splendid. *Info*: Carrickfergus. Tel. (028) 9335-1273. Generally Monday through Saturday from 10am to 5pm and Sunday from 2pm until 6pm, sometimes later (check before you visit). Admission is £2.70 for adults, less for seniors, students, and children; family tickets are available.

As you drive on the A2 between Larne and Ballycastle, watch for the **Glens of Antrim**. Nine of them in all, they are deep, heavily forested glades, some of them with quasi-tropical greenery. The prettiest of these is **Glenariff**, and its **Glenariff Forest Park.** You have a choice of numerous walking paths, featuring cascading waterfalls, beautiful wild flowers, and dense undergrowth. Trails vary from a half-mile stroll up to a nine-mile scenic trek. *Info*: on the B14 near Carnlough.

Next, head for Cushendun. Look for signposts directing you to **Torr Head Road**. This ribbon-like road snakes around the northeastern tip of Northern Ireland, a scarce 12 miles from Scotland at its closest point. It is a very narrow road, but well-maintained. On a clear day the views are stunning, and you might enjoy pulling off the road and listening to the surf crashing against the rocks below you.

Torr Head Road ends about two miles southeast of **Bonamargy Friary** near Ballycastle. Built in the 16th century, it is largely intact and will provide an interesting few minutes of wandering. Perhaps you'll be fortunate enough to see an ancestor of mine, Julia McQuillan, the mysterious (and ghostly) Black Nun of Bonamargy Friary. Look in the corner of the graveyard for a large cross that marks the site of the final resting place of soldiers washed ashore during both world wars. *Info*: south of Ballycastle on the A2. Admission free.

If you want to stay in a place with an old world feel, try either **Whitepark House** in Ballintoy, Tel. (028) 2073-1482; or, if you decide to visit the famous Bushmills Distillery (see below), consider the **Bushmills Inn Hotel**, Tel. (028) 2073-3000, which dates from the 16th century.

Sunday

From Ballycastle, watch for signs directing you to the B15 and **Carrick-a-Rede Rope Bridge**. The rope bridge is suspended 80 feet above the ocean across a chasm 60 feet wide. Now, neither of those may seem high or long, until you are in the middle of this swaying rope bridge. Hold tight, move slowly, and you're sure to leave with a pleasant memory and feeling a little bolder for the effort. Access is via a scenic half-mile walk up a slight incline. *Info: Info*: near Ballintoy. Tel. (028) 2076-9839 Open daily from March through October with hours generally from 9:30am to 5pm, later during the summer (check before you visit). Admission is £2.50 for adults, less for seniors, students, and children; family tickets are available.

In the nearby town of Bushmills, you'll find **Bushmills Distillery.** It is thought that the Bushmills distillery is the oldest in the world. The Bushmills Distillery produces their famous brand of Irish whiskey here on the northern coast of Ulster. Guided tours are conducted to give you a "flavor" for their process, including a wee nip at the end! *Info*: Bushmills. Tel. (028) 7073-1521. Open with hours generally from 9:30am to 5:30pm during the summer, five times throughout the day during the winter (check before you visit). Admission is £2.50 for adults, less for seniors, students, and children.

When you've completed your distillery tour, watch for signs directing you to **Giant's Causeway**, less than one mile away. Giant's Causeway is one of two things: it is either an incredibly interesting work of nature, or it might be, as the legends say, the handiwork of the giant Finn McCool who was trying to build a stepping-stone bridge to Scotland to find a wife. Either way, the sight is fascinating. Geologists believe that Giant's Causeway is a group of 40,000 symmetric hexagonal stone columns formed millions of years ago by rapidly cooling molten lava. Stop first at the Visitors Center. You can either walk or ride an inexpensive shuttle to the stones. *Info*: on the B146 just off the A2 between Ballintoy and Bushmills. Tel. (028) 7073-1855. Open daily with hours generally from 10am to 5pm, later during the summer (check before you visit). Admission is £2 for adults, less for seniors, students, and children; family tickets are available.

Further west along the coast road between Portrush and Bushmills, you come to **Dunluce Castle**. Dunluce is perched atop a natural basalt tower that rises abruptly out of the ocean. Surrounded on three sides by the ocean, and on the fourth by a gorge, Dunluce Castle was once considered an impregnable fortress. Its picture

graces the cover of almost every tourist brochure for Northern Ireland. *Info*: Near Portrush. Tel. (028) 2073-1938 Open daily with hours generally Monday through Saturday 10am to 6pm and Sunday 2pm to 6pm later during the summer and earlier during the winter (check before you visit). Admission is £1.50 for adults, less for seniors, students, and children; family tickets are available.

Finish off your weekend with a visit to one of Northern Ireland's most beautiful cliff-studded beaches: **Portrush Whiterocks Beach**. Miles of sandy beaches guarded by cliffs with names like Giant's Head, the Wishing Arch and Elephant Rock. *Info*: near Dunluce Castle.

A WONDERFUL WEEK IN ULSTER & NORTHERN IRELAND

I have paired Ulster and Northern Ireland together to provide you a great week in this northernmost portion of the Emerald Isle. All the best sights in this province are here, like the ancient **Grianan of Ailigh** and the picturesque castles of **Dunluce** and **Donegal**. The beautiful Irish coastline offers the unique **Giant's Causeway** and the fun rope bridge of **Carrick-a-Rede**. Walk among cascading waterfalls in **Glenariff Forest Park**, or visit great museums in and around **Belfast**.

RECOMMENDED PLAN: You'll spend a day in Belfast, a couple of days in other areas of Northern Ireland seeing splendid natural and man-made wonders, then we'll move to the sights in Ulster: castles, beaches, parks and forts.

Belfast
Let's start your tour of Northern Ireland in Belfast. Your first stop should be the **Ulster Museum**. This museum is Northern Ireland's version of the Smithsonian and features an eclectic collection of important Irish historical artifacts, natural history, and art. My favorite exhibit is the paraphernalia recovered from the *Girona*, a Spanish ship that sunk in the cold waters off the Antrim Coast in

Don't Miss ...

- **Glenariff Forest Park** – ancestral home of the leprechauns
- **Carrick-a-Rede Rope Bridge** – take a walk on the wild side!
- **Giant's Causeway** – miraculous stones
- **Dunluce Castle** – one of the most photographed castles on the Emerald Isle
- **Grianan of Ailigh** – 3,000-year-old stone ring fort

1588 after their ill-fated expedition against England. Jewelry, weaponry, articles of clothing, and personal effects are among the collection. *Info:* Stranmillis Road. Tel. (028) 9038-3000. Open Monday through Friday 10am to 5pm, Saturday 1pm to 5pm, Sunday 2pm to 5pm. Admission is free.

The Ulster Museum is located on the grounds of the **Botanic Gardens**. This is a nice place to stroll and enjoy the beauty of the flowers, plants, and shrubs.

The central area of Belfast is Donegall Square, and the central attraction of the square is the **Belfast City Hall**. Columned and domed, the building was erected in 1907. The entrance for the general public is located around back. You are free to go in and walk around the open public areas. As you'd suspect, it's marbled and grand. The statue of the woman out front of City Hall is Queen Victoria. On the west of the capitol is a war memorial, and on the east is a monument to those who perished on the Titanic, which was built in Belfast. *Info*: Donegall Square. Tel. (028) 9032-7000. Open Monday through Friday from 9am to 5pm. Admission is free.

For a pint of Guinness and a peek into the Victorian past, stroll west of City Hall down Howard Street to Queen Victoria Street and you'll find the **Crown Liquor Saloon**, a genuine

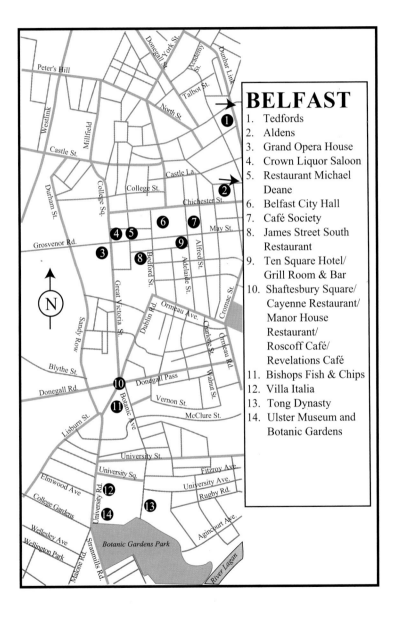

BELFAST

1. Tedfords
2. Aldens
3. Grand Opera House
4. Crown Liquor Saloon
5. Restaurant Michael Deane
6. Belfast City Hall
7. Café Society
8. James Street South Restaurant
9. Ten Square Hotel/ Grill Room & Bar
10. Shaftesbury Square/ Cayenne Restaurant/ Manor House Restaurant/ Roscoff Café/ Revelations Café
11. Bishops Fish & Chips
12. Villa Italia
13. Tong Dynasty
14. Ulster Museum and Botanic Gardens

Victorian-era saloon that hasn't changed much since the early 19th century. Gaslights glisten, mosaics on the floor shine, *snugs* (small, semi-private booths with high walls) beckon patrons to share their most intimate secrets, brass fixtures shine brightly, and the ornate mirrors are a sight to behold. The building is so important that the National Trust of Northern Ireland maintains it. No fear, though – it is a working pub run by an independent company. *Info:* Tel. (028) 9024-9476. Donegall Square District: 46 Great Victoria Street. Open daily.

Belfast's Times Square

Shaftesbury Square is formed by the confluence of Great Victoria Street, Dublin Street, Botanic Avenue, Bradbury Place, and Donegall Road – sort of a Times Square of Belfast, complete with a large electronic billboard. There are lots of restaurants, bookies, pubs, movie theaters, the main post office, and a fun place to watch the panorama of Belfast street life.

Across the street from the Crown Liquor Saloon is the **Grand Opera House**. Built in 1895, this beautiful Victorian Theater was restored to all its finery in 1980. The restoration was faithful to the original heavy gilding and ornamental plasterwork. Productions range from plays and operas to ballet. *Info:* Great Victoria Street, Tel. (028) 9024-1919. Tickets range from £3 to £20 for adults and less for children and seniors.

Head out on the A2 from Belfast toward Bangor. Just after you go through the town of Hollywood (still on the A2), watch for the signpost directing you to the **Ulster Folk Park and Transport Museum**. Perhaps the finest recreation of its kind on the Emerald Isle, the Ulster Folk and Transport Museum features cottages, chapels, schoolhouses, and farms all brought from their original sites and transported here from all over Ulster. They have been painstakingly reconstructed and extensively equipped with period furnishings. The museum gives you a glimpse of the 18th- and 19th-century lives of the Ulster folk, from priests to peasants, farmers to fiddlers. The Transport Museum is a look at the history of transportation in Ulster. You can easily spend three or four hours here. *Info*: Bangor. Tel. (028) 9042-8428. Open daily with hours generally from 10am to 5pm, later during the summer and earlier in the winter (check before you visit). Admission is £5.50 for adults to either the Folk Park or the Transport Museum, £7 for a combined ticket for adults, less for seniors, students, and children; family tickets are available.

Elsewhere in Northern Ireland

Head north of Belfast on the A2 for **Carrickfergus Castle**. This 12th-century castle has an impressive five-story keep which originally housed the well for the castle's drinking water as well as a dungeon. On the third floor is the Great Hall. The keep is also home to a Cavalry Regimental Museum, with several fine examples of ancient weaponry. The views from the top of the keep are splendid. *Info*: Carrickfergus. Tel. (028) 9335-1273. Generally open Monday through Saturday from 10am to 5pm and Sunday from 2pm until 6pm, sometimes later (check before you visit). Admission is £2.70 for adults, less for seniors, students, and children; family tickets are available.

As you drive on the A2 between Larne and Ballycastle, take in the incredible seascapes, as well as the famous **Glens of Antrim**. Nine of them in all – home to the wee folk called leprechauns — they are deep, heavily forested glades, some of them with quasi-tropical greenery. The prettiest of these is **Glenariff**, and its **Glenariff Forest Park.** Known as the "Queen of the Glens," Glenariff Forest Park is billed as an "area of outstanding natural beauty," and it truly is. You have a choice of numerous walking paths, featuring cascading waterfalls, beautiful wild flowers, and dense undergrowth. The beautiful, moist gorges support a wide variety of plant life. Several walking trails are available from a half-mile stroll up to a ten-mile scenic trek. The three-mile waterfall trail is the most popular and, I think, the prettiest. At the edge of the car park is a sign detailing the various hiking paths available in the park. The various paths range from several hundred yards to 10 miles, with something for everyone, it seems. *Info*: on the B14 near Carnlough.

Next, head for Cushendun. Look for signposts directing you to **Torr Head Road**. This ribbon-like road snakes around the northeastern tip of Northern Ireland, a scarce 12 miles from Scotland at its closest point. It is a very narrow road, but well-maintained. If you venture out on Torr Head Road, you'll be richly rewarded for your daring. On a clear day the views are stunning, and you might enjoy pulling off the road and listening to the surf crashing against the rocks below. If you do – hold onto your hat; or better yet, leave it in the car. Otherwise, it may become part of the flotsam below.

Torr Head Road ends about two miles southeast of **Bonamargy Friary** near Ballycastle. The friary was founded in the 1500s by Rory McQuillan, and thrived for several centuries before its destruction by the (dratted) McDonnells, arch-enemies of my kinsmen the McQuillans. Take a few minutes and wander among the ruined walls of this Franciscan friary. See if you can find the small round stone cross of one of my ancestors: **Julia McQuillan**, the Black Nun (it's easy to find - it's marked). Legend has it that Julia still roams the deserted friary, cursing the McDonnells. Look in the corner of the graveyard for a large cross that marks the site of the final resting place of soldiers washed ashore during both world wars. *Info*: south of Ballycastle on the A2. Admission free.

If you want to stay in a place with an old world feel, try either **Whitepark House** in Ballintoy, Tel. (028) 2073-1482; or, if you decide to visit the famous Bushmills Distillery (see below), consider the **Bushmills Inn Hotel**, Tel. (028) 2073-3000, which dates from the 16th century.

From Ballycastle, watch for signs directing you to the B15 and **Carrick-a-Rede Rope Bridge**. The rope bridge is suspended 80 feet above the ocean across a chasm 60 feet wide. Now, neither of those may seem high or long, until you are in the middle of this swaying rope bridge. Hold tight, move slowly, and you're sure to leave with a pleasant memory and feeling a little bolder for the effort. Access is via a scenic half-mile walk up a slight incline. *Info*: near Ballintoy. Tel. (028) 2076-9839 Open daily from March through October with hours generally from 9:30am to 5:00pm, later during the summer (check before you visit). Admission is £2.50 for adults, less for seniors, students, and children; family tickets are available.

In the nearby town of Bushmills, you'll find **Bushmills Distillery.** It is thought that the Bushmills distillery is the oldest in the world. The Bushmills Distillery produces their famous brand of Irish whiskey here on the northern coast of Ulster. Guided tours are conducted to give you a "flavor" for their process, including a wee nip at the end! *Info*: Bushmills. Tel. (028) 7073-1521. Open with hours generally from 9:30am to 5:30pm during the summer, five times throughout the day during the winter (check before you visit). Admission is £2.50 for adults, less for seniors, students, and children.

When you've completed your distillery tour, watch for signs directing you to **Giant's Causeway,** less than one mile away. Giant's Causeway is one of two things: it is either an incredibly interesting work of nature, or it might be, as the legends say, the handiwork of the giant Finn McCool who was trying to build a stepping-stone bridge to Scotland to find a wife. Either way, the sight is fascinating. Geologists tell us that Giant's Causeway is a group of 40,000 symmetric hexagonal stone columns formed millions of years ago by rapidly cooling molten lava. They are absolutely fascinating and probably unlike anything you have ever seen.

Stop first at the **Visitors Center.** It is well done, and helps you understand the scientific explanation for the geological oddity you're about to see. From the Visitors Center, you have two options to reach the Causeway. The first (my preference) is a clifftop walk of about a mile and a half to some very steep steps descending to the shore below. You actually overshoot the main attraction by several hundred yards, but the scenery is well worth it. You can come back that way, or do the more direct shot from the rocks up a fairly steep hill back to the Visitors Center. A shuttle bus runs constantly between the two points, and is available for £1 each way. The second way is to head straight down the hill by foot or shuttle. *Info*: on the B146 just off the A2 between Ballintoy and Bushmills. Tel. (028) 7073-1855. Open daily with hours generally from 10am to 5pm, later during the summer (check before you visit). Admission is €2 for adults, less for seniors, students, and children; family tickets are available.

Further west along the coast road between Portrush and Bushmills, you come to **Dunluce Castle**. Ancestral home of my own McQuillan clan, Dunluce is perched atop a natural basalt tower that rises abruptly out of the ocean. Surrounded on three sides by the ocean, and on the fourth by a gorge, Dunluce Castle was once considered an impregnable fortress. Initially a McQuillan stronghold, it was lost to the MacDonnell Clan who lived there until 1639, when the kitchen (and numerous cooks!) crashed into the ocean! After that, the lady of the castle was no longer interested in living there. Its pic-

Best Romantic Ruin

Between Giant's Causeway and Dunluce Castle on the A2, watch for the romantic ruins of **Dunseverick Castle**, on the ocean-side of the road. The smallish ruins on a rocky promontory are all that is left of the gate house; the castle is long gone. Dunseverick was once the capital of the ancient Irish kingdom of Dalriada. But alas! Dunseverick fell – not as the victim of war or famine, but rather as the result of treachery, unrequited love, and vengeance.

ture graces the cover of almost every Northern Ireland tourist brochure. *Info*: Near Portrush. Tel. (028) 2073-1938 Open daily with hours generally Monday through Saturday 10am to 6pm and Sunday 2pm to 6pm, later during the summer and earlier during the winter (check first). Admission is £1.50 for adults, less for seniors, students, and children; family tickets are available.

Next, head for one of Northern Ireland's most beautiful cliff-studded beaches: **Portrush Whiterocks Beach**. Miles of sandy beaches guarded by cliffs with names like Giant's Head, the Wishing Arch, the Lion's Paw and Elephant Rock, it provides a pleasant stroll and scenic sunsets. Surfers from all over Ireland and Europe come here to surf — and there are usually plenty who come to watch the surfers! *Info*: near Dunluce Castle.

Next, set your sights on **Derry** (also called Londonderry). To begin your tour of the city, you should climb up on the **City Walls** and take a stroll. It should take you no more than an hour to complete the mile-long circuit, but it will provide you with a bird's-eye view of the city and its major sights. Historical markers along the walk help you learn a little of the history of this fair city.

At the northwestern corner of the city walls, you'll find the **Tower Museum**. This award-winning museum (it has won both British *and* Irish Museum-of-the-Year awards) is a must-see on your tour of Derry. It takes its visitors on a tour through Derry's sometimes-turbulent history. Effective (and interesting) high-tech presentations march you through the highlights of Derry's history. There are also a number of ancient artifacts, including a dug-out boat that was found in the area that has been carbon dated to approximately 520 AD! *Info*: O'Doherty's Tower. Tel. (071) 372411. Open daily from 10am to 1pm, and 2pm to 4:30pm. Admission is free.

In the southeastern corner of the walled city you'll find one of the more popular sites in Derry: **St. Columb's Cathedral**. Inside this 17th-century Protestant cathedral you'll find exquisite stone and wood carvings. Beautiful stained glass windows, dark wood and tall open-beamed ceilings make for an interesting visit. *Info*: Open April to October Monday through Saturday from 9am to 5pm, and 9am to 4pm Monday through Saturday from November through March. Admission is £1.

What's in a Name?

Today, those who favor Northern Ireland remaining part of the United Kingdom call the city **Londonderry**; those who wish Northern Ireland to become part of the Irish Republic (the Republicans) call it **Derry**.

Just outside the city walls at the north end of the city, you'll find the **Harbour Museum**.

This small museum has a number of exhibits that feature Derry's maritime history. One of the more interesting exhibits is a memorial to American sailors who perished in WWII. *Info:* Harbor Square. Tel. (071) 37731. Open Monday through Friday from 10am to 1pm and from 2pm to 4:30pm. Admission is free.

Ulster

From Derry, head northwest out of the city on the A2. Watch for the R238, and/or signs directing you toward Buncrana. Proceed through Buncrana following the signs for Malin, beyond which is **Malin Head,** the northernmost point of the Emerald Isle. The views, especially those along the southern shoreline, are breathtaking, and it's hard to beat the incredible sunsets from this particular vantage point. If the weather cooperates, you'll be able to see the Scottish island of **Islay,** on the northeast horizon.

Continue around the Inishowen Peninsula until you return to the A2. Take the A2 northwest to the N13, then south toward Letterkenny. Watch for signposts directing you to the **Grianan of Ailigh.** Follow the signs for about two miles up a winding lane to the top of an 800-foot hill and you're at Grianan of Ailigh – an impressive stone ring fort that was once the stronghold of the O'Neills. Archaeologists speculate that the fort dates from the Iron Age, making it approximately 3,000 years old! It is a circular structure with three terraced rings one inside the other. On the inside a series of stone walks bring you to the top of the 17-foot tall walls. Their base is a *mere* 13 feet. The structure you see today was restored from a somewhat disheveled state about 100 years ago. Sweeping views greet you from the top. I have been to the Grianan of Ailigh during nice weather as well as stormy weather. Regardless of whether it is shrouded in mist or basking in bright sunlight it is an impressive sight indeed.

If you want to learn more about this curious structure, back down on the N13, at the foot of the hill upon which the Grianan Ailigh presides, is the **Grianan Ailigh Heritage Centre**. It is an interpretive center focused on the Grianan of Ailigh. It offers dioramas and a scale model of the fort. *Info*: Near Letterkenny. Tel. (077) 68080. Open daily 10am to 10pm. Admission for adults is €5, less for seniors, students, and children; family tickets are available.

Back on the N13, head toward Letterkenny. From Letterkenny, head northwest on the N56 to Termon, then on the R255 toward Dunlewy. Near Churchill, you'll find **Glenveagh National Park.** In a land of incredible beauty, Glenveagh National Park can hold its own, and then some. Glenveagh Lough is simply gorgeous, as is Glenveagh Castle, and it boasts a set of gardens that are exquisite. You cannot drive through the park, but walking paths are available. A 45-minute tour of the castle is also interesting. *Info*: Near Churchill. Tel. (074) 37090. Open mid-March through early November daily from 10am to 6:30pm. Admission to the park is €2.50 for adults, less for seniors, students, and children; family tickets are available. Admission to the castle is the same.

From Glenveagh, take the R250 southwest toward Killybegs. Continue west from Killybegs on the R263 to get to the **Slieve League Mountains**. The cliffs of Slieve League Mountains are the highest in Ireland, sloping nearly 2,000 feet into the ocean.

Several cliff walks are available in the area. One of them, "One Man's Pass," feels not unlike a high-wire act, and is not for the faint of heart or people suffering from fear of heights. Not as abrupt or scary as the Cliffs of Moher, they are still very impressive.

Your next stop will be **Donegal,** with its tourist shops, including McGinty's Sweater Shop and Magee's Tweed Shop. Take a few moments to walk the town square. Stop in at **Donegal Castle,** in the center of town just off the square. Tours of the castle yield wonderful views of ornate Persian rugs, splendid French tapestries and information panels tell the history of the castle. *Info*: Donegal, Tirchonaill Street. Tel. (073) 22405. Open mid-March through October daily from 10am to 6pm. Admission is €3.70 for adults, less for seniors, students, and children; family tickets are available.

After exploring Donegal, head south on the N15 toward Ballyshannon. At Ballyshannon, take the N3 into Belleek for an elegant treat at **Belleek Pottery**. Belleek china is that creamy-looking china you'll see throughout Ireland. Half-hour tours of the factory are available during the week. There is a museum and also a lovely display area/shop where you can marvel at the elegance of Belleek pottery, and of course you can purchase some of their goods if you wish. *Info:* Belleek. Tel. (028) 6865-9300. Open Monday through Friday with hours generally from 9am to 6pm, sometimes later (check before you visit). Saturdays they open an hour later. Sundays they are generally open from 2pm to 6pm. During the winter, they are not open on Saturdays or Sundays. Admission is £4 or €6 for adults, less for seniors, students, and children; family tickets are available.

From Belleek, take the A47 about four miles east to the ruins of **Castle Caldwell**. Watch for the entrance to the ruins of Castle Caldwell on the right-hand side of the road. Its ivy-covered walls are fascinating. The woods around the area are a national bird-watching preserve. The most intriguing artifact here is the tombstone of **Denis McCabe**, a fiddler of some ability. While on a pleasure cruise on the lake in 1770, Denis fell overboard and drowned. The epitaph chiseled into his headstone gives us a clue as to the reason for his demise:

> *"Beware ye fidlers of ye fidlers fate*
> *Nor tempt ye deep least ye repent too late.*
> *Ye ever have been deemed to water*
> *Foes then shun ye lake till it with whiskey flows.*
> *On firm land only exercise your skill,*
> *That you may play and safely drink your fill.*

–To the memory of Denis McCabe, Fidler, who fell out of the St. Patrick Barge belonging to Sir James Calldwell Bart and Count of Milan and was drowned off this point August 17, 1770.

Poor Denis!

The headstone and plaque are at the entrance to Castle Caldwell. The headstone is weather-worn and barely legible, but the attached plaque tells the sad tale.

From Castle Caldwell, follow the A47 until it dead-ends into the A32. Turn left and follow the signposts to Omagh. About three miles north of Omagh on the A5 you'll come to the **Ulster American Folk Park**, This particular folk park presents an interesting angle. They have reconstructed a typical 18th-century County Tyrone village, as well as an American settlement from the same period. Their attempt is to compare and contrast the life Irish emigrants left for the life they found in America. *Info*: Camphill, County Tyrone. Tel. (028) 8224-3292. Open Easter through September Monday to Saturday 10:30am to 4:30pm, Sunday from 11am to 5pm; Admission is £4.50 for adults, less for seniors, students, and children; family tickets are available.

8. IRELAND IN TWO WEEKS

If you have two weeks to spend on the Emerald Isle and want to see it all, follow this itinerary – I'll take you to the best ruins, incredible cathedrals, superb museums and some of the most memorable scenery in Ireland (or the world, for that matter). You'll find details on **Dublin** and each of **Ireland's four provinces** covered here. Please refer to the maps in the earlier chapters for locations of sights in this chapter.

RECOMMENDED PLAN: Take two days in Dublin, and another couple of days in the countryside outside of Dublin. Then head south for two days seeing the sights in the southeast part of Ireland. Continue clockwise around the country, seeing the sights in the southwest and central part of Ireland for a couple of days. Then head for Ireland's west coast for three days. Finish up in Northern Ireland.

Dublin & Surrounding Areas

Start your first full day in Dublin with a stop at **St. Patrick's Cathedral**. Considered the National Cathedral of the Church of Ireland, St. Patrick's was founded in 1191, but its history goes back much further. St. Patrick himself once performed baptisms on this sight, making it the oldest Christian site in Dublin. Originally built outside the Dublin city walls, the location earned St. Patrick's the reputation of being the "church of the people."

It's hard to believe that Oliver Cromwell showed his contempt for this magnificent structure by demanding that his horses be stabled inside the cathedral.

Be sure and look for the **Door of Reconciliation**, a memorial to incredible courage. In 1492, two of Ireland's most powerful men, the Earl of Kildare and the Earl of Ormond, had been warring. The Earl of Ormond sought sanctuary in the Chapter House on the grounds of St. Patrick's, and a standoff ensued. Tired of the war, the Earl of Kildare approached the Chapter House and chopped a hole in the door. As an act of reconciliation and to show his willingness to lay down arms (figuratively as well as literally, apparently!), he thrust his arm through the

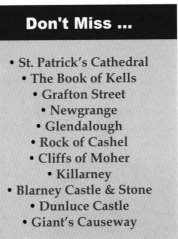

Don't Miss ...

- **St. Patrick's Cathedral**
- **The Book of Kells**
- **Grafton Street**
- **Newgrange**
- **Glendalough**
- **Rock of Cashel**
- **Cliffs of Moher**
- **Killarney**
- **Blarney Castle & Stone**
- **Dunluce Castle**
- **Giant's Causeway**

hole and grasped the hand of his enemy, ending the war. *Info:* Patrick Street. Tel. (01) 475-4817. Open daily 9am to 6pm. Admission is €4.50 for adults, less for seniors, students, and children; family tickets available.

Just west of St. Patrick's Cathedral is **Francis Street** – known as Dublin's **Antiques Row**. Although you'll find antique shops elsewhere in Dublin, nowhere is there the concentration as thick as you'll find here on Francis Street. Visitors will be enticed by many of the small shops, some of whose owners are as precious and delightful as the antiques they peddle.

Head east until you come to St. Stephen's Green, and you'll find **Grafton Street**, a long pedestrian open-air mall. Grafton Street is a fascinating blend of antique, jewelry, and upscale shops, with a generous mix of *buskers*, street entertainers, ranging from musicians to magicians, jugglers to Marionette masters, and a host of other talented individuals. The naturally demonstrative nature of the buskers comes through delightfully as they sense an audience gathering around them. Be sure and check out the very upscale department store **Brown Thomas** (aka BT), as well as **Weirs Jewelers**.

Grafton Street is quite an experience. Give yourself plenty of time to stroll along the crowded sidewalks and sample a wee bit of this aspect of Irish culture. Don't rush your visit on Grafton Street – there is so much to see and do, so many stores to investigate.

At the north end of Grafton Street, don't miss the **Molly Malone Statue**, standing at the corner of Suffolk and Grafton Streets. Molly Malone is a featured character in an old Irish folk song. The bodice on Molly's dress is so scandalously low (even for a statue!) that she has been dubbed variously *The Tart with the Cart* and *The Dish with the Fish!*

Your next stop is the **National Gallery of Ireland** – the finest art gallery on the island. If you are hoping to see works of art by Irish painters, you won't be disappointed. I suppose every major Irish artist - and many not-so-major artists - are represented here. Don't miss the room devoted to impressionist Jack Butler Yeats, brother of Irish writer William Butler Yeats. In addition, there is a fine European collection, including works by such notables as **Rembrandt, Degas, El Greco, Goya, Monet, Reynolds, Rubens, Titian, Van Dyck**, and others. One of the museum's most extraordinary aspects is a four-story circular staircase lined with paintings of three centuries' worth of notable personalities in Irish history, a kind of wall of fame.

Guided tours are offered on Saturday afternoons at 3pm and Sundays at 2:30pm, 3:15pm, and 4pm. You can easily spend three or four hours in the gallery; there are that many works of art to consider. If you find yourself here around lunchtime, there is an award-winning self-serve restaurant available to meet your gastronomical needs. *Info:* Merrion Square West. Tel. (01) 661-5133. www.nationalgallery.ie. Open Monday through Saturday 9:30am to 5:30pm (Thursday until 8:30pm), Sunday from noon until 5:30pm. Admission is free.

From the National Gallery head one street east to Kildare Street and the **National Museum of Ireland**. The National Museum of Ireland has a number of fascinating displays which take you through the history of Ireland from the Bronze Age (2200 BC to 700 BC) to the present. The *Treasury Exhibition* is worth a visit, even though it is the only part of the museum requiring a modest admission fee. It includes the lovely Tara Brooch (8th-century), the Ardagh Chalice (8th-century), and the silver and bronzed Cross of Cong (12th-century), and much more.

An exhibit that will give you a good sense of Ireland's struggle for independence is highlighted by *Ar Thóir na Saoirse*, which is Gaelic for "The Road to Independence." It is a permanent exhibit that deals with the major personalities and events that took place from 1916 to 1922 as Ireland finally forged her independence. *Info:* Kildare Street. Tel. (01) 677-7444. www.museum.ie/archae-ology. Open Tuesday through Saturday 10am to 5pm and Sunday from 2pm to 5pm. Admission is free (except for special exhibits).

After finishing your tour of the National Museum, head over to **Trinity College** for one of the highlights of your trip to Dublin: the **Book of Kells**. Without a doubt, the most important holding at Trinity College is the Book of Kells, the ornately illustrated four Gospels written by the monks of the Kells monastery in County Meath. Written (drawn?) in the 9th century, the Book of Kells is four volumes of elaborate ornamental drawings of the four Gospels. The title pages of each Gospel are particularly elaborate. There are also gorgeous pictures depicting many scenes from Christ's life, including his temptation and arrest.

The Book of Kells is kept in a glass case in a room with muted lighting. Two Gospels are shown at a time, and the pages are turned each day. The pages are calfskin made from 185 calves! As you look at the incredible craftsmanship and stunning artwork of the books, it's hard to imagine that these lovely works were once hidden under a roll of sod to protect them from the ravages of invaders! *Info:* Trinity College Colonnades. Tel. (01) 677-2941. Generally open daily 9:30am to 5pm; Sunday hours are shorter during the off-season. Admission is €8 for adults, less for seniors, students, and children; family tickets available.

After you view of the Book of Kells, you are treated to a fascinating stroll through the lavish **Long Room of the Old Library** on your way out. This impressive room is over 200 feet long and 40 feet wide. For nearly 200 years, Trinity College has been receiving a copy of every book published in Ireland and England, and many of them are on display here in the Old Library. Included in the holdings of the library are first editions of some of Shakespeare's works, as well as copies of the original printing of the *Proclamation of 1916* (Ireland's equivalent of the Declaration of Independence).

After being wowed by the Book of Kells and the Long Library, head straight to **Grafton Street** for a fun and memorable evening of mirth and frivolity. Half-way down (or half-way up, depending on your approach) Grafton Street at the intersection of Grafton and Duke Streets, you'll spot a tourist sign directing you to the **Dublin Literary Pub Crawl**. Local actors take turns entertaining, informing, shocking, and delighting their guests with tales of Ireland's most note-

worthy writers: **Brendan Behan, James Joyce, W. B. Yeats, Oscar Wilde, Oliver Goldsmith, George Bernard Shaw**, and others. Each session is conducted by a two-some. Four or five pubs are part of the tour, as are the grounds of Trinity College. You'll experience a rollicking good time, full of literary one-liners, a little irreverence, lots of laughs, (a little bawdy at times), and plenty of good, (mostly) clean fun. *Info:* Duke Street. Tel. (01) 670-5602. www.dublinpubcrawl.com. Operating May through September: nightly at 7:30pm, and Sundays at noon. October through April: Sundays at noon, Thursday through Saturday 7:30pm. Admission is €7.50.

During your pub crawl, you may have filled up on pub grub or assorted snacks, but if you are still hungry, head for **Pasta Fresca**, just off Grafton Street, for great made-on-the-premises pasta. For a fabulous dinner, head over to Merrion Street and **Restaurant Patrick Guilbaud**. The restaurant is housed in an old Georgian home that has been exquisitely renovated. You'll feel most comfortable if you are dressed in a coat and tie, or dress. And if you're not in the mood for dressing up (or couldn't get reservations), for Restaurant Patrick Guilbaud, try **Gallagher's Boxty House**. Gallagher's offers a more casual dining experience than Restaurant Patrick Guilbaud, and features traditional Irish meals. See *Best Sleeps & Eats* chapter for more details on each place.

A trip to Ireland would not be complete unless you try their world-famous Guinness beer. And there is no better place than the sprawling, 60-acre **Guinness Storehouse and Brewery**, where Dubliners swear the beer tastes better! For the uninitiated,

Guinness is a dark, heavy, bitter beer with a creamy head served at room temperature. For many, it is an acquired taste, but all beer lovers should try it at least once.

Arthur Guinness founded the brewery on the banks of the River Liffey in 1759, and his descendants have carried on his work. The brewery produces an amazing four million pints of Guinness beer *per day*. Tours of the brewery itself are no longer conducted, but a fine audiovisual presentation on the history of the brewery is available in the Hop Store. At the close of the presentation, a complimentary sample of Guinness is available to those who wish to sample the dark brew. *Info:* Crane Street. Tel. (01) 453-8364 (information line) or (01) 408-4800 (for reservations for large groups, or to talk to the Hop Store). Open April through August daily from 9:30am until 6pm, September through March daily from 9:30am to 5pm. Admission is €9 for adults, less for seniors, students, and children; family tickets available.

From the Guinness Storehouse, stroll east along the River Liffey for about six blocks until you come to the **Ha'penny Bridge**, and then cross over to the other side of the bridge. Ha'penny (pronounced hay'-penny) Bridge is the only strictly pedestrian bridge in Dublin, and it derives its name from the toll charged to use the bridge in earlier days.

Once on the north side of the bridge, continue east another block to **O'Connell Street**, and turn left (north). The first thing that dominates your view of O'Connell Street is the **Spire of Dublin,** a 393-foot stainless steel pole. The Irish have a penchant for nicknaming their monuments, and this one is no exception. The Spire of Dublin is often called, among other things, *the Stiffy by the Liffey, the Pointless Point*, and (my favorite) *the Stiletto in the Ghetto*.

Once you've overcome your surprise at the Spire of Dublin, head north on O'Connell Street toward the Spire. Before you arrive at it, on your left you will come to the **General Post Office**, better known as the **GPO**. This is probably the best-known building in Dublin. It is the main post office, and as such everyone is familiar with it. But its mark on history goes much beyond postal service: it was the flash point of the 1916 Easter Rising, which ended in

Ireland gaining her independence from England. It was from the seized GPO that Irish rebel leaders proclaimed their message of a new republic. The ensuing battle destroyed most of the area around O'Connell Street. Some of the GPO's massive stone columns still bear the scars of flying bullets. The words of the **1916 proclamation** read by the rebel leaders on that fateful Easter can morning are inscribed in a green marble plaque in the GPO. *Info:* Tel. (01) 872-8888. Open Monday through Saturday 8am until 8pm, Sundays from 10:30am to 6:30pm.

POBLACHT NA H EIREANN.

THE PROVISIONAL GOVERNMENT
OF THE
IRISH REPUBLIC
TO THE PEOPLE OF IRELAND.

IRISHMEN AND IRISHWOMEN In the name of God and of the dead generations from which she receives her old tradition of nationhood, Ireland, through us, summons her children to her flag and strikes for her freedom.

Having organised and trained her manhood through her secret revolutionary organisation, the Irish Republican Brotherhood, and through her open military organisations, the Irish Volunteers and the Irish Citizen Army, having patiently perfected her discipline, having resolutely waited for the right moment to reveal itself, she now seizes that moment, and, supported by her exiled children in America and by gallant allies in Europe, but relying in the first on her, own strength, she strikes in full confidence of victory

We declare the right of the people of Ireland to the ownership of Ireland, and to the unfettered control of Irish destinies, to be sovereign and indefeasible. The long usurpation of that right by a foreign people and government has not extinguished the right, nor can it ever be extinguished except by the destruction of the Irish people. In every generation the Irish people have asserted their right to national freedom and sovereignty, six times during the past three hundred years they have asserted it in arms. Standing on that fundamental right and again asserting it in arms in the face of the world, we hereby proclaim the Irish Republic as a Sovereign Independent State, and we pledge our lives and the lives of our comrades-in-arms to the cause of its freedom, of its welfare, and of its exaltation among the nations.

The Irish Republic is entitled to, and hereby claims, the allegiance of every Irishman and Irishwoman. The Republic guarantees religious and civil liberty, equal rights and equal opportunities to all its citizens, and declares its resolve to pursue the happiness and prosperity of the whole nation and of all its parts, cherishing all the children of the nation equally, and oblivious of the differences carefully fostered by an alien government, which have divided a minority from the majority in the past.

Until our arms have brought the opportune moment for the establishment of a permanent National Government, representative of the whole people of Ireland and elected by the suffrages of all her men and women, the Provisional Government, hereby constituted, will administer the civil and military affairs of the Republic in trust for the people.

We place the cause of the Irish Republic under the protection of the Most High God, Whose blessing we invoke upon our arms, and we pray that no one who serves that cause will dishonour it by cowardice, inhumanity, or rapine. In this supreme hour the Irish nation must, by its valour and discipline and by the readiness of its children to sacrifice themselves for the common good, prove itself worthy of the august destiny to which it is called.

Signed on Behalf of the Provisional Government,
THOMAS J. CLARKE.
SEAN Mac DIARMADA, THOMAS MacDONAGH,
P. H. PEARSE, EAMONN CEANNT,
JAMES CONNOLLY. JOSEPH PLUNKETT.

Near the GPO, catch a bus for your next stop today. Watch for buses 13, 19 or 134, and hop on for a short ride to the **National Botanic Gardens**. This is a real treat and worth the short bus ride. Visitors have enjoyed these gardens for over 200 years. The gardens boast over 20,000 plant species spread over 45 acres, but the oversized arboretum threatens to steal the show. The green houses – over 400 feet of them – house an astounding variety of exotic plants and trees, such as orchids, banana trees, and palm trees. *Info:* Glasnevin Road. Tel. (01) 837-7596 or (01) 837-4388. Generally open Monday through Saturday from 9am until 6pm, Sundays from 11am to 6pm; slightly shorter hours during the winter. Admission is free.

After viewing the Botanic Gardens, catch any bus labeled *An Lar* (Irish for City Center). You'll be dropped off across the street from the GPO. Nearby is the **Garden of Remembrance**, a memorial to those who gave their lives for Ireland's independence. This is a peaceful and contemplative place where visitors think about

Irish patriots who gave their lives for a free Ireland. The square features an ornamental pond in the form of a crucifix, and the setting is very serene and peaceful. Just beyond the small pond is a statue that looks like children chasing geese and making them fly away. It is in reality a statue of the children of Lir, who were turned into swans by their wicked stepmother (according to legend). *Info:* Parnell Square. Generally open daily from 9:30am to 7pm, shorter during the winter months. Admission is free.

From the Garden of Remembrance, head over to the **Dublin Writer's Museum**. Ireland has always loved its writers and poets, and there has always been a special place for them in the heart of every Irish man and woman. Now there is a museum for them, too. The Dublin Writer's Museum opened in 1991 and is one of Dublin's top attractions. It is one of the most elegant, tasteful and well thought-out museums in Ireland. Be sure to check out the permanent exhibits that feature famed Irish authors such as **Samuel Beckett, Brendan Behan, George Bernard Shaw, Jonathan Swift,** and **Oscar Wilde**. Paintings, photographs, letters, and memorabilia are all part of the various exhibits. *Info:* 18/19 Parnell Square. Tel. (01) 872-2077. Open Monday through Saturday from 10am to 5pm, and Sundays from 11am to 5pm. Open later during the summer. Admission is €6.70 for adults, less for seniors, students, and children; family tickets available.

Once you've finished your day's sightseeing, hop on the DART at Pearse, Tara or Connolly Street stations and head out to **Howth** and the **Abbey Tavern**. Here you'll find a good meal and a delightful traditional Irish music show. Before or after dinner, be sure and walk the short distance to the quay and walk along the seashore, **enjoying a wonderful sunset over the Irish Sea**. Through the years, some of my most stunning sunset photos of Ireland were taken here.

About a 45-minute drive north of Dublin you'll find **Newgrange,** one of Ireland's most impressive ancient sights. The Newgrange burial mound is an enormous, well-preserved grave dating back to nearly 3,000 BC. At 8:58am on December 21 of each year, the rising sun strikes an aperture in the roof of the passage grave. The sunlight is directed down into the passage grave, and as the sun rises its rays slowly move down the passage until they arrive in the main burial chamber, illuminating it.  The rest of the year the effect is simulated by shining a light down the passage and into the burial chamber, as though it was really December 21, simulating the path the sun's rays take. Including the roundtrip drive from Dublin, a little time in the Visitors Center and time at Newgrange, you easily spend five or six hours on this excursion. *Info:* Entrance to the Visitors Center is just south of Slane off the N2. Tel. (041) 988-0300. Open March through November, with hours generally from 9:30am to 5pm, sometimes later (check before you visit). Admission is €5.80 for adults, less for seniors, students, and children; family tickets available.

Relatively close to Newgrange are two other sights you should definitely spend a few minutes perusing: the Hill of Tara and Monasterboice. About six miles north of Drogheda on the N1, watch for the first Dunleer exit north of Drogheda, then follow the signs to **Monasterboice**. It is not signed particularly well from the N1, but watch for the lonely round tower off the west side of the N1 and make your way over to it. This site offers one of the premier exhibits of finely preserved high crosses in Ireland. It is the monastic settlement of Monasterboice, which takes its name from the Irish *Mainstir Buithe*, which means "St. Buithe's Abbey."

·St. Buithe founded a monastery on this site during the 5th century. In 1097, the round tower suffered a devastating fire. The monastery was eventually abandoned in the 12th century. The site consists of the ruins of two churches, a round tower, and three high crosses.

Two of the high crosses at Monasterboice are among the best examples of high crosses in the world. One of them, the **Cross of Muiredach**, is remarkably well preserved. An inscription at the base of the cross says, "A prayer for Muiredach by whom this cross was made." This 10th-century High Cross stands almost 17 feet tall, and has scenes depicting Adam and Eve, Cain and Abel, Christ as the Judge, and Michael weighing souls. It also contains a depiction of the crucifixion. **Tall Cross** (21 feet high) depicts the sacrifice of Isaac by Abraham, the Vigil at the Tomb, Judas' kiss of betrayal, and the crucifixion.

One other cross, the **North Cross**, only partially survived the years. Scholars speculate that these crosses served more than an artistic outlet for some sculptor; they believe the crosses were used by monks to teach their non-reading followers about the scriptures. The forlorn round tower that keeps a silent vigil over Monasterboice is nearly 110 feet tall, even without its peaked cap, which was lost many centuries ago. *Info:* There is no charge to visit Monasterboice. Just park your car in the small carpark across the street, and let yourself in the gate.

After examining Monasterboice, head toward Navan and the **Hill of Tara**. Eight miles south of Navan just off the N3 (watch for the signpost) is the Hill of Tara, one of the most significant historic, religious, secular, and mythical sights in Ireland. It is the ancient site of the coronation of the Celtic kings of Ireland. Atop this legendary hill is a statue of St. Patrick, and a small pillar called the *Lia Fial*, the stone believed to have been used as an ancient coronation stone. Legend has it that when the High King of Ireland (called the *Ard Ri*) was crowned at this sight, if the coronation was acceptable to the pagan gods, the Lia Fial roared mightily. The pagan Celtic kings would probably roll over in their graves if they knew the statue of this zealous Christian missionary had been erected on the hill of their ancient coronations. Today, little else is on the Hill of Tara except grass-covered mounds and the occasional grazing sheep – the new kings of Tara. *Info:* Near Navan. Open May through September from 10am to 5pm, sometimes longer. Admission is €2 for adults, less for seniors, students, and children; family tickets are available.

South of Dublin near the town of Enniskerry you'll find **Powerscourt Gardens and Waterfall**. Without knowing it, you've probably seen pictures of Powerscourt Gardens before - they are popular scenes used to depict the beauty of Ireland. Powerscourt gardens were originally laid out beginning in 1745, and were revised to their present grand design in the mid-1800s. They cascade in a series of terraces down a slope from the house. The gardens are filled with verdant greenery: sculpted shrubs, trees, and many varieties of flowering plants, set among statues, fountains, and walkways. From the top of the terraces, the views

sweep across the breath-taking **Dargle Valley**, culminating in outstanding views of Great Sugar Loaf Mountain and Kippure Mountain. In addition to the views, Powerscourt offers a tea-room, garden center and small shop. You could easily spend half a day wandering through the various gardens of Powerscourt.

Three miles south of the gardens is **Powerscourt Waterfall**. The highest waterfall in Ireland, the water cascades more than 400 feet off the edge of the mountain. It serves as a favorite picnic area for tourists and locals alike. *Info:* Enniskerry. Tel. (01) 204-6000. The gardens are open March through October daily from 9:30am until 5:30pm. Admission is €9 for adults, less for seniors, students, and children; family tickets are available. The waterfall is open all year from 9:30am until 7pm. Admission to the waterfall area is €4.50 for adults, less for seniors, students, and children; family tickets available.

If you really enjoyed the floral magnificence of Powerscourt and would like more of the same, head south to Ashford and **Mt. Usher Gardens,** and then over to Tully and the **Japanese Gardens**. You'll be treated to even more floral splendor.

After enjoying the beauties of Powerscourt, head further south to **Glendalough**."The glen of the two lakes" – *Glen Da Locha* – is perhaps one of the most serene places in the world. Two lakes grace the valley with their elegance and beauty - they are called simply Upper Lake and Lower Lake. Heavily forested mountains encompass the valley. Add to the natural beauty some exquisite and ancient ruins, and this is a wonderful place to visit. But don't rush your visit here; take your time and see all there is to see. A webwork of walking paths laces the woods all around Glendalough, and if you're interested in that aspect of touring, they offer wonderfully serene views.

The best place to begin your tour of Glendalough is at the visitors center. Here they have a fine audio-visual presentation on Glendalough and its history. Near the visitors centre you'll find some of the finest religious ruins in Ireland. Towering above the trees, the well-preserved 100-foot tall **Round Tower** stands as a mute witness of past oppressors and as a sentry against future invaders. Built in the 10th century, the only entrance is a doorway a mere 25 feet above the ground!

The **Cathedral** located at Glendalough is in relatively good shape, given its age (11th century) and the history of conquest this valley has had. The nave, chancel, and small sacristy are still intact. Nearby is **St. Kevin's Kitchen**, and this small church has a high-pitched stone roof. It is thought this structure was also built in the 11th century. And don't miss **St. Kevin's Cross**, (it would be hard to), an 11-foot granite cross 1,300 years old.

Other ruins of interest in Glendalough include **St. Savier's Church** (12th century), **Church of our Lady** (the oldest ruin in the lower valley), and the **Priest's House**, site of burials for priests. On the east end of Upper Lake you'll find an old fort dating from the late Bronze or early Iron age. *Info:* Near Laragh. Tel. (0404) 45325. Visitors Center open mid-March through May daily with hours generally from 9:30am to 6pm, sometimes later (check before you visit). Admission is €2.90 for adults, less for seniors, students, and children; family tickets available.

Southeastern Ireland

As you head further south in Leinster, you'll come to Kilkenny. The best sights in Kilkenny are **St. Canice's Cathedral** and **Kilkenny Castle** – be sure you don't miss them.

After seeing the impressive stonework of **Kilkenny Castle**, the next thing you will see will be the richly landscaped grounds. They are immaculate with hardly a blade of grass or mum out of place. The castle sits along the banks of the River Nore, and is surrounded by acres upon acres of manicured lawns, fountains, and flowers. When you've had your fill of the grounds, venture into the castle. A one-hour guided tour includes visits to a number of the castle's rooms, including the drawing and dining rooms, the library, and some of the bedrooms, which are imposing: each has ample numbers of antiques, tremendous tapestries, and plenty of paintings. Many of the furnishings you'll see are original to the castle, and the library has a number of books that have been here for hundreds of years!

By far the most impressive room in the castle is the remarkable **Long Gallery**, a cavernous room 45 meters long and 9 meters wide, with a ceiling about 60 feet high. Its walls  are decked out with the portraits of the Butler family - 500 years' worth! In addition, splendid 17th-century tapestries grace several of the walls. Look closely at those tapestries - they are linen, silk, and wool, and took 65 Parisian artisans three months to weave them! *Info:* The Parade, Kilkenny. Tel. (056) 21450. Open daily with hours generally from 9:30am to 5pm, with longer summertime hours (check before you visit). Admission is €4.50 for adults, less for seniors, students, and children; family tickets are available.

Not far from Kilkenny Castle is **St. Canice's Cathedral**, an impressive gray granite house of worship. Modeled after many of the English churches of the period (13th century), St. Canice's stands firm and straight despite the efforts of a number of plunderers, including Cromwell's forces. *Info:* Corner of Dean and Parliament Streets, Kilkenny. Tel. (046) 64971. Open Monday through Saturday with hours generally from 9:30am to 6pm, and Sunday from 2pm to 6pm, although winter hours are more abbreviated (check before you visit). Admission is €2.

Southeast of Kilkenny and two miles south of Thomastown on the N9 you'll find **Jerpoint Abbey**, considered one of the finest monastic ruins in Ireland. Spend a few minutes walking among the ample ruins, imagining what the life of a monk in the late 12th century would have been like at this monastery. The ruin is large - it is nearly the exact length and width of a football field. There are a series of interesting sculptures in the cloister. Judging from the flowing robes on many of them, they may represent some of the monks who served at Jerpoint Abbey. There are several **interesting tombs** in the church, including one of Bishop Felix O'Dulaney. The bishop's effigy is interesting: it depicts a snake biting the crosier (a hooked staff, like a shepherd's crooked stick) held by the good bishop. The small visitor's center provides a history of the monastery. The monastery is a wonderful subject for photographers, amateur as well as professional. It is impressive, and is well worth the small admission fee. *Info*: Near Thomastown. Tel. (056) 24623. Open March through November daily generally from 9:30am to 6pm, although winter hours are more abbreviated (check before you visit). Admission is

Best Remote Castle Ruin

On the road between Kilkenny and Thomastown (the R700), watch for signs directing you to Graiguenamanagh Abbey. Turn there, and watch for a weathered signpost directing you to **Coolhill Castle**. After several twists and turns on a very narrow single-lane road, you'll come to a grand castle. This fascinating ruin standing as a forlorn sentinel in the middle of a farmer's field is a mere shadow of its former self. But there is enough of its ancient round structure left to help you imagine what a magnificent place it must have been at one time - someone's pride and joy. Long since abandoned, the castle now stands guard over rolling fields, grazing sheep, and landscape that appears to be stitched together by a giant hand.

€2.90 for adults, less for seniors, students, and children; family tickets are available.

At the northern edge of Wexford you'll find the small village of Ferrycarrig, and the **Irish National Heritage Park**. This fun and educational park traces Ireland's heritage from the Stone Age through the conquest of the Anglo-Normans. Thirty acres are filled with a myriad of life-size structures – dwellings, forts, a monastery, Norman castle, etc., to give you an idea of how the ancient Irish lived, worked, and were buried. Actors in period dress answer questions and share their skills at weaving, pole lathing, and pottery through frequent demonstrations. This is a lot of fun and very interesting. In about two hours you'll get a good overview of about 4,000 years of Irish history. *Info*: Ferrycarrig. Tel. (053) 20733. Open March to November from 10am to 7pm (last admittance at 5pm). Admission is €7.50 for adults, less for seniors, students, and children; family tickets are available.

> ## Hotel Splurge Alert!
>
> You might consider saving your pennies to stay at one of Ireland's best hotels: **Mount Juliet**, near Thomastown (www.mountjuliet.ie, Tel. (056) 777-3000). Even if you don't stay, drive through the grounds and dream of what it would be like to stay there!

Follow the signposts from Wexford toward the beautiful fishing village of Kilmore Quay (the N25 to the R739), where you'll find thatched-roof cottages and pleasant villagers. Along the way, watch for the signposts directing you to Tacumshin; follow those signs to Tacumshin, and you'll be treated to a picturesque sight – the **Tacumshin Windmill**. This old thatched windmill, reminiscent of those Holland is famous for, was built in 1846 and used until 1936. *Info*: Stop into the small store that is in front of the

windmill, and the proprietor will unlock the door so you can go inside and view the inner workings of the windmill.

The word for **Kilmore Quay** is picturesque. It is a radiant little village with thatched roofs and whitewashed cottages. Sitting on a small peninsula on the Celtic Sea, the sea views are fabulous, the air is fresh, and the local villagers are warm and cheerful.

The **Ring of Hook Drive** is as peaceful a drive through the Irish countryside as you are likely to take. From Wellington Bridge, take the R733 toward Fethard-on-the-Sea. From there, follow the signs for the Ring of Hook lighthouse and the Celtic Sea. It's a great place to take plenty of pictures.

The Ring of Hook ends at **Duncannon**, just across the harbor from Waterford. At the edge of town you'll find Duncannon Fort. For many years Duncannon was a site of military importance, particularly as protection against marauding ships of (take your choice) Vikings, Anglo-Normans, Irish rebels, the Spanish Armada, Napoleon's navy, etc. No matter who controlled this site, they kept the three-acre fort fortified and ready to greet any foes that ventured her way. *Info*: Duncannon. Tel. (051) 389454, (051) 389188. Open daily June through September from 10am to 5:30pm. Admission is €4 for adults, less for seniors, students, and children; family tickets are available.

Between Arthurstown and Wellington Bridge you'll find the ruins of **Tintern Abbey.** A plaque on the site says, "Founded in 1200 by William Earl Marshall. This abbey was called 'Tintern de Voto' after Tintern Abbey in Wales, from where its monks came." The abbey is largely intact, and has recently undergone extensive renovation. The remains consist of a vaulted chapel, nave, tower, and chancel. *Info*: Open mid-June through late September daily from 9:30am to 6:30pm. Admission is €2.10 for adults, less for seniors, students, and children; family tickets are available.

Little **Ballyhack** sits at the mouth of Waterford Harbor on the R733. It has been an incredibly popular locale for artists and photographers from all over the world. This stereotypical Irish fishing village offers plenty to paint, sketch, or photograph: fishing boats, old **Ballyhack Castle**, and the assorted local residents, full of character. Ballyhack Castle was originally part of the preceptory (a religious house) of the Knights Templar; today its ivy-covered and weathered rock walls keep watch over the harbor. A short car ferry ride that will set you back €5 across the harbor will take you to another picturesque Irish fishing village in County Waterford: **Passage East**, which competes with Ballyhack for its share of photographers and artists.

Three miles north of Ballyhack on the R733 are the imposing ruins of **Dunbrody Abbey** and **Dunbrody Castle**. The Abbey was built in the late 12th century, and the castle (adjacent to the Abbey) is of similar vintage. The ruins are set back from the main road about 150 yards, and on sunny days especially, it makes for marvelous pictures. Sitting next to the peacefully flowing Barrow River, the Abbey must have been a wonderfully serene setting for its former inhabitants to do whatever it was they did at the Abbey. Stop in at the small visitor's center across the street from the ruins. It encompasses a museum, tearoom, and gift shop. *Info*: near Campile. Tel. (051) 88603. Visitor center open May through September Monday through Friday from 10am to 6pm, Saturday and Sunday 10am to 8pm. Admission is €2 for adults, less for seniors, students, and children; family tickets are available.

Southwestern Ireland

Your next stop is Waterford and its world-renowned **Waterford Crystal Factory**. To get there from Wexford, take the N25 west, and follow the signs directing you to the factory. The crystal factory includes an extensive showroom and an hour-long tour that will change the way you look at lead crystal for the rest of your life. Several years ago, Waterford Crystal was commissioned to create the trophy for the Super Bowl winners; a replica of the trophy is on display, and it is incredible. You'll easily spend several hours here. *Info*: Cork Road, Waterford. Tel. (051) 875788. Open daily with hours generally from 8:30am to 5pm. Admission is a little steep (but well worth it) at €9 for adults, less for seniors, students, and children; family tickets are available.

Head from Waterford toward Cahir on the N24. Once there, you'll probably recognize **Cahir Castle** since it has been used as a setting for several medieval movies (including *Excalibur*). Built in 1142, the castle sits on a rocky outcropping of the River Suir. You can readily see how its picturesque setting and imposing presence must have been awe-inspiring in its day. (Heck, it's awe-inspiring now!) Strong walls and turrets, a protective moat, and trained archers would have made this an impregnable fortress indeed. The castle features a massive square keep, spacious internal courtyards, and a wonderful "Great Hall." The castle is well worth an hour of so of your time to stop and explore. *Info:* Cahir Town. Tel. (052) 41011. Open daily with hours generally from 9:30am to 5:30pm, although hours vary slightly throughout the year (check before you visit). Admission is €2.90 for adults, less for seniors, students, and children; family tickets are available.

Exquisite Antiques

Take a breather from medieval castles and review a few items from the 17th through 20th centuries: check out **Fleury Antiques** in the main town square. It is sort of like visiting an exquisite museum where you can take pieces home (if you are willing to pay the price). *Info:* The Square, Cahir. Tel. (052) 41226.

From Cahir, it's a short ride northeast on the N8 to the **Rock of Cashel**. Save plenty of film for one of the most awe-inspiring sites in Ireland. The setting for this chapel/ round tower/cathedral is on a mound towering some 200 feet above the surrounding plains. The ruins are amazingly well preserved, and the visitors' center at the foot of the Rock of Cashel is informative. Whether you experience bright sunshine, a dull day or a bit of rain while at the Rock of Cashel, it is still well worth the visit. Personally, I find that the lowering clouds give the ruins a bit of a mysterious and brooding quality. So regardless of the weather, visit this important and awe-filled site. Incredible views of the surrounding Tipperary plains await visitors to the site. *Info:* Cahir. Tel. (062) 61437. Open daily with hours generally from 9:30am to 5:30pm, although they close a little later in the summer and a little earlier in the winter (check before you visit). Admission is €5.30 for adults, less for seniors, students, and children; family tickets are available.

Backtrack a bit through Cahir on the N8. At Fermoy, take the N72 east to Mallow, then south on the N20 to your next stop: **Blarney Castle** and **Blarney Stone**. Before my first visit to Ireland, I had no idea the Blarney *Stone* was part of Blarney *Castle*. The famous stone is located atop the ancient keep underneath its battlements. To kiss the stone – which legend says grants the kisser the gift of *blarney* (flattery) – you lay on your back and slide down and under the battlements. One hundred and twenty-ish steps up a spiral staircase will precede your kiss of the Blarney Stone.

Stop and spend some time on the grounds in the various gardens and walks – they may well be as memorable as your kiss of the Blarney Stone. *Info*: Blarney. Tel. (021) 438-5252. Open Monday through Friday, with hours generally from 9am to 6:30pm, sometimes later (check before you visit). They are also open year round on Sunday from 9:30am to 5:30pm. Admission is €8 for adults, less for seniors, students, and children; family tickets are available. (Children under 8 are free).

If you want to spend the night in the area, try **Claragh B&B** just outside of Blarney for a delightful Irish hostess and a comfortable B&B (Tel. (021) 488-6308, Waterloo Road).

From Blarney, head south through Cork to the seaside resort of Kinsale. You'll take the N27 south out of Cork to the R600 into Kinsale. The town is a tidy affair of narrow winding streets, brightly painted Georgian homes, quays, sea breezes, and in-

triguing ruins. Take some time to stroll through the town. Hungry? Stop in at **Fishy, Fishy** for some fine seafood fare (Market Place, Tel. (021) 477-4453).

While in Kinsale, check out nearby **Charles Fort**. This hilltop fort is nearly 400 years old, and covers approximately 12 acres. The star-shaped, 17th-century stone fort is quite impressive. Guided tours are offered during the summer months. *Info*: near Summer Cove. Tel. (021) 477-2684. Open mid-March through October daily with hours generally from 10am to 5pm, sometimes later (check before you visit). Open during the winter on Saturday and Sunday only. Admission is €3.50 for adults, less for seniors, students, and children; family tickets are available.

West Coast of Ireland

From Kinsale, head back into Cork, then west on the N22 to Killarney. There is so much to see and do in and around Killarney that is well worth your time. Start your tour of Killarney at **Ross Castle**. Ross Castle is about one and a half miles from the town center. As you head out of town towards Muckross House, watch for the signpost directing you to Ross Castle. Turn right and continue a mile or so along a tree-lined street until you reach the castle.

Ross Castle sits along the shores of Lough Leanne, and is one of the finest examples of 14th-century castles in Ireland. A 40-minute tour takes you into the rooms that have been restored to their former (austere) beauty. While none of the furnishings is original to the castle, the owners have tried very hard to furnish the castle in period furnishings. *Info*: Ross Road. Tel. (064) 35851. Open daily generally from 10am to 6pm, closing a little earlier in early spring and winter (check before visiting). Admission is €5.30 for adults, less for seniors, students, and children; family tickets are available.

From Ross Castle, get on the N71 and head for **Muckross House and Gardens**. This beautiful Victorian mansion was built for a Member of the British Parliament over 150 years ago. As impressive as the house is, I feel the gardens and estate are the real selling point for this attraction. In the courtyard in front of the house you'll find a number of jaunting car drivers anxious to show you the beauties of the Muckross estate during a leisurely horse-drawn carriage ride.

Also located on the Muckross House estate is the **Muckross Traditional Farms**. These three working farms display a representation of the lifestyles of the rural Kerry folk before the advent of electricity. In addition to actors in period dress performing a bevy of old crafts and chores, there are ducks, chickens, and a variety of other farm animals. *Info*: N71, Killarney. Tel. (064) 3 1440. Open daily with hours generally from 9am to 6pm, sometimes later during the summer (check before you visit). Admission for adults is €5.75 for either sight, or a combined ticket is €8.65 for adults, less for seniors, students, and children; family tickets are available.

From Muckross, head southwest on the N71 on a portion of the **Ring of Kerry**. Shortly after you leave Muckross House, you'll see a sign for Torc Waterfall and a small parking area. A few minutes' walk from your car brings you to a **splendid waterfall**. The water that comes crashing over the 60-foot cliff comes there innocently enough from a small lake called the **Devil's Punchbowl**. Admire the waterfall, then take the path that ascends higher up the mountain. About 15 minutes higher up the mountain and you are treated to stunning panoramic views of the Lakes of Killarney.

Back on the Ring of Kerry, within a few minutes you will come to **Ladies' View**, an area of wonderful views back toward Killarney. During the latter part of the nineteenth century, Queen Victoria was a frequent visitor to the Killarney area. This spot on the Ring of Kerry was a point where her Ladies in Waiting often stopped to stretch their legs and see the views on their trips into the countryside.

A few miles further along the Ring of Kerry and you'll come to signs directing you to **Staigue Fort**, an impressive (and largely

A Trip Back in Time!

Take a side trip back in time: continue west on the Ring of Kerry to Waterville, and arrange a boat trip out to **Skellig Michael**, the largest of three picturesque islands jutting abruptly out of the ocean off the west coast of Ireland. The island has the **ruins of a 9th-century monastic settlement** perched on its craggy ridges. More than 650 stone steps hewn out of the mountain lead to the settlement. You'll find six old beehive huts, stone walls, two oratories, two churches and other remains. The settlement was abandoned in the 13th century. There is a lighthouse that silently and solemnly stands vigil on the island. *Info*: local boat operators will take you out, including Michael O'Sullivan, Tel. (066) 947-4676; Dermot Walsh, Tel. (066) 947-6115; Des Lavelle, Tel. (066) 947-6124; Declan Freehan, Tel. (066) 947-9182; and Joe Roddy, Tel. (066) 947-4268. Call ahead at least a day for your reservations and to get departure times and locations.

intact) circle fort dating from the Iron Age. Archaeologists estimate its age at roughly 2,500 years old. The fort is a massive circular structure whose walls are 13 feet thick at the base and nearly seven feet thick at the top. *Info*: Castlecove off the N70. Open year-round. Admission is €1 donation in an honor box (you're on your honor to contribute!).

Head back towards Killarney and watch for signs directing you to **Kenmare**, one of Ireland's more picturesque towns. Walk among the multi-colored shops, pubs and restaurants to get a flavor of this corner of southwest Ireland. Stop by **Black Abbey Crafts** on Main Street for an enchanting and surprising collection of crafts, or pop into **Quill's** for a bit of Irish fashion.

Kenmare sits at the entrance to the **Beara Peninsula**, an often overlooked gem. The Beara peninsula is every bit as beautiful and scenic as The Ring of Kerry, but with far fewer cars, tour buses, souvenir shops and tourists. It is what I imagine the Ring of Kerry was 25 years ago.

To tour the Beara Peninsula, head south from Kenmare on the N71. In addition to pastoral views and beautiful seascapes, you'll find such sights as **Dunboy Castles**. About a mile before you arrive at Castletownbere on the Eyeries Road, watch for the signpost pointing you to Dunboy Castles. The first is an old manor house that must have once been quite an exquisite place in its day. A few hundred yards beyond that you'll find the ruins of a 15th-century O'Sullivan castle. A grand castle at one time, today it is a series of grass-covered mounds and arches that beg to be explored and photographed. *Info*: Entrance to the manor house and castle ruins are via an honor box at a gate. Admission is €5 per car (or €1 per person or €1 per cyclist).

Back on the N71, head for Ballylickey and watch for signposts directing you to **Gougan Barra Forest Park**. This is an isolated area of extreme and spectacular beauty. As you near the Forest Park you'll encounter a beautiful lake at the base of towering hills. On a small peninsula in the lake is a lovely little church that has become a memorable venue for many marriages. One mile

beyond the lake you'll find the Forest Park. Numerous walks wend through moss-covered trees. You may either walk along one of the many walking paths or drive through the park for a number of miles. A great hotel to use as a base for touring this part of Ireland is **Earl's**  **Court** in Killarney. See *Best Sleeps & Eats* chapter for details.

Head back toward Killarney, and on through on the N71, through town and out on the N22 toward Tralee and Limerick. At Tralee, take the N86, following the signs for the **Dingle Peninsula.** Your first stop during your tour of the Dingle Peninsula the town of **Dingle** – signposted in Irish as *An Daingean*. Dingle is located on the southern coast of the Dingle Peninsula on the N86. The shops are inviting, so take a few minutes to stroll about. Be sure and visit the **Cearolann Craft Village**, where you can purchase silver, leather, knitted goods, and many other Irish crafts. For €8 you can also ride out into the harbor to see a popular local tourist attraction – Fungi, the Dingle Dolphin.

Between Ballyferriter and Ballydavid, watch for signposts directing you to **Gallarus Oratory**, and there you'll find an incredibly well-preserved church - one of the earliest in Irish history. The mortar-free masonry has been watertight for over 1,000 years. The inside of the church is about 10 feet by 15 feet. *Info*: Ballydavid. Tel. (66) 915-5333. Open daily.

Connor Pass is a thrilling and beautiful mountainous drive. Be sure and stop at the carpark at the apex of the pass and check out the views. Whether you're looking toward Tralee or back toward Dingle, the views are incredible.

Remember that the Dingle Peninsula is a *Gaeltacht* (Irish-speaking) area. Many signs, including those on the doors of rest rooms, may only be marked in Irish. If you guess, you'll probably guess wrong: *Mná* is for women, and *Fir* is for men. Pretty much the opposite of what most of us would guess!

After your tour of the Dingle Peninsula, head toward Limerick on the N21/N20. On your way to Limerick, stop in the town of **Adare** and stroll a bit. Several ancient monasteries, pleasant restaurants and a magnificent hotel (**Adare Manor**) are waiting to be explored.

As you enter **Limerick**, one of the most prominent sights you'll see is the 13th-century **King John's Castle** on the Shannon River.

 Head for it, and enjoy the short but informative slide show about the history of Limerick. Following that is a short tour of the castle. There's not much to go into, mostly just the outside walls remain. Several years ago, while beginning restoration work on one of the walls,

workers unearthed a pre-Norman village the castle had been built on top of! Currently archaeologists are working on the find, and tourists are welcome to get some up-close views of the work in progress. *Info*: corner of Castle Street and The Parade, Limerick. Tel. (061) 411201. Open daily with hours generally from 9:30am to 5:30pm, though they close earlier in the winter (check before you visit). Admission is €7.50 for adults, less for seniors, students, and children; family tickets are available.

From St. John's, head south a few blocks on Nicholas Street and turn right on Patrick Street. A block or so on your left is the **Hunt Museum Collection**. This wonderful museum offers a unique collection of Irish art and craftsmanship extending from the Neolithic period to contemporary times. Exhibits include European and Irish religious art, ancient (and exquisite) gold jewelry and Christian brooches, as well as everyday medieval items such as pottery, crucifixes, forks, and spoons. In addition to the collection of Irish antiquities, the museum has a fine assortment of Stone and Bronze Age implements from Egypt, Germany, England, and Spain.

The most impressive exhibit here is that of Celtic and medieval treasures. There is also a wonderful selection of early Christian art, including three dozen ancient crucifixes, Bishop's crosiers (hooked staffs), and other religious trappings. Be sure to check out the silver coin they have on display there – legend has it that this little piece of silver was one of 30 used as payment for betraying a certain Jewish carpenter/preacher about 2,000 years ago. *Info*: Patrick Street. Tel. (061) 312833. Open Monday through Saturday from 10am to 5pm, Sunday from 2pm to 5pm. Admission is €6.50 for adults, less for seniors, students, and children; family tickets are available.

Take the N18 north out of Limerick toward Ennis. On the outskirts of Limerick, you'll find **Bunratty Folkpark and Castle**. Bunratty Castle is a magnificently restored 15th-century castle. Originally the home of the Earls of O'Brien, it was considered one of the most outstanding structures of its day. As you enter the castle, look for the "murder holes" – portals in the roof where various boiling concoctions were dumped on the heads of unsuspecting invaders. Consider taking part in the banquet here; period costumes, traditional Irish songs, harp music, and lots of fun are in store for you as you feast like the orignal lord of the castle would have! *Info*: Bunratty Castle, N18 near Limerick.Tel. (061) 360788. The banquet is held twice nightly throughout the year, at 5:30pm and 8:45pm. The late banquet usually fills up first. Prices for the banquet are €52 for all. Children 5 and under dine free.

Adjacent to Bunratty Castle is the Bunratty Folk Park. The Folk Park is a wonderful recreation of 19th-century Ireland complete with artisans replicating the various vocations of that time period: candle makers, blacksmiths, millers, basket weavers, etc. It's a lot of fun and very informative. *Info*: on the N18. Tel. (061) 361511. Generally open 9:30am to 6:30pm, shorter during the winter. Admission is €9.50 for adults, less for seniors, students, and children; family tickets are available.

Continuing on, head straight for the dramatic **Cliffs of Moher**, which run along the coast for about five miles. One route is to take the N18 west through Ennis, then head northwest on the N85 to Ennistymon. From there, follow the R478 to the Cliffs of Moher. These sea cliffs have awed, intrigued, and astounded visitors and locals alike for centuries with their 700-foot drops to the sea. Breathtaking views await you at these wonders of nature. Your first stop should be at the visitors center at the edge of the parking lot. Here you'll learn a little of the history of the area, and they will give you information on the best cliff-side walks avail-

able. In the past, visitors could walk right out to the edge of the cliffs and peer over the dizzying edge. Large stones along the path now block your ability to do that, and signs ask visitors not to venture too close to the edge. The Irish name for the cliffs is *Aillte an Mhothair*, which means "Cliffs of Ruin." *Info*: Visitors Center is open daily from 9:30am until 5:30pm (9am to 8pm during the summer). Admission is free, although the carpark costs €5.

From the Cliffs of Moher, head to **Galway**. Galway is one of the busiest and most enjoyable of Ireland's cities. **Eyre Square** is the ideal place to begin your exploration of Galway City. It's often busy with tourists and business people. It's not a large park, but it is a pleasant one. The gardens in the park are a memorial to John F. Kennedy. The late American president visited Galway on his trip to Ireland less than six months before his assassination in 1963. Watch for the statue of a little man sitting atop a rock; it is in honor of Irish-language poet Padraic O'Conaire.

From Eyre Square, head down William Street and turn right on Abbeygate Street, then left on Market Street. Look for the **Lynch Memorial Window**, a black marble skull and cross-bones memorializing the actions of one James Lynch Fitzstephen. As mayor of Galway at the time, James Lynch Fitzstephen had the unimaginable task of sentencing his own son to death for murdering a visitor to the city. When no one could be found to carry out the sentence, Mayor Lynch did the unhappy job himself. From these unfortunate circumstances arose the term "lynch law."

Back out on Shop Street, you'll be on a pedestrianized walkway like Grafton Street in Dublin. You'll find some wonderful shops, entertaining pubs, and delicious diners along with the people watching opportunities. Dip into **Kenny's Books** and peek at thousands of Irish books, old and new. If you've not yet purchased a Claddagh ring, try **Fallers**, one of the best jewelers in Ireland.

If it is ancient Ireland you are most interested in, I suggest you spend one day on the **Aran Islands**, specifically **Inishmore**. The island is approximately five miles long and two miles wide. Winding rock walls, ancient ruins, prehistoric forts, and megalithic tombs greet visitors in stony silence. You can walk the rocky roads, rent bicycles in Kilronan, or take one of the many minibuses or jaunting cars that are available. While on Inishmore, be sure and visit **Dun Aengus.** This semicircular stone-walled fort ends dramatically and abruptly at the edge of a precipitous 300-foot drop to the ocean. Archaeologists estimate the age of Dun Aengus as 4000 years old, but why it was built and who they were protecting themselves against is still a mystery. Massive walls, some 20 feet tall and 18 feet wide, encircle the fort. The structure is 150 feet across, so you can imagine the kind of effort it must have taken to erect this fortress. The fort is located about four miles from Kilronan, so it is a little far to walk. Ride a bicycle or catch a ride on one of the minibuses. *Info:* Open daily during the summer from 10am to 6pm, and during the winter from 11:30am to 3:30pm. Admission is €2 for adults, less for seniors, students, and children; family tickets are available.

Near Dun Aengus, you'll come across the impressive ruins of **The Seven Churches.** These ancient houses of worship conjure up myriad thoughts about who, and how, these ancients worshipped. *Info:* Admission is free.

Closer to Kilronan you'll find **Black Fort**, an ancient fort estimated to have been built around 3,000 BC. As with many of the other ruins on the Aran Islands, Black Fort has also stymied the best efforts of archaeologists trying to determine its purpose. *Info:* Admission is free.

The ferry is the least expensive means of getting to the Aran Islands: €20 round trip for adults, €10 for children. The ferry takes 90 minutes from Galway, and 30 minutes from Inverin. Following are the ferry companies that ply the waters to the Aran Islands:

* **Doolin Ferries**, Tel. (091) 567283
* **Island Ferries**, Tel. (091) 568903
* **Inis Mor Ferries**, Tel. (091) 566535

You can catch a ferry to the Aran Islands in Galway, Inverin or Rossaveal.

If you take a short drive north of Galway on the N84, you'll come to the small town of **Cong**. Check out the ruins of **Cong Abbey**, dating from the 12th century. The abbey and its clerics were the benefactors of Turlough Mor O'Connor. He also commissioned the **Cross of Cong**, a beautiful work of religious art. It stood proudly at Cong Abbey for centuries, but has since been moved to the National Museum in Dublin, as it is considered one of Ireland's religious masterpieces. Take the time to look at some of the gravestones. There are some old and interesting ones here – many of which unfortunately serve as flagstones for the paths and are badly worn.

Two Great Castle Hotels!

If you want an exquisite (if expensive) lodging experience, spend the night at **Ashford Castle** on the edge of Cong (www.ashford.ie, Tel. (094) 954-6003, US toll free 800/346-1001). Or try the **Ballynahinch Castle Hotel** in Recess, the former getaway for a wealthy maharajah (www.ballynahinch-castle.com, Tel. (095) 31006).

From Cong, take the R345 to the N59, and head west to **Kylemore Abbey**. You've probably seen pictures of it before – it is one of the most photographed abbeys in Ireland. Nestling snugly along the shores of Kylemore Lake, it was originally built as a residence for a wealthy Member of Parliament in the late 1800's, although now it serves as a secondary school for girls. Unfortunately, very little of the Abbey itself is open to the public – only one or two rooms in addition to the entry hall. *Info*: Near Letterfrack. Tel. (095) 41113. Open daily with hours generally from 10am to 4pm, until 6pm spring and summer (check before you visit).

Several hundred yards from the Abbey, around the shores of the lake, is a lovely little Gothic Chapel that's worth walking to and looking at: it reminds me of a dollhouse.

Continue your sightseeing with a circular tour of the Connemara countryside by driving west on the N59 to **Clifden**. The steeples of the local Catholic and Protestant churches lift skyward above the town, and beyond them are even higher *natural* steeples – the

Twelve Bens – that rise majestically in the distance. Interesting shops on Main Street in Clifden include O'Hehir's Woolen Shop, Market Street, Lavelle Art Gallery, and Clifden Art Gallery.

Stop in at **Destry's Restaurant** on the main street in Clifden, a great sandwich shop, when hunger calls.

From Clifden, head east on the N59 until you come to Oughterard. Just outside town are the ruins of **Aughnanure Castle**. A former stronghold of the feared O'Flaherty Clan (the west gate to Galway City once held the inscription: "From the fury of the O'Flahertys, good Lord deliver us."), the castle makes for a great visit. Their castle is a six-story tower house with several squat round towers. *Info*: near Oughterard. Tel. (091) 552214. Open from the end of March through October 31 daily from 9:30am to 6pm. Admission is €2.75 for adults, less for seniors, students, and children; family tickets are available.

From the castle, go west on the N59 to Maam Cross, north to Maam, then west a mile or two on the N59 to the R335 to Louisburgh. Resting offshore at the mouth of Clew Bay is the 4,000-acre **Clare Island**. By far its most famous occupant over the centuries was **Grace O'Malley**, the "Uncrowned Queen of the West." She was recognized as a gutsy pirate full of daring and bravado, and more than one ballad has been sung to her feats. The ruins of

Best Local Hike

Take the N59 to the R335 to Murmisk and the Croagh Patrick Information Center for a great hike. **Croagh Patrick** is that rather abrupt 2,500-foot peak on the south side of the road overlooking Clew Bay. Croagh Patrick is known as Ireland's "Holy Mountain." It is the legendary peak where tradition holds that **St. Patrick** rid Ireland of snakes. Croagh Patrick is an impressive mountain, and the site of yearly pilgrimages by many Catholic faithful. There is a good hiking path up Croagh Patrick The well-worn path ascends to the top of the mountain with many places to stop and rest along the way. The views from the top are stunning.

her home, **Carrigahooley Castle** as well as **Clare Island Abbey**, where Grace was buried, are found on the island. *Info*: Clare Island. Ferries leave from Roonagh Pier, near Louisburgh.

Back on the R335 heading west and you'll come to the resort town of **Westport**. Westport is at the head of Clew Bay, an island-studded estuary on this western edge of Ireland. Irish and tourists alike head for Westport to savor her shops, and there are many to be visited. Check out James Murtagh Jewelers on Bridge Street for Celtic jewelry, or slip into Matt Molloy's Pub for a Guinness or two.

Beyond Westport, take the N5 east to the N4, then north toward Sligo. Just south of Sligo on the N4, watch for signs directing you to the 17th-century **Parke Castle**. The drive, along the lovely shores of **Lough Gill**, is particularly pleasant. The castle sits along the shoreline of the lake, and is particularly impressive at night, when it is basked in bright halogen lights. This 17th-century house was partially built using stones taken from the ruins of a nearby castle. In so doing, the English owner incurred the ire of the native Irish for his thoughtlessness. *Info*: Near Sligo. Tel. (071) 916-4149. Open mid-March through October daily from 10am to 6pm, Admission is €2.75 for adults, less for seniors, students, and children; family tickets are available.

From Parke's Castle, take the R286 back toward Sligo. In Sligo, catch the N15 north. Five miles north of Sligo on the N15 you'll find the ruins of the monastic settlement of **Drumcliffe**. The only remaining artifacts are a series of gravestones, the remains of a round tower, and an elaborately carved high cross, both of which sit right next to the N15.

Perhaps the most interesting aspect of your visit here is the grave of revered Irish writer W. B. Yeats in the nearby Protestant graveyard. His simple epitaph reads:

> *Cast a cold eye*
> *On life, on death.*
> *Horseman, pass by!*

Just beyond Drumcliffe, watch for signs directing you to **Lissadell House**. Once inside the mansion, you'll be awed by the lovely architecture and plentiful *objets d'art*. You'll enjoy the half-hour tour that spins the history of Lissadell House for you, complete with the tales of some of her most intriguing owners. *Info*: Drumcliffe, off the N15. Tel. (071) 916-3150. Open daily mid-March through September from 10:30am to 6pm. Admission is €6 for adults, less for seniors, students, and children; family tickets are available.

Between Sligo and Bundoran is the large, flat-topped mount called by some "Table Mountain." Deep ravines ring the edges of the steep slopes of **Benbulben**. Traces of stone-age settlements have been uncovered on the top of Benbulben's tabletop summit.

Continuing north on the N15, watch for signs directing you to **Creevykeel Court Tomb**. It is one of the finest examples of a classic court tomb in existence today in Ireland. Archaeologists estimate it has been here since 3,000 BC. Upright stones mark the circular ritual court, and lead to a burial chamber. *Info*: On the N15 between Cliffony and Castlegal.

Back on the N15, head north to the Ballyshannon, where you'll take the N3 into Belleek for an elegant treat at **Belleek Pottery**. Belleek china is that creamy-looking china you'll see throughout Ireland. Half-hour tours of the factory are available during the week. There is a museum and also a lovely display area/shop where you can marvel at the elegance of Belleek pottery, and of course you can purchase some of their goods if you wish. *Info*: Belleek. Tel. (028) 6865-9300. Open Monday through Friday with hours generally from 9am to 6pm, sometimes later (check before you visit). Saturdays they open an hour later. Sundays they are generally open from 2pm to 6pm. During the winter, they are not open on Saturdays or Sundays. Admission is £4 or €6 for adults, less for seniors, students, and children; family tickets are available.

From Belleek, take the A47 about four miles east to the ruins of **Castle Caldwell**. Its ivy-covered walls are fascinating. The woods around the area are a **national bird-watching preserve**. The most intriguing artifact here is the tombstone of Denis McCabe, a fiddler of some ability. The epitaph chiseled into his headstone gives us a clue as to the reason for his demise:

> *Beware ye fidlers of ye fidlers fate*
> *Nor tempt ye deep least ye repent too late.*
> *Ye ever have been deemed to water*
> *Foes then shun ye lake till it with whiskey flows.*
> *On firm land only exercise your skill,*
> *That you may play and safely drink your fill.*

–To the memory of Denis McCabe, Fidler, who fell out of the St. Patrick Barge belonging to Sir James Calldwell Bart and Count of Milan and was drowned off this point August 17, 1770.

Poor Denis!

Continue on the A47 to the R232 and head over to the town of **Donegal,** with its pleasant town square and its tourist shops, including **McGinty's Sweater Shop** and **Magee's Tweed Shop**. Take a few moments to walk the town square. Stop in at **Donegal Castle**, in the center of town just off the square. Tours of the castle yield wonderful views of ornate Persian rugs, splendid French tapestries and information panels tell the history of the castle. *Info*: Donegal, Tirchonaill Street. Tel. (073) 22405. Open mid-March through October daily from 10am to 6pm. Admission is €3.70 for adults, less for seniors, students, and children; family tickets are available.

After exploring Donegal, head north on the N15 toward Letterkenny. At Stranorlar, take the N13 north and watch for signposts directing you to the **Grianan of Ailigh.** Follow the signs for about two miles up a winding lane to the top of an 800-foot hill and you're at Grianan of Ailigh - an impressive stone ring fort that was once the stronghold of the O'Neills. Archaeologists speculate that the fort dates from the Iron Age, making it approximately 3,000 years old! It is a circular structure with three terraced rings one inside the other. On the inside a series of stone walks bring you to the top of the 17-foot tall walls. Their base is a *mere* 13 feet. The structure you see today was restored from a somewhat disheveled state about 100 years ago. Sweeping views

174 OPEN ROAD'S BEST OF IRELAND

greet you from the top. I have been to the Grianan of Ailigh during nice weather as well as stormy weather. Regardless of whether it is shrouded in mist or basking in bright sunlight it is an impressive sight indeed.

If you want to learn more about this curious structure, back down on the N13, at the foot of the hill upon which the Grianan Ailigh presides, is the **Grianan Ailigh Heritage Centre**. It is an interpretive center focused on the Grianan of Ailigh. It offers dioramas and a scale model of the fort. *Info*: Near Letterkenny. Tel. (077) 68080. Open daily 10am to 10pm. Admission for adults is €5, less for seniors, students, and children; family tickets are available.

Eat at the Kee's Hotel

After you've visited the Grianan of Ailigh and you want a great meal, watch for **Stranorlar** and the **Kee's Hotel** (Main Street, Tel. (074) 913-1018). The hotel restaurant is an exceptional gem, serving a nice variety of traditional Irish dishes, from spring Donegal lamb to Irish beef.

Northern Ireland

From the Grianan Ailigh, head north on the N13, which changes to the A2. Watch for the R238, and/or signs directing you toward Buncrana. Proceed through Buncrana following the signs for Malin, beyond which is **Malin Head,** the northernmost point of the Emerald Isle. The views, especially those along the southern shoreline, are breathtaking, and it's hard to beat the incredible sunsets from this particular vantage point. If the weather cooperates, you'll be able to see the Scottish island of **Islay**, on the northeast horizon.

Circle the peninsula and head back to **Derry** (called Londonderry by those in favor of remaining a part of the United Kingdom). To begin your tour of the city, you should climb up on the **City Walls** and take a stroll. It should take you no more than an hour to complete the mile-long circuit, but it will provide you with a bird's-eye view of the city and its major sights. Historical markers along the walk help you learn a little of the history of this fair city.

Remember, once you cross into Northern Ireland, you are in the U.K. – you must use **British pounds** here, not Euros!

At the northwestern corner of the city walls, you'll find the **Tower Museum**. This award-winning museum (it has won both British *and* Irish Museum-of-the-Year awards) is a must-see on your tour of Derry. It takes its visitors on a tour through Derry's sometimes  turbulent history. Effective (and interesting) high-tech presentations march you through the highlights of Derry's history. There are also a number of ancient artifacts, including a dug-out boat that was found in the area that has been carbon dated to approximately 520 AD. *Info*: O'Doherty's Tower. Tel. (071) 372411. Open daily from 10am to 1pm, and 2pm to 4:30pm. Admission is free.

In the southeastern corner of the walled city you'll find one of the more popular sites in Derry: **St. Columb's Cathedral**. Inside this 17th-century Protestant cathedral you'll find exquisite stone and wood carvings. St. Columb's Cathedral is a wonderful architectural example of what has come to be known as *Planter's Gothic*, and it features beautiful stained glass windows, dark wood and tall open-beamed ceilings. *Info*: Open April to October Monday through Saturday from 9am to 5pm, and 9am to 4pm Monday through Saturday from November through March. Admission is £1.

From Derry, take the coast road (the A2) and between Portrush and Bushmills you come to **Dunluce Castle**. Ancestral home of my own McQuillan clan, Dunluce is perched atop a natural basalt tower that rises abruptly out of the ocean. Surrounded on three sides by the ocean, and on the fourth by a gorge, Dunluce Castle was once considered an impregnable fortress. Initially a McQuillan stronghold, it was lost to the MacDonnell Clan who lived there until 1639, when the kitchen (and numerous cooks!) crashed into the ocean! After that, the lady of the castle was no longer interested in living there. Its picture graces the cover of almost every tourist brochure for Northern Ireland. *Info*: Near Portrush. Tel. (028) 2073-1938. Open daily with hours generally Monday through

Ruins with a View!

Between Giant's Causeway and Dunluce Castle, watch for the romantic ruins of **Dunseverick Castle** on the ocean-side of the road. Legend has it that medieval intrigue, murder and revenge were the cause of the fall of Dunseverick.

Saturday 10am to 6pm and Sunday 2pm to 6pm, later during the summer and earlier during the winter (check before you visit). Admission is £1.50 for adults, less for seniors, students, and children; family tickets are available.

In the nearby town of Bushmills, you'll find **Bushmills Distillery.** It is thought that the Bushmills distillery is the oldest in the world (at least the oldest *legal* distillery). The Bushmills Distillery produces their famous brand of Irish whiskey here on the northern coast of Ulster. Guided tours are conducted to give you a "flavor" for their process, including a wee nip at the end! *Info*: Bushmills. Tel. (028) 7073-1521. Open with hours generally from 9:30am to 5:30pm during the summer, five times throughout the day during the winter (check before you visit). Admission is £2.50 for adults, less for seniors, students, and children.

When you've completed your distillery tour, watch for signs directing you to **Giant's Causeway**, less than one mile away. Giant's Causeway is one of two things: it is either an incredibly interesting work of nature, or it might be, as the legends say, the handiwork of the giant Finn McCool who was trying to build a stepping-stone bridge to Scotland to find a wife. Either way, the sight is fascinating. Geologists believe that Giant's Causeway is a group of 40,000 symmetric hexagonal stone columns formed millions of years ago by rapidly cooling molten lava. Stop first at the Visitors Center. You can either walk or ride an inexpensive shuttle to the stones. *Info*: on the B146 just off the A2 between Ballintoy and Bushmills. Tel. (028) 7073-1855. Open daily with hours generally from 10am to 5pm, later during the summer (check before you visit). Admission is £2 for adults, less for seniors, students, and children; family tickets are available.

While in this part of Northern Ireland, for a lodging treat spend the night at **Whitepark House** in Ballintoy, Tel. (028) 2073-1482, a lovely B&B over 250 years old.

From Bushmills, take either the B15 or the B146 and watch for signs directing you to **Carrick-a-Rede Rope Bridge**. The rope bridge is suspended 80 feet above the ocean across a chasm 60 feet wide. Now, neither of those may seem high or long, until you are in the middle of this swaying rope bridge. Hold tight, move slowly, and you're sure to leave with a pleasant memory and feeling a little bolder for the effort. Access is via a scenic half-mile walk up a slight incline. The rope bridge is installed each March and taken down each September by salmon fishermen who need access to the fishery on the small island. *Info*: near Ballintoy. Tel. (028) 2076-9839 Open daily from March through October with hours generally from 9:30am to 5pm, later during the summer (check before you visit). Admission is £2.50 for adults, less for seniors, students, and children; family tickets are available

After shakily walking the rope bridge, head for Ballycastle. Just east of town on the A2, you'll find **Bonamargy Friary**. Built in the 16th century, it is largely intact and will provide an interesting few minutes of wandering. Perhaps you'll be fortunate enough to see an ancestor of mine, Julia McQuillan, the mysterious (and ghostly) Black Nun of Bonamargy Friary. Look in the corner of the graveyard for a large cross that marks the site of the final resting place of soldiers washed ashore during both world wars. *Info*: south of Ballycastle on the A2. Admission free.

About two miles beyond Bonamargy Friary on the A2 you'll find **Torr Head Road**. This ribbon-like road snakes around the north-eastern tip of Northern Ireland, a scarce 12 miles from Scotland at its closest point. It is a very narrow road, but well-maintained. On a clear day the views are stunning, and you might enjoy pulling off the road and listening to the surf crashing against the rocks below you. If you do step out of your car, hold onto your hat; or better yet, leave it in the car. Otherwise, it may become part of the flotsam below.

178 OPEN ROAD'S BEST OF IRELAND

Torr Head road ends in Cushendun. As you proceed south on the A2 between Cushendun and Carnlough, take in the incredible seascapes, as well as the famous **Glens of Antrim**. Nine of them in all – home to the leprechauns — they are deep, heavily forested glades, some of them with quasi-tropical greenery. The prettiest of these is **Glenariff**, and its **Glenariff Forest Park**. You have a choice of numerous walking paths, featuring cascading waterfalls, beautiful wild flowers, and dense undergrowth. The three-mile waterfall trail is the most popular and, I think, the prettiest. At the edge of the car park is a sign detailing the various hiking paths available in the park. Trails vary from a half-mile stroll up to a nine-mile scenic trek. *Info*: on the B14 near Carnlough.

Continue south on the A2 toward Belfast. Along the way, you'll encounter **Carrickfergus Castle**. This 12th-century castle has an impressive five-story keep which originally housed the well for the castle's drinking water as well as a dungeon. On the third floor is the Great Hall. The keep is also home to a Cavalry Regimental Museum, with several fine examples of ancient weaponry. The views from the top of the keep are splendid. *Info*: Carrickfergus. Tel. (028) 9335-1273. Generally Monday through Saturday from 10am to 5pm and Sunday from 2pm until 6pm, sometimes later (check before you visit). Admission is £2.70 for adults, less for seniors, students, and children; family tickets are available.

Finish off your two weeks on the Emerald Isle in **Belfast**. Your first stop should be the **Ulster Museum**, Northern Ireland's version of the Smithsonian, featuring an eclectic collection of important Irish historical artifacts, natural history, and art. My favorite exhibit is the paraphernalia recovered from the *Girona*, a Spanish ship that sunk in the cold waters off the Antrim Coast in 1588 after their ill-fated expedition against England. Jewelry, weaponry, articles of clothing, and personal effects are among the collection. *Info:* Stranmillis Road. Tel. (028) 9038-3000. Open Monday through Friday 10am to 5pm, Saturday 1pm to 5pm, Sunday 2pm to 5pm. Admission is free.

The Ulster Museum is located on the grounds of the **Botanic Gardens**. This is a nice place to stroll and enjoy the beauty of the flowers, plants, and shrubs.

The central area of Belfast is Donegall Square, and the central attraction of the square is the **Belfast City Hall**. Columned and domed, the building was erected in 1907. The entrance for the general public is located around back. You are free to go in and walk around the open public areas. As you'd suspect, it's marbled and grand. The statue of the woman out front is Queen Victoria. On the west of the capitol is a war memorial, and on the right is a monument to those who perished on the Titanic, which was built in Belfast. *Info*: Donegall Square. Tel. (028) 9032-7000. Open Monday through Friday from 9am to 5pm. Admission is free.

Head out on the A2 from Belfast toward Bangor. Just after you go through the town of Hollywood (still on the A2), watch for the signpost directing you to the **Ulster Folk Park and Transport Museum**. Perhaps the finest recreation of its kind on the Emerald Isle, the Ulster Folk and Transport Museum features cottages, chapels, schoolhouses, and farms all brought from their original sites and transported here from all over Ulster. They have been painstakingly reconstructed and extensively equipped with period furnishings. The museum gives you a glimpse of the 18th- and 19th-century lives of the Ulster folk, from priests to peasants, farmers to fiddlers. The Transport Museum is a look at the history of transportation in Ulster. You can easily spend three or four hours here. *Info*: Bangor. Tel. (028) 9042-8428. Open daily with hours generally from 10am to 5pm, later during the summer and earlier in the winter (check before you visit). Admission is £5.50 for adults to either the Folk Park or the Transport Museum, £7 for a combined ticket for adults, less for seniors, students, and children; family tickets are available.

9. BEST SLEEPS & EATS

Ireland offers a broad spectrum of **accommodations** – from low-budget hostels and B&Bs (€) to exquisite five-star hotels (€€€). Some are simple country homes, some luxurious hotels, and some are historic castles!

In recent years, **food** in Ireland has undergone somewhat of a renaissance. In the past, food critics described the food in Irish restaurants as unimaginative, bland, and relatively unexciting. (Supporters of Irish food called it "simple.") The Irish food industry took the criticism to heart. Chefs trained in Europe were brought in, and the food took on a decidedly European – and delectable — flavor.

THE SKINNY ON IRISH LODGINGS

Many accommodation prices in Ireland are listed as **per person sharing** (sometimes abbreviated *pps*) – in other words, each person staying in the room pays that price. Some of the hotels charge a flat rate for the first two people staying in the room, with a small supplement for additional guests. When you make your reservations, be sure and clarify whether the price is for the room or per person sharing. Some B&Bs and hotels charge a "single supplement" when only one person stays in a double room. This amount is added to the per person sharing rate.

Many hotels in Ireland tack on a **service charge** (gratuity) to the cost of their rooms. These charges range from 10-15%. The proceeds are divided among the hotel staff - from the maids to the front desk personnel. It's a good idea to check if there is a charge and how much it is when you make your reservations.

Guaranteeing a reservation at a hotel in Ireland with a credit card may mean just that – *guaranteeing* a reservation. At some of the upscale hotels in Ireland, if you cancel a reservation within fourteen days of your intended day of arrival, and you guaranteed the reservation with a credit card, you will still pay for one night's lodging whether you stay or not. And a few have even implemented a policy whereby if you cancel within seven days, you must pay for the entire time you had booked! With the rates at luxury hotels ranging from €300 per night to over €1,000 per night, that's a pretty expensive cancellation. So be sure and ask about the hotel's cancellation policy.

The price range for hotels in this book are:

€ = up to $74 per person sharing (pps)
€€ = $75-149 pps
€€€ =$150+ pps

THE SKINNY ON IRISH RESTAURANTS

As an island nation, Ireland is particularly proud of their **seafood**. Salmon, scallops, prawns, lobster, sea trout, mussels, and oysters are generally plentiful, especially in seaport towns such as Galway, Kinsale, Westport, Dublin, Wexford, and Waterford.

Dublin

An Irish specialty that should not be missed is **Irish soda bread**. This flavorful brown bread is made from stone-ground wheat flour. Its crust is, well, crusty, and covers soft and succulent dough on the inside. It is used to accompany just about any meal, but more particularly it is served with seafood platters of salmon, mussels, or scallops.

My price range for restaurants, **per meal per person**, are:

€ = up to $16
€€ = $17-49
€€€ = $50+

DUBLIN

BEST SLEEPS
The very best hotels and restaurants are **south of the Liffey**.

Berkeley Court Hotel €€€
Plush, elegant, extraordinary. Five-star hotel with beautiful furnishings and appointments. From the magnificent lobby to the superb rooms, you'll be transported into a world of luxury that only a handful of hotels in Ireland can offer. The large bedrooms are light and airy, with comfortable, classic furniture. Several restaurants and a lounge. *Info:* www.jurys-dublin-hotels.com/berkeleycourt_dublin. Tel. (01) 665-3200. Ballsbridge District: Lansdowne Road. 200 rooms.

Conrad Hotel €€€
Part of the Hilton Hotels Group. Top quality is the rule here. Ample-sized rooms, very nicely decorated with quality furnishings and soft salmon-colored decor. The Conrad is also one of the few hotels in Ireland that is air conditioned. Most of the rooms have relatively boring views, but the rooms in the front of the hotel overlook the National Concert Hall across the street. When there is a concert (most nights), the Concert Hall is lit up and makes for a stunning view out your bedroom window. Spacious and lavish suites, among the nicest in all of Ireland. Two restau-

rants, one pub, gym and spa. *Info:* www.conraddublin.com. Tel. (01) 676-5555, US toll free 800/Hilton. South Grafton Street District: Earlsfort Terrace. 191 rooms.

Brooks Hotel €€€
Popular hotel on the south side of the Liffey. It's hard to tell whether it's the super-friendly staff or the immaculate, comfortable rooms that make it so popular, but both contribute to the excellence of Brooks Hotel. Located just a few blocks off Grafton Street. Restaurant, bar, gym and sauna. *Info:* www.sinnotthotels.com/brooks. Tel. (01) 670-4000. South Grafton Street District: 59-62 Drury Street. 98 rooms.

Shelbourne Meridien Hotel €€€
The nicest of the nice in Dublin. From the rich dark wood to the lovely antique Waterford crystal chandelier in the Lord Mayor's lounge, to the flawless service, you'll be delighted with every aspect of your stay at the Shelbourne. While not as flamboyant as some of the other brass-and-crystal hotels you'll find in Dublin, it is all grace and grandeur, refinement and splendor. The rooms and the furnishings, the fine equestrian art, and the ambiance are as rich and lovely as you'll find in Dublin. Restaurant, lounge, swimming pool, sauna and Jacuzzi. *Info:* www.shelbourne-hotel.com. Tel. (01) 663-4500. South Grafton Street District: 27 St. Stephen's Green. 190 rooms.

Westbury Hotel €€€
Contemporary lobby with marble, brass and crystal aplenty. Comfortable sofas and chairs throughout the lobby. Smallish but lavishly decorated rooms. Great location: just a half block off Grafton Street (even though their address is given as Grafton Street), it is in the hub of activity in Dublin. Free parking for guests is included. Two restaurants, lounge, bar and gym. *Info:* www.jurys.com/ireland/doyle_westbury.htm. Tel. (01) 602-8900, US toll free 800/423-6953. Grafton Street District: Grafton Street. 204 rooms.

Eliza Lodge Guesthouse €€
Delightful, newer, award-wining guesthouse. Located just west of the Ha'penny Bridge on Wellington Quay at the edge of the

Temple Bar area. The rooms are comfortably furnished and brightly painted. Although the rooms are a bit on the small side, the service of the staff and management more than makes up for it. Great value for your accommodations in Dublin. *Info:* www.dublinlodge.com. Tel. (01) 671-8044. Temple Bar District: 23/24 Wellington Quay. 18 rooms.

Longfield's Hotel €€

Lovely comfortable rooms, a safe neighborhood, a great location close to shopping and sights, and personable, outgoing staff. One of the nicest small hotels in Dublin. Located a few blocks east of St. Stephen's Green, Longfield's is a converted Georgian townhouse. The rooms are nice size - although not huge - with tall ceilings and light colors. Number 10 Restaurant is in the basement of Longfield's, and it is one of the best restaurants in Dublin. (See the *Best Eats* section.) *Info:* www.longfields.ie. Tel. (01) 676-1367. South Grafton Street District: 10 Fitzwilliam Street Lower. 28 rooms.

Schoolhouse Hotel €€€

Unique, warm and welcoming. Featuring large rooms with comfortable furnishings. The Ballsbridge area where the hotel is located is a nice, quiet area of Dublin, but close enough to downtown to walk (10 minutes), or catch the DART, which is just three blocks away. One restaurant. *Info:* www.schoolhousehotel.com. Tel. (01) 667-5014. Ballsbridge District: 2-8 Northumberland Road. 31 rooms.

Stauntons On The Green €€

A series of converted Georgian townhouses on the south side of St. Stephen's Green. Large, individually and elegantly decorated rooms. The rooms at the front of the house overlook St. Stephen's Green and those at the back of the hotel overlook flower gardens. *Info:* www.stauntonsonthegreen.ie. Tel. (01) 478-2300. South Grafton Street District: 83 St. Stephen's Green South. 38 rooms.

Temple Bar Hotel €€

Don't let the unconvincing exterior dissuade you from staying at the Temple Bar Hotel. The hotel itself is very nice and comfortable. The rooms are good sized and comfortably if not lavishly decorated. The bathrooms are upgraded and modern. Restaurant and bar. *Info:* www.templebarhotel.com. Tel. (01) 677-3333. Temple Bar District: Fleet Street. 108 rooms.

Waterloo House €€
Waterloo house features large, high-ceilinged rooms that feel almost spacious, even with several beds in them. The breakfast is excellent, and the location is nice – as they advertise, close to the hustle and bustle, but much quieter. Some of the rooms are nicer than others, so if you get there early in the day, ask to select your room. *Info:* www.waterloohouse.ie Tel. (01) 660-1888. Ballsbridge District: 23 Waterloo Road. 17 rooms.

Ariel House €€
One of the warmest welcomes and most pleasant stays you can have in Ireland. Three Victorian townhouses. The front sitting room is furnished with comfortable leather chairs surrounded by antiques all situated before a lovely fireplace. Twenty of the thirty rooms are furnished almost exclusively with furniture from the Victorian era. There are an additional 10 rooms added onto the back of Ariel House that are strictly functional. While Ariel House is several miles from downtown Dublin, it is only 100 yards from the Lansdowne DART station, about a three-minute ride to downtown. *Info:* www.ariel-house.net. Tel. (01) 668-5512. Ballsbridge District: 50-52 Lansdowne Road. 40 rooms.

Oliver St. John Gogarty's Youth Hostel €
Comfortable Dublin hostel. The small cafe provides an inexpensive continental breakfast. Located in the trendy Temple Bar District, Dublin's answer to Paris's Left Bank. The place to stay for budget accommodations in Dublin. *Info:* www.olivergogartys.com. Tel. (01) 671-1822. Temple Bar District: 18-21 Anglesea Street. 27 rooms, 130 beds.

Avalon House Youth Hostel €
Probably the busiest hostel in Dublin. Offers the most amenities of any of Dublin's hostels. There is a small cafe, as well as a Bureau de Change, self-catering kitchen facilities, laundry service, TV room, luggage storage, and secure bicycle storage. Linens are provided in the rate. All single rooms are ensuite (have bathrooms), but the larger rooms and the dormitory rooms share

community bathrooms. Men and women share the same shower facilities, but don't worry — each shower has its own locking stall. *Info*: www.avalon-house.ie. Tel. (01) 475-0001. South Grafton Street District: 55 Aungier Street. 185 beds.

BEST EATS
L'Ecrivain €€€
L'Ecrivain means "the writer" in French, and the walls of this restaurant are decorated with paintings that pay homage to a number of Irish writers. A traditional French restaurant, L'Ecrivain offers a set dinner menu with a surprisingly wide selection, including crisp confit of duck and rack of lamb. They also have an excellent four-course set lunch menu. Their extensive wine list is considered one of the best in Dublin. For dinner, a jacket is required and a tie is suggested. *Info*: Tel. (01) 661-1919. St. Stephens Green District: 109 Lower Baggot Street. Closed Sundays. Reservations required.

Le Coq Hardi €€€
Located in a converted Georgian home, Le Coq Hardi is perhaps the best place in Ireland for French cuisine. The restaurant is expensively and elegantly decorated with rosewood and brass, and linen, fine china, and crystal make for elegant table settings. Try the house special: coq hardi, baked chicken breast stuffed with potatoes, mushrooms and a variety of seasonings wrapped in bacon, and flamed at your table. Dress is jacket and tie. *Info*: Tel. (01) 668-9070. Ballsbridge District: 35 Pembroke Road. Closed Sundays. Reservations required for dinner.

Number 10 €€€
In the Longfield's Hotel, this is my favorite restaurant in Dublin. Great lunch and breakfast menus as well, but dinner is the main event: try the confit of French duck or ravioli stuffed with fresh crab. Superb service. *Info*: Tel. (01) 676-1367. Ballsbridge District: 10 Fitzwilliam Street Lower. Reservations recommended.

Restaurant Patrick Guilbaud €€€
The only eatery in Ireland with a second Michelin star, the food is truly marvelous in a classic old Georgian home setting. For something special try the roast quail or the poached Connemara

lobster, or the even more expensive *Menu Surprise* (chef's choice). *Info*: Tel. (01) 676-4192. Ballsbridge District: 21 Merrion Street. Closed Sundays and Mondays. Reservations required.

Abbey Tavern Restaurant €€
North of Dublin (take the DART to Howth station), this popular tavern features burning peat in the fireplace and 16th-century stone walls. Good seafood and pub fare, good beer and nightly Irish music. *Info*: Tel. (01) 839-0307. Howth: Abbey Street. Closed Sundays. Reservations recommended.

High-End But Budget!

Dublin

If you'd like to dine at Restaurant Patrick Guilbaud but are reluctant to spring for it, consider having lunch there. Lunch prices are significantly less than dinner, but the atmosphere, food and service are all the same. Reservations required.

The Imperial Chinese Restaurant €€
Serene ambiance and excellent food. They have several set menus offering a variety of entrees; a la carte specialties include Peking duck, king prawns, and fried squid. *Info*: Tel. (01) 677-2580. Grafton Street District: 13 Wicklow Street. Open daily. Reservations strongly recommended.

Fitzer's Cafe €€
Nice, cheery cafe located on Dawson Street. Relaxed and easy atmosphere. The lunch menu items include chicken breast and ricotta cheese, and prawns and fried potatoes. The dinner menu offers such treats as duck liver and sweet potatoes, and roast duck stuffed with pistachio nuts. *Info*: Tel. (01) 677-1155. Grafton Street District: 51 Dawson Street. Open daily.

Latchford's Bistro €€
This family-run bistro has a warm, comfortable atmosphere topped only by the excellent cuisine. Very popular with the locals. Latchford's specializes in a contemporary French/Italian menu ranging from roast pheasant in a lentil and orange sauce (outstanding) to noisettes of lamb to fillet of salmon, or you can choose their set dinner menu. Save room for dessert – the sticky

toffee gateau on a raspberry coulis is to die for! *Info*: Tel. (01) 676-0784. St. Stephen's Green district: 99 - 100 Lower Baggot Street. Closed Sunday. Reservations are recommended.

Cafe En Seine €€
Trendy cafe on Dawson Street. This art deco, quasi-Parisian restaurant attracts bohemians and the business set, avant-garde types to traditionalists. Contemporary jazz music greets you as you step into this long restaurant. They specialize in sandwiches and soups. It's worth a stop if only to stroll through and do a little people watching. Offerings include sandwich au poulet, le grand plateau, and fillet mignon. *Info*: Tel. (01) 667-4369. Grafton Street District: 40 Dawson Street. Open daily.

The Orchid Restaurant €€
This is a wonderful Chinese restaurant in south Dublin. The Orchid offers a set menu as well as á la carte selections. On the á la carte menu, you can select from such savory dishes as Cantonese roast duck, Szechwan spicy chicken, and sweet and sour pork. *Info*: Tel. (01) 660-0629. Ballsbridge District: 120 Pembroke Road. Open daily. Reservations necessary on the weekends.

Pasta Fresca €€
A light and cheerful atmosphere and superb made-on-the-premises pasta delight patrons. There always seems to be diners here, especially at lunchtime and dinnertime. All the pasta dishes are great, but try the fettuccine pasta fresca or the bistecca al Pepe. *Info*: Tel. (01) 475-2597. Grafton Street District: 2 - 4 Chatham Street (near the Westbury Hotel). Closed Sundays.

Bewley's €
Sort of a cross between McDonald's and a bistro, Bewley's is a very busy cafeteria on Grafton Street. A convenient place to stop for a bite to eat while you're shopping. It's worth going to either the mezzanine or the James Joyce Room upstairs to look out on the Grafton Street crowd below. Be sure and ask for a table near the window. The fare is simple, consisting mainly of sandwiches. They have a few other dishes such as Chicken Creole and Irish oak smoked salmon. *Info*: Tel. (01) 677-6761. Grafton Street District: 78 - 79 Grafton Street. Open daily.

Oliver St. John Gogarty's €
"Pub grub" is popular in Ireland, and the traditional Irish food served at Oliver St. John Gogarty's pub is among the best. The crowded, noisy atmosphere doesn't detract a bit from the decent food. Most nights they have traditional Irish music in a small bar upstairs, and there is often Irish music on the first floor also. *Info*: Tel. (01) 288-4707. Temple Bar District: 58 - 59 Fleet Street. Open daily.

Gallagher's Boxty House €
Come here for hearty authentic Irish food; a 'boxty' is a potato, an Irish staple. Beyond potatoes, try the Irish stew, corned beef and cabbage, or their poached salmon. Nice fireplace and antique pine tables complete the atmosphere. *Info*: Tel. (01) 677-2762. Temple Bar District: 20-21 Temple Bar. Closed Sundays. No reservations.

Dublin

Leinster

LEINSTER

BEST SLEEPS
Kildare Country Club €€€
Sensational. Elegant. Relaxed. Rejuvenated. Affectionately known as the K Club. In addition to luxurious rooms, world-class service and a superb adventure, you can choose from their spa, pool, Jacuzzi, steam rooms, gym, etc. If those don't catch your interest, you may horseback ride or shoot clay pigeons. Whether you come to golf or just to be pampered, you'll never forget your time at the K Club! *Info*: www.kclub.ie. Tel. (01) 601-7200. East of Dublin: Straffan, County Kildare.

Mount Juliet Club €€€
Stunning. There are not enough superlatives to effectively describe Mt. Juliet to you. First you drive through acres and acres of the beautifully manicured greens and fairways of the Jack Nicklaus-designed Mt. Juliet Golf Club. Next comes the leisure center and spa, then Hunter's Yard and the Rose Garden Lodges. Finally you come to the main Mt. Juliet manor house, a home that was built in 1750. Regardless of which accommodation choice

190 OPEN ROAD'S BEST OF IRELAND

you select, you'll be treated to a luxurious night's sleep. In addition to the gorgeous rooms, A wide variety of sports activities are available, including golf, swimming, tennis, croquet, horseback riding, fishing, trap shooting, and archery. If your travel plans include a helicopter, there is a helipad on the estate. One restaurant and bar. *Info:* www.mountjuliet.ie. Tel. (056) 777-3000. South of Thomastown. 59 rooms.

Rathsallagh House   €€€
On this site in 1798, a lovely Queen Anne house burned down, leaving only the stables. Pity the house, but rejoice that the stables were spared, because they have been converted into a romantic hide-away. Two types of rooms – large and spacious, and smaller but warmer. Rathsallagh House is set in over 500 acres of emerald greenery, and the feeling is one of getting away from it all. About 45 minutes from downtown Dublin. No children under age 12 are allowed. Golf course, swimming pool, restaurant, snooker. *Info*: www.rathsallagh.com. Tel. (045) 403112. Dunlavin, County Wicklow. 31 rooms.

Tinakilly Country House   €€€
Feels more like being at (a very expensive) home than staying in a hotel. Antiques abound, from the sitting room with its blazing fire to the spacious antique-laden rooms, most with lovely views of the Irish Sea. Many rooms have four-poster beds. The house is so impressive that it often overshadows the exquisite setting of the house – verdant green grounds overlooking the turquoise waters of the Irish Sea. One restaurant. *Info:* www.tinakilly.ie. Tel. (0404) 692. Rathnew, County Wicklow. 29 rooms.

Butler Court Guest Accommodation   €€
Modern, clean rooms, comfortable furnishings and an infectiously delightful hostess. Each of the rooms opens out onto a pleasant courtyard where you can relax after a day's sightseeing. Within easy walking distance of downtown Kilkenny and Kilkenny Castle. *Info:* www.butlercourt.com. Tel. (056) 776-1178. Patrick Street, Kilkenny. 10 rooms.

Hibernian Hotel   €€
Looks like a converted bank building – because it is. But what a

conversion! Everything about this hotel – from the spacious lobby to the elegant rooms – is beautiful and welcoming. The staff seem to work to out-do one another to make you feel welcome and comfortable. The hotel restaurant – Jacobs Cottage – is excellent and the fare splendid. As a special bonus, the hotel is centrally located and very near the main sites to see in Kilkenny. One restaurant and two bars. *Info*: www.kilkennyhibernianhotel.com. Tel. (056) 7771-8881. 1 Ormonde Street, Kilkenny. 46 rooms.

Hodson Bay Hotel €€
Scenic views from the shores of Lough Ree. Average-sized but pleasantly and comfortably furnished rooms. Half of the rooms offer beach and lake views that are memorable. The other half of the rooms overlook Athlone golf course. Several years ago they built a new addition to the hotel, and those rooms are the nicest. Nearby activities include golf at the nearby Athlone 18-hole golf course to swimming, to a leisurely beach to play and/or relax on. Two restaurants and one bar, golf, swimming, beach. *Info*: www.hodsonbayhotel.com. Tel. (090) 644-2000. Athlone, County Westmeath. 182 rooms.

Hunter's Hotel €€
Underwhelming on the outside, Hunter's nonetheless offers old-world charm and ... creakiness ... on the inside. Originally a coaching inn during the early 19th century. Individually decorated antique-clustered rooms possess their own special character and personality. Take a moment to stroll through their wonderful gardens, but mind the signs: "Gentlemen and ladies will not, and others shall not, pick the flowers." The restaurant at Hunter's Hotel is considered one of the best south of Dublin. One restaurant. *Info*: www.hunters.ie. Tel. (0404) 40106. Rathnew, County Wicklow. 16 rooms.

Kelly's Resort Hotel €€
Resort-town hotel. Sits right on a wide sandy beach. The rooms are wonderful, bordering on elegant. All are tastefully furnished and spacious. Ask for a room overlooking the bay, or perhaps you'd like the rooms that open out into the hotel's gardens. One restaurant and spa. *Info*: www.kellys.ie. Tel. (053) 913-2114. Rosslare, County Wexford. 99 rooms.

Lemongrove House €
You'll get a warm Irish welcome from Colm and Ann McGibney. Five ensuite and four standard rooms to choose from, and all are furnished smartly and are warm and comfortable. The rooms feature views of the countryside. Located at the northern edge of Enniscorthy (north of Wexford). The McGibneys are well acquainted with the surrounding area, and will be happy to help you plan your adventures. *Info*: www.euroka.com/lemongrove/rates.html. Tel. (054) 36115. Blackstoops, Enniscorthy. 9 rooms.

Hillside House B&B €
Peace, tranquility, and a genuine warm Irish welcome. There is a sitting room for guests with a wonderful fireplace. Each room is large, individually decorated, and quite pleasant. *Info:* www.hillsidehouse.net. Tel. (055) 21726. Tubberduff, Gorey, County Wexford. 8 rooms.

The Reefs Bed And Breakfast €
Sitting just across the road from the Irish Sea, this is an enjoyable and relaxing place to stay. Walk across the road and sit on the shoreline of the Irish Sea to enjoy the sunset over that lovely body of water. I have often used The Reefs as the B&B for my last evening in Ireland. It provides lovely, serene seascapes, a pleasant "last remembrance" of Ireland, and is only 20 minutes from the airport. *Info*: www.skerrieshomepage.f2s.com/reefs.html. Tel. (01) 849-1574. Balbriggan Coast Road, Skerries, Co. Dublin. 4 rooms.

BEST EATS
Brunel Restaurant €€€
A touch of elegance complemented by serenity and dining excellence. The menu is wide-ranging, and main courses are augmented by fresh produce that is grown on the estate. They have gained some renown of late for their treatment of lamb. Other menu items include seafood (of course), Irish beef, and several vegetarian dishes. Aside from any of the lamb dishes, you might consider their excellent beef tenderloin with spring vegetables and champignon. *Info*: (0404) 69274. Restaurant for Tinakilly House. Rathnew. Open daily. Reservations recommended.

Marlfield House Restaurant €€€

19th-century country home. The chef uses only the freshest ingredients, from the herbs and produce grown in their own garden to the fish or meat harvested from the surrounding rivers, ocean, and countryside. Seafood is a specialty; if you're lucky, one of the starters may be the crab and salmon sausage with spring onions and a light mustard sauce. If not, you won't be disappointed in such entrees as baked salmon stuffed with asparagus or roast breast of Barbary duck with onions braised in a cream, white wine, and wild mushroom sauce. *Info*: Tel. (055) 21124. Gorey, County Wexford. Open daily.

Mount Juliet Hotel Restaurant €€€

Elegant, bordering on opulent. Wedgwood china, starched Irish linen, and gleaming silverware punctuate your dining experience. The meal? Equally as exquisite. French with an Irish flair, the presentation of your fare is as spectacular as it is tasteful. The menu changes, but you might expect the likes of baked escalope of salmon, roast breast of Barbary duck with fruit sauce, or roast rack of spring lamb. Jacket and tie are requested. *Info*: Tel. (056) 73000. Thomastown. Open daily. Reservations recommended.

Galley Cruising Restaurant €€

Looking for a different dining experience in Ireland? Then try dining while sightseeing on the Galley Cruising Restaurant in New Ross. Depending on the tides and the weather, you'll cruise on the rivers Suir, Nore or Barrow. Fish caught locally is the specialty. *Info*: Tel. (051) 421723. The Quay at New Ross. Open Easter through October for lunch, afternoon tea, or dinner.

The Granary Restaurant €€

A series of booths enable you to quietly enjoy the pleasant atmosphere you'll find here, not to mention the food. It won't take much imagination on your part to figure out that the restaurant once served as a granary, as the heavy pillars and massive beams are still very evident. Sample the Kilmore crab claws in garlic butter with Cashel bleu cheese melted over fresh treacle bread. Follow that with a sumptuous serving of Kilmore scallops poached in white wine. Vegetarian meals are also available. *Info*: Tel. (053) 23935. Westgate, Wexford. Closed Sundays.

Hunter's Hotel Restaurant €€

Don't let the exterior of Hunter's Lodge put you off, as you'll miss a dining treat if you do. The owners are proud of the traditional meals prepared here for their hotel guests as well as those who journey here specifically for a meal. The menus vary day to day, but you'll always find quality, such as oak-smoked trout fillet, and Irish lamb and beef, all complemented with vegetables fresh from Hunter's Hotel's gardens. *Info*: Tel. (0404) 40106. Newrath Bridge, Rathnew. Open daily.

Quaglino's €€

A fine Italian restaurant. If you are in the mood for seafood, you might find an appetizing morsel or two like smoked salmon, poached Dublin Bay prawns, or perhaps even baked oysters in a light garlic butter sauce. If it is traditional Italian fare you have an appetite for, try the veal and eggplant parmagiana, and numerous pasta dishes. If you can't make up your mind between Italian and seafood, why not compromise, and try the seafood fettuccine? *Info*: Tel. (042) 933-8567. 88 Clanbrassil Street, Dundalk. Open daily.

The Tree of Idleness €€

Come see this Greek-Cypriot restaurant on the waterfront. Located in an old Victorian house, the owner has managed a winning combination: fine Greek food, a marvelous wine list, stunning dessert selection, and a pleasant atmosphere. Try the spinach ravioli stuffed with crab mousse or the fillet of Irish beef or pheasant with grapes and chestnuts. *Info*: Tel. (01) 286 3498. On the waterfront, Bray, County Wicklow. Closed Mondays.

An Caisean Ui Cuain €

This bar has succeeded in mixing traditional and trendy Irish atmosphere. The food is branded "pub grub," and is tasteful and substantial. Officially, Monday evenings feature traditional Irish music, but with the artsy crowd that frequents An Caisean ui Cuain, impromptu live music can break out spontaneously at any time. *Info*: Tel. (056) 65406. 2 High Street, Kilkenny Town. Open daily.

An Sos Cafe €

Flight attendant-recommended. Easily missed if you're not looking for it. As you are zooming along the N1 between Drogheda and Dundalk, slow down as you go through the hamlet of Castlebellingham and watch for the thatch-roofed cottage known as *An Sos* Cafe. This charming cafe run by Julie McMahon specializes in breakfast and a warm welcome. *Info*: Tel. (042) 72149. Castlebellingham. Open daily.

Archer's Pub €

Check out Archer's Pub when you're in Wexford. You'll have a choice of a substantial meal or a lighter snack, depending on the time of day. Pub grub is generally available from noon until 3pm Monday through Saturday, and the rest of the time you can choose from such entrees as cod or monkfish, prawns in garlic butter, or a variety of roasts (lamb or beef). They generally offer at least one vegetarian dish most of the time. *Info*: Tel. (053) 22316. Redmond Square, Wexford. Open daily.

MUNSTER

BEST SLEEPS

Note: because of the popularity of **Killarney** as a tourist destination, I've listed it separately in its own subsection beginning on page 199.

Adare Manor €€€

This is the way 18th-century royalty lived. Located in the spotless town of Adare. Exquisite furnishings, including crystal chandeliers, many antiques, stained-glass, and rich mahogany furniture. Spacious, individually decorated rooms include many with hand-crafted fireplaces and elegant furnishings. Large, high-quality bathrooms. Restaurant, garden, gym, sauna, snooker, game room, riding, fishing, shooting. *Info*: www.adaremanor.com. Tel. (061) 396566. Adare, County Limerick. 63 rooms.

Dromoland Castle €€€

"A fantasy come true," "A piece of heaven," "Exceeded every

expectation I had" – these were the last three entries in the guest book on the morning after I stayed at Dromoland Castle. Grace and charm. Dromoland Castle is set amid 370 acres of woodlands, parks, and golf fairways and greens. Spacious and tastefully decorated rooms. All rooms come with nightly turndown service, warm robes, and chocolates on your pillow. One restaurant, indoor swimming pool, spa, sauna, fitness center, beauty salon, tennis, snooker, golf, riding, fishing, shooting, bicycles. *Info*: www.dromoland.ie. Tel. (061) 368144. Newmarket-on-Fergus, County Clare. 100 rooms.

Park Hotel Kenmare €€€
Built in 1897, renovated luxuriously since then. From the turned-down beds, bathrobes and slippers, and a clean windshield in the morning "... to get a clear view of our Emerald Isle," you'll be delighted you stayed. The rooms are nice-sized; the ones in the back are the nicest, offering views of Kenmare Bay and most of the 11 acres of gardens. The halls are filled with antiques and portraits. One restaurant, croquet, tennis. *Info*: www.parkkenmare.com. Kenmare, County Cork. Tel. (064) 41200. 50 rooms.

Sheen Falls Lodge €€€
Built around a 17th-century baronial manor house. Sitting amid 300 acres of park-like surroundings, the Sheen Falls Lodge is a popular resort spot. The hotel has been expensively and richly decorated, from leather couches to mahogany paneling, from marble to crystal to roaring fireplaces. The rooms are of exceptional size, and each has views of Kenmare Bay or the Sheen Falls on the Sheen River. One restaurant, croquet, tennis, gym, sauna, spa, beauty salon, riding, shooting, fishing, golf. *Info*: www.sheenfallslodge.ie. Tel. (064) 41600. Kenmare, County Kerry 66 rooms.

Anam Cara €€€
A bit of creative heaven where writers, poets and artists go to find inspiration. *Anam Cara* means *Soul Friend* in Irish, and peaceful tranquility truly encompasses all who stay here. Overlooking picturesque Coulagh Bay, above a peaceful series of cascades and pools along the Kealincha River. The rooms vary in size and feature various types of furnishings. Each room has a desk or

work area suitable for working on creative projects. Writers and artists are asked to provide a project plan for their time at Anam Cara. While at the retreat, 10am to 5pm is reserved for working on those projects. *Info*: www.anamcararetreat.com. Tel.(027) 74441. Eyeries, Beara Peninsula. 5 rooms.

Ballymakeigh House €€

Regal country estate. Inside, there's a mixture of hospitality, fresh flowers, and starched linen to complement your stay. Renovated, ensuite bedrooms are individually decorated and comfortably furnished. But the warm Irish welcome seems to be what brings 'em back. Enjoy your meals in a plant-filled solarium that looks out on the lovely grounds. *Info*: www.ballymakeighhouse.com. Tel. (024) 95184. Killeagh, County Cork. 5 rooms.

Isaac's Hotel €€

Isaac's Hotel pays homage to Ireland's many writers. Each room proudly displays a portrait of an Irish writer along with a quote or two of their work. All of the rooms in this Victorian mansion are large and well appointed. Tasteful and comfortable furnishings are found in each room. As a bonus, Isaac's is located on a street that is lively and fun in the evenings, with hotels, restaurants, pubs and lots of things going on. *Info*: www.isaacs.ie/hotel_isaacs_cork/index.htm. Tel. (021) 450-0011. 48 MacCurtain Street, Cork City. 36 rooms.

Iskeroon B&B €€

A lovely, edge-of-the-world B&B nestled in a cove above a secluded harbor. While the rooms are all standard – meaning the bathroom for each is across the hall – each guest is provided with a bathrobe to cross to their respective bathrooms. There is one bathroom per guest room, so you are not sharing bathrooms with others. Each of the rooms has a lovely view of the cove below the B&B. Enjoy the walking path down to their private pier. *Info*: www.iskeroon.com. Tel. (066) 947-5119. Bunavalla, Caherdaniel. 3 rooms and a self-catering apartment.

Jury's Cork Inn €€

Centrally located. Simple but pleasantly furnished rooms. The bathrooms are a little small, but they are modern, well lit and adequate. A number of handicap-accessible rooms are available. *Info*: www.jurys.com. Tel. (021) 494-3000. Downtown Cork District: Anderson's Quay, Cork. 133 rooms.

Sallyport House B&B €€

Elegance and beauty. From the warmth of the fire in the sitting room to the luxurious furnishings in each of the bedrooms to the dining room overlooking lovely gardens, you'll feel just a little special for having stayed here. The rooms are tastefully decorated with antiques and reproductions. Each room is generous size. Sallyport House is a non-smoking facility, and the owners ask that you not bring children under 13. *Info*: www.sallyporthouse.com. Tel. (064) 42066. Kenmare, County Kerry. 5 rooms.

Blenheim House €

Beautifully restored Georgian residence just outside Waterford. Built in 1763, it has been furnished throughout with lovely antiques. The rooms are comfortable, tastefully decorated, and well-furnished. Located at the end of a country lane on its own park-like setting. *Info*: homepage.eircom.net/~blenheim. Tel. (051) 874115. Blenheim Heights, Waterford. 6 rooms.

Claragh House €

Which is lovelier: Claragh House or your hostess Cecilia Kiely? Warm and genuine, Cecelia will make your stay memorable. The rooms at Claragh House are simply and tastefully decorated. A ten-minute drive from downtown Blarney, Claragh House is well signposted from the center of town. Open from April through October. *Info*: www.claragh.com. Tel. (021) 488-6308. Waterloo Road, Blarney, County Cork.

Moran's Seaside Farmhouse B&B €

Pleasant B&B perched on a hill high above one of Ireland's prettiest coves. Two of the four rooms have large picture windows that look out on this idyllic scene. While the rooms aren't exceptionally large, each is comfortably furnished and accented with knotty pine doors, dressers and closets. The sunroom overlooks the beautiful cove just a few hundred yards below the house. *Info*: Tel. (066) 947-5208. Bunavalla, Caherdaniel. 4 rooms.

KILLARNEY BEST SLEEPS
Aghadoe Heights Hotel & Spa €€€

Idyllic location, overlooking the Lakes of Killarney. Each of the rooms is large and comfortable, and those with views of the lake are especially wonderful. Spacious rooms, top-flight service, ideal location, superb restaurant, sauna, solarium, fitness rooms and an indoor swimming pool – what more can you ask? *Info:* www.aghadoeheights.com. Tel. (064) 31766. Lakes of Killarney, Killarney, County Kerry. 74 rooms.

Cahernane House €€€
Tranquil, serene hide-away. Originally the 17th-century home of the Earls of Pembroke, it now provides wonderful get-aways to those who are fortunate enough to stay there. The rooms are spacious and elegant. The restaurant will provide a romantic, enjoyable meal. *Info:* www.cahernane.com/location.html. Tel. (064) 31895. Muckross Road, Killarney, County Kerry. 48 rooms.

Carrig Country House €€€
For Victorian elegance on the Ring of Kerry, spend a night or two at Carrig Country House. Beautiful furnishings, wonderful views and perfect hospitality greet you upon arrival. Sitting on the shores of Caragh Lake, it is hard to imagine a more idyllic setting. All of the rooms are large, have antique furnishings and marvelous views. *Info:* www.carrighouse.com. Tel. (066) 976-9166. Caragh Lake, Ring of Kerry. 15 rooms.

Hotel Ard Na Sidhe €€€
Built in 1880 by an English woman who called Ard Na Sidhe the "House of the Fairies." With lots of antique furnishings and an inviting open fireplace, the hotel feels like a regal baronial manor. Beautiful gardens. Spacious and tastefully furnished rooms with a bevy of antiques. It is approximately 17 miles from Killarney - watch for the signposts on the Killarney-Killorglin Road. One restaurant. *Info:* www.iol.ie/khl/eur1.htm. Tel. (066) 976-9105. Caragh Lake, Killorglin, County Kerry. 20 rooms.

Hotel Dunloe Castle €€€
White rail fences and beautiful horses grazing contentedly are your first view of this hotel. A country inn serving families, the

hotel provides a variety of activities for families. Those splendid horses you saw are available for horseback riding. There is a playground and playroom available, as well as a swimming pool, sauna, fitness center and tennis court. The rooms are comfortable with modern pine furnishings, and many have outstanding views of the Gap of Dunloe. *Info*: www.iol.ie/khl/eur1.htm. Tel. (064) 44111. Killarney, County Kerry. 120 rooms.

Hotel Europe €€€

A lovely five-star hotel on the shores of Lough Leanne. Comfortable, and those rooms at the back of the hotel offer the prettiest views of the lake and the mountains. Amenities include a boutique, beauty salon, fishing, boating, cycling, indoor swimming pool, fitness center, and a sauna. In addition, Hotel Europe is within minutes of six championship golf courses. Hotel Europe is open from mid-march through the end of October. *Info*: www.iol.ie/khl/eur1.htm. Tel. (064) 71300. Killarney, County Kerry. 206 rooms.

Earl's Court €€

This gets my vote for the best lodging in Ireland for your money. Soft music and a lovely antique-laden sitting room greet you upon arrival. All the rooms and suites are large and elegant, and like the rest of Earl's Court, many of the furnishings are antiques. You will most likely have the opportunity to meet Simba, the owners' giant, docile golden retriever. Let his restful repose remind you of the rest and relaxation that awaits you at Earl's Court. *Info*: www.killarney-earlscourt.ie. Tel. (064) 34009. Woodlawn Junction, Muckross Road, Killarney, County Kerry. 24 rooms.

Hotel Killarney Ryan €€

About a mile from the Killarney city center. A wide variety of activities are available. Their fitness center includes an indoor swimming pool, Jacuzzi, sauna, and a sports hall, with facilities for basketball, volleyball, soccer, and ping-pong. A miniature golf course and tennis courts round out their athletic offerings. The rooms are average sized and are pleasant and comfortable, clean and close to town. *Info*: Tel. (064) 31555. Cork Road, Killarney, County Kerry. 164 rooms.

Killarney Court Hotel €€

A short walk into town from Killarney Court Hotel. Nice-sized, clean and comfortable rooms. Extraordinarily pleasant and helpful staff. One restaurant, Jacuzzi, steam room and gym for unwinding at the end of the day. *Info*: www.killarneycourthotel.com. Tel. (064) 370370. Tralee Road, Killarney, County Kerry. 96 rooms.

Killarney Great Southern Hotel €€

A turf fire burning in the fireplace, dark oak floors, crystal chandeliers, plush rugs, and marble pillars greet you here. Built in 1854 as a railway hotel. Set in the midst of 36 acres of gardens; the gardens wend their way around the hotel, and offer nice views from some of the public rooms as well as some of the bedrooms. The rooms are of average size, well-maintained, and nicely furnished. One restaurant, indoor swimming pool, sauna, Jacuzzi, steam room, fitness center, and tennis court. *Info*: www.gsh.ie. Tel. (064) 38000. Town Centre, Killarney. 172 rooms.

Killarney Royal Hotel €€

Sterling service makes you feel at home. Each room is large and comfortably furnished. Speaking of comfort, each room also comes with fluffy bathrobes and towel warmers – nice touches to add to your comfort. The restaurant is one of the best around. *Info*: www.killarneyroyal.ie. Tel. (064) 31853. College Street, Killarney, County Kerry. 29 rooms.

The Lake Hotel €€

A beautiful setting for a lovely hotel. The hotel features large rooms and comfortable furnishings. About half the rooms have lake views (stunning) and the other half have woodland views (equally as stunning). Two restaurants, Jacuzzi, gym, library. *Info*: www.lakehotel.com. Tel. (064) 31035. Lake Shore, Killarney, County Kerry. 85 rooms.

Riverside Hotel €€

Overlooking the River Flesk and the MacGillicuddy Reeks mountains. Large and comfortable rooms, a warm welcome from the staff and pleasant stay. An easy 10-minute walk brings you into the heart of the town, close enough to be convenient, but also far enough away to be out of the hustle and bustle of Killarney. One restaurant and one bar. *Info*: www.riversidehotelkillarney.com. Tel. (064) 39200. Muckross Road, Killarney, County Kerry.

Carriglea Guesthouse €

Overlooking the Lakes of Killarney, Carriglea provides a pleasant place to stop for the night. Built in 1832, the original home was a Georgian mansion, and a new addition was added during the Victorian era. It has a beautiful sitting room that overlooks the Irish countryside. The bedrooms are spacious and tastefully decorated, generously endowed with antiques, many of them original to the house. *Info*: www.carrigleahouse.com. Tel. (064) 31116. Muckross Road, Muckross, Killarney. 9 rooms.

Crystal Springs Guest House €

About one mile from downtown Killarney. Exceptionally clean and comfortable, each of the bedrooms is large and comfortably furnished. All have top quality furnishings. The dining room is a nice large area that overlooks the ruins of a nearby mill. *Info*: www.crystalspringsbb.com. Tel. (064) 33272. Ballycasheen Cross, Killarney. 8 rooms.

Friar's Glen Country House €€

Nestled amid 27 acres of some of the prettiest scenery in Killarney. Friar's Glen is a short distance from Muckross House. Each of the bedrooms has large windows that look out onto the grounds and Killarney National Park. Each room is tastefully decorated and furnished with comfortable furniture. All the bathrooms are large, well lit and tiled. There are large windows in the dining room that look out onto the grounds of Killarney National Park. *Info*: www.friarsglen.ie. Tel. (064) 37500. Mangerton Road, Muckross. 10 rooms.

BEST EATS

Note: because of the popularity of **Killarney** as a tourist destination, I've listed it separately in its own subsection beginning on page 205.

Arbutus Lodge Restaurant €€€

Considered one of the finest restaurants in Ireland. Traditional Irish food prepared with care and presented with an artistic flair all topped by outstanding service. From seafood to steak, lobster to lamb, all the meals are cooked with fresh ingredients, many of them from Arbutus Lodge's own kitchen garden. Try their pan-fried mussels with a walnut and garlic dip, or perhaps the spiced beef with chutney or fillet of steak. *Info*: Tel. (021) 501237. Middle Glanmire Road, Montenotte, Cork City. Closed Sundays. Reservations required.

Munster

Earl of Thomond Room €€€
Superb. Spectacular. Romantic. High ceilings, rich dark wood, gorgeous crystal chandeliers, crisp starched linen tablecloths, gleaming china, and an Irish harpist, singer or fiddler all contribute to an elegant and opulent dining experience. Typical offerings include picatta of milk-fed veal, in classic "Nicoise" style, pan-fried fillet of John Dory set upon a nage of leeks and mushrooms, and terrine of Dromoland estate venison with fig chutney. *Info*: Tel. (061) 368144. Newmarket-on-Fergus, County Clare. Open daily. Reservations required.

Longueville House Presidents' Restaurant €€€
Award-winning restaurant in an elegant country house. Fresh ingredients from the nearby gardens, streams and hills. Impeccable service. All combine to make an exceptional dining experience. Guests are tempted by a variety of exceptional offerings, including an ever-popular *Surprise Taste Menu*, which is a seven-course treat. Or try the roast of Longueville lamb with a gratin of turnips, pan-fried medallions of monkfish, or Kilbrack pork. For dessert, Longueville House is renowned for their pyramid of chocolate with an enchanting orange sauce. *Info*: Tel. (022) 47156. Mallow, County Cork. Open daily. Reservations required.

Doyle's Seafood Bar €€
Doyle's combines a homey atmosphere with fresh and exceptionally well-prepared

Best Medieval Feast!

Medieval banquets are hosted at several venues in Ireland, but I think the best is at **Bunratty Castle**. You'll meet the Lord of the castle and savor a tasty medieval feast without utensils. *Info*: Tel. (061) 360788. Bunratty Castle, N18 near Limerick. Two dinners served daily.

seafood. One of their specialty dishes is millefeuille of warm oysters with Guinness sauce, a dish that has received international attention. Other dishes include baked lemon sole, mussels in herb and garlic sauce, and fried scallops. *Info*: Tel. (066) 915-1174. 4 John Street, Dingle, County Kerry. Closed Sundays.

Fishy, Fishy Cafe €€

Slightly upscale seafood restaurant in Kinsale. Bustling, noisy atmosphere, and good seafood. Select from lobster, crab, crayfish, cod, monkfish, squid, John Dory or haddock. Local cheeses and home made breads add to the variety. If the weather's nice, enjoy your lunch at their outside tables. *Info*: Tel. (021) 477-4453. Market Place, Kinsale, County Cork. Open daily for lunch only.

The Inn Between Restaurant €€

A wonderful little restaurant with a thatched roof and great food. Warm and comfortable any time of the year, the Inn Between Restaurant is a nice place to pause for a bite to eat and meet some of Adare's fine citizens. Dine outside in the courtyard on nice days. Try their Irish stew or any of their home made soups. *Info*: Tel. (061) 396633. Adare, County Limerick. Open daily.

Jim Edwards Pub and Restaurant €€

Jim Edwards Pub and Restaurant has successfully bridged the gap between the two enterprises of pub and restaurant. Noted for excellent seafood as well as fine steaks. The decor is simple, and the food is quite good. Try the fillet of Irish beef, or any of the local seafood specialties. *Info*: Tel. (021) 477-2541. Market Quay, Kinsale, County Cork. Open daily.

The Lime Tree €€

Wonderful restaurant in a converted 1830s schoolhouse. It has been called cozy, but with lots of yellow paint and large mirrors, I found it more energetic than cozy. Paintings done by local artists adorn the walls. The menu has a wide variety of offerings, including one of the specialties of the house: Kenmare salmon cooked on an oak plank. Another favorite is the Kenmare seafood potpourri "en papillote." For dessert, try the mascarpone covered with sweetened strawberries, raspberries, and blackberries.

It is exquisite to say the least. *Info*: Tel. (064) 41225. Kenmare. Open daily. Reservations recommended.

Munster

An Fear Gorta - The Tea Rooms €
The little burg of Ballyvaughan is located about an hour's drive northwest of the Cliffs of Moher on the N67. If you've come to see the famous cliffs and find yourself in Ballyvaughan (perhaps on your way to Galway?), this might be a nice place to stop for a casual bite to eat. Scones, pastries, Irish cheeses, soups, salads, and a few light seafood lunches are available. *Info*: Tel. (065) 77023. Ballyvaughan, County Clare. Open during the summer, closed Sundays.

The Estuary Restaurant €
Family-style restaurant at the edge of Waterford. This pleasant restaurant features a good variety of beef, chicken and sea food dishes. Inside, you'll find pine tables, candles and lots of conversation. The soft yellow walls and are bedecked with the artwork of local artists. When the weather is nice, picnic tables on the back lawn are available for your dining pleasure. *Info*: Tel. (051) 873082. Dunmore Road, Waterford, County Waterford. Open daily.

Lemon Tree Restaurant €
On The Square in Blarney. You'll find a dozen or so tables, hardwood floors and a pleasant, chatty atmosphere. The lunch menu features soups, salads, sandwiches and Irish stew. The dinner menu is a bit more substantial, and you will find such meals as oven-baked chicken breast filled with smoked salmon garnished with deep-fried leeks and accompanied by a white wine, cream and chive sauce. *Info*: Tel. (021) 538-5542. The Square, Blarney, County Cork. Open daily.

KILLARNEY BEST EATS
Foley's Town House €€€
While the specialty at Foley's is seafood, there is also a good selection of beef and lamb dishes. Typical offerings include crab claws in garlic butter, lobster bisque, smoked salmon, fillet of steak, herb-stuffed fillet of pork with creamy apricot sauce, or roast duckling. Add to these dishes an appetizing dessert cart

and a surprisingly good wine list, and you have a winner. *Info*: Tel. (064) 31217. 23 High Street, Killarney, County Kerry. Open daily.

Gaby's Seafood Restaurant €€€
Considered by many to be the best seafood restaurant in Killarney. Fresh local produce enhances the offerings of the day. The seafood portion of the menu changes daily, depending on the success of the local fishermen. Possible offerings include salmon salad, Kerry seafood platter, and Lobster Gaby in cognac, wine, and cream sauce. They have an extensive wine list. Gaby's has garnered many local and national awards over the years. *Info*: Tel. (064) 32519. 27 High Street, Killarney, County Kerry. Closed Sundays.

The Lake Room €€€
The main restaurant for Aghadoe Heights Hotel. Classical cuisine served in a dining room that overlooks the Lakes of Killarney make a nice combination. Dine in elegance on milk-fed veal or peach sauce and a trellace of sea trout or the braised lamb shank with lentil cassoulette. Info: Tel. (064) 31766. Lakes of Killarney, Killarney, County Kerry. Open daily. Reservations recommended.

Bricín Restaurant €€
Located above an Irish crafts store on High Street (the continuation of Main Street) in downtown Killarney. It oozes class and elegance, and is a most pleasant place to eat. Soft lighting and candle-lit tables set in small private snugs provide the feel of a romantic night out. The menu changes now and again, but you are likely to find darné of salmon poached simply in wine, lemon and butter, of a rack of Kerry lamb roasted with a rosemary and wine sauce. *Info*: Tel. (064) 34902. 26 High Street, Killarney, County Kerry. Closed Sundays.

Cronins €€
A great family-friendly cafe with fast and friendly service. A good variety of soups, salads and sandwiches are available, including a children's menu. Try the Irish stew, but save room for their delicious Danish Apple pie – it's to die for! *Info*: Tel. (064) 35857. College Street, Killarney, County Kerry.

The Cooperage €€

Very stylish, modern restaurant with good service and great food. The Killarney fashionable are often seen here, enjoying the food and soft jazz music. The menu changes and features modern Irish dishes such as grilled monkfish with basil pesto and cracked pepper, or the roast rack of Donegal spring lamb. Vegetarian dishes are also available. *Info*: Tel. (064) 37716. Old Market Lane, Killarney, County Kerry. Open daily.

The Flesk Restaurant €€

A pleasant conversational environment will greet you here, along with a varied menu that gives you a good selection to choose from. The choices range from beef to lamb to fish and even a few vegetarian choices. The menu changes frequently, but you might find such items as large wild Killarney Lake salmon with light hollandaise sauce, or roast half Irish farm chicken with herb stuffing and a delicious red wine and mushroom sauce. *Info*: Tel. (064) 31128. Main Street, Killarney, County Kerry. Open daily.

West End House Restaurant €€

London's Savoy Restaurant's loss is your gain. The former chef at that regal restaurant delights West End House guests. Try the monkfish fillet on spring onion sauce with new potatoes and seasonal salad or the home made lobster ravioli. *Info*: Tel. (064) 32271. Lower New Street, Killarney, County Kerry. Closed Mondays.

The Bean House €

The Bean House is a nice place to stop and have a sandwich, soup and/or salad. A spot of tea is also available, and you'll enjoy the pleasant and laid-back atmosphere. *Info*: Tel. (064) 32113. 8 High Street. Killarney, County Kerry. Open daily.

The Laurels Pub €

Award-winning Main Street pub in Killarney. Inside, you'll find a series of tables and booths, all comfortably situated for conversation and dining. Open-beam ceilings and a peat-burning fireplace provide just the right atmosphere for your dining and visiting. The Laurels has earned a good reputation for the quality of their pub grub, and you'll find a variety of soups, salads and sandwiches here. (I found their Irish stew to be extraordinary!) *Info*: Tel. (064) 31149. Main Street, Killarney, County Kerry. Open daily.

O'Connor's Pub €

A great, busy pub for enjoying traditional Irish music and good pub grub. Sandwiches and soup are the main meal fare here. Irish comics and an occasional play are also seen here. *Info*: Tel. (064) 30200. 8 High Street, Killarney, County Kerry. Open daily.

CONNACHT

BEST SLEEPS
Ashford Castle €€€
Exquisite! Ashford Castle – photo shown on the first page of this chapter – has been highlighted repeatedly on television (several times on *The Lifestyles of the Rich and Famous*), was one of the hotels President Ronald Reagan stayed in and was the hotel Pierce Brosnan chose for his wedding reception. This 13th-century Norman castle in the midst of 350 acres is a sight to behold. Inside, you'll find scores of high-quality antiques and old portraits, rich paneled walls and luxurious carpets. The public rooms are elegant. The bedrooms are all different, and are probably the largest you'll find in Ireland for each class of room. All have antiques aplenty, plush carpets, and marvelous bathrooms. Thick robes, slippers, mineral water, and a bowl of fruit greet you upon arrival. Restaurant, gardens, tennis, grounds, fishing, walking trails, golf. *Info*: www.ashford.ie. Tel. (094) 954-6003, US toll free 800/346-1001. Cong, County Galway. 83 rooms.

Save on Hotels

Want to stay in some of Ireland's best hotels but can't quite bring yourself to pay that much? Consider coming during the **off-season**. Though the weather may be a little cooler, the rooms at even some of the most expensive hotels are much more within reach of the average traveler.

Ballynahinch Castle Hotel €€€
Ancestral home of the Martin Clan of Connemara, Ballynahinch Castle has been converted into a four-star hotel. Spacious rooms with elegant and comfortable furnishings, feature beautiful views of either the mountains or the lake. The service is impeccable. Shooting, riding, croquet, gardens and walking trails are also available to visitors. One restaurant. *Info*: www.ballynahinch-castle.com. Tel. (095) 31006. Recess, Connemara. 40 rooms.

Connacht

Lough Inagh Lodge €€€
Once the hunting lodge for Ballynahinch Castle, now a fine hotel with a reputation for excellence all its own. Turf fires, period antiques, and a wonderful, friendly atmosphere. Large, tastefully decorated rooms, all with lovely views of either Lough Inagh or the mountains and countryside. Lough Inagh Lodge caters to families, with a discount available for children. One restaurant. *Info*: www.loughinaghlodgehotel.ie. Tel. (095) 34706. Recess, Connemara. 12 rooms.

Rosleague Manor €€
About nine miles out of Clifden between Clifden and Westport. Elegant Georgian manor house overlooking Ballinakill Bay. Thirty acres of lush lawns and gorgeous gardens available for guests to stroll through. The house features antiques, turf fires, and old portraits. Spacious bedrooms furnished thoughtfully with antiques and comfortable furniture are complemented by nice bathrooms with modern fixtures. The rooms have wonderful views. One restaurant, sauna, billiards, tennis. *Info*: www.rosleague.com. Tel. (095) 41101. Letterfrack, Connemara. 18 rooms.

Ardilaun House Hotel €€
Located in a quiet residential neighborhood. One of the best places to stay in the Galway City area. The rooms are of varying sizes, decorated in soft colors, and are comfortably furnished. Restaurant, pub, tennis, fitness center, sauna. *Info*: www.ardilaunhousehotel.ie. Tel. (091) 521433. Taylor's Hill District: Taylor's Hill, Galway City. 90 rooms.

Coopershill House €€

Regal home sitting in the midst of 500 verdant acres. But don't let this intimidate you. Once inside the doors, you'll feel as comfortable as if you are long-lost and well-loved family coming for a visit. Spacious bedrooms are generously endowed with antiques, old portraits, and four-poster beds in most rooms. Complement those amenities with fresh flowers from the gardens and mineral water and you've all the trappings for a restful stay. Tennis court, snooker table. *Info*: www.coopershill.com. Tel. (071) 916-5108 Riverstown, County Sligo. 8 rooms.

The Quay House €€

Peace and tranquility and a genuine warm Irish welcome. Large, tastefully and expensively decorated rooms. The rooms at the front of the house overlook Clifden Harbor. If you've an extra few minutes, see if you can eat lunch with - or at least chat with - one of the owners, Paddy or Julia Foyle. They are both truly delightful. One restaurant. *Info*: www.thequayhouse.com. Tel. (095) 21369. Beach Road, Clifden. 10 rooms.

Sunnybank Guesthouse €€

Overlooking Clifden. The converted Georgian house (circa 1814) boasts large, tastefully decorated rooms with high ceilings. The rooms are quite comfortable. In addition to fine sleeping accommodations, Sunnybank also offers a nice fitness package for their guests. They have an outdoor swimming pool (it's heated), sauna, solarium, and tennis courts. Sunnybank Guesthouse is the recipient of a number of industry awards, including one for outstanding breakfasts. *Info:* www.sunnybankhouse.com. Tel. (095) 21437. Westport Road, Clifden, Connemara. 11 rooms.

Fairgreen Hotel €€

Modern hotel located about a one-minute's walk from Eyre Square, the center of Galway. The rooms are large and comfortably if not elegantly furnished. This would be a nice place to stay if you like to be right in the middle of the hustle and bustle of Galway. One restaurant, sauna, indoor pool, gym. *Info*: www.fairgreenhotel.com. Tel. (091) 513100. Fairgreen Road, Galway. 42 rooms.

Brookside Youth Hostel €

At the edge of Clifden. The furnishings, rooms, and about everything else here are basic (some might say Spartan!), but they'll meet your needs if you're looking for a no-frills hostel. Two self-catering kitchens are available for guests. Linens are included. *Info*: www.hostelz.com/hostel/18168-Brookside-Hostel. Tel. (095) 21812. Hulk Street, Clifden, Connemara. 35 beds.

Connacht

Roncalli House €

A pleasant facility warmed by a turf fire and a sincere welcome. Highly recommended B&B. The six bedrooms all have their own bathrooms. The two rooms at the front of the house have nice views of Galway Bay. The rooms are pleasant, light, and airy, and feature soft pastels or tasteful floral prints. You're within a short walk of downtown Galway, as well as Galway Bay. *Info*: www.roncallihouse.com/location.htm. Tel. (091) 584159. Lower Salthill District: 24 Whitestrand Avenue, Galway. 6 rooms.

Ross House €

Sitting on a quiet cul-de-sac in the Lower Salthill area of Galway is Mrs. Sadie Davy's Ross House B&B. Features four ensuite bedrooms that are tastefully decorated. The dining room is elegant yet simple. Sadie is quite proud of the breakfasts she whips up, and you will enjoy them, as many of her return guests have enjoyed them. Located about 200 yards from Galway Bay, and many guests enjoy walking along the Galway Bay Esplanade. It is also convenient to downtown Galway. *Info*: www. rosshousebb.com/eng/Booking_Bed_Breakfast.php. Tel. (091) 587431. Lower Salthill District: 14 Whitestrand Avenue, Galway. 4 rooms.

Sea Breeze B&B €

Highly recommended Galway B&B. You'll receive a warm and genuine greeting from Colette and Joe O'Donnell. This is not a "purpose built" B&B (a home built specifically to serve as a B&B), so it feels more like you are staying in an Irish home than in a B&B. Enhance those qualities with Colette's cooking and Joe's company, and you have a winning combination. Only open during the summer months. So, be sure and call ahead to make your reservations. *Info*: Tel. (091) 581530. Lower Salthill District: 13 Whitestrand Avenue, Galway. 4 rooms.

BEST EATS

Connaught Room and George V Room €€€

Two of the most elegant restaurants in Ireland are located in the same place – Ashford Castle. If you are romanced by the hotel, you will be positively seduced by the dining experience here. The Connaught Room is a small, intimate restaurant overlooking the grounds of the estate. Rich, dark paneling, an exquisite Waterford crystal chandelier and an open fireplace are the perfect touches to put you in the mood for a wonderful dinner. In addition to the Connaught Room, there is the equally lovely George V Room. With an open fire, gorgeous chandeliers, and beautiful light oak paneling that gives the room less of a regal feel and more of a traditional Irish feel, which is the perfect complement to the traditional Irish cuisine featured here. *Info*: Tel. (094) 954-6003. Cong, County Galway. Open daily. Coat and tie required. Reservations required.

Cromleach Lodge €€€

Panoramic views and incredible food. Christy and Moira Tighe have created a culinary dining destination with few peers. The menu, Irish in focus, changes daily and never fails to delight. Try the pan-fried wild salmon on smoked haddock brandade with light mustard sauce. Vegetarians will enjoy offerings like Mediterranean vegetables, goat's cheese and basil pesto in a puff of pastry shell. *Info*: Tel. (071) 916-5155. Near Castlebaldwin, County Sligo. Open daily. Reservations highly recommended.

Owenmore Restaurant €€€

Romantic setting. Elegant, efficient service. Splendid food. Beautiful views. All are a recipe for restaurant success. Typical offerings at the restaurant of Ballynahinch Castle include poached breast of guinea fowl with herbs and vegetables, and pan-fried pork fillet with sherry and mushroom sauce. Desserts are terrific; try the three-chocolate mousse with puree of fresh fruit. Jacket and tie are requested. *Info*: Tel. (095) 31006. Recess, Ballynahinch, County Galway. Open daily.

Asgard Tavern and Restaurant €€

Another fine Westport seafood restaurant overlooking Clew Bay. Typical dishes include poached fillet of salmon hollandaise, lobster in brandy cream, and peppered beef fillet on a warm salad. There are also several vegetarian dishes available, although it's not a wide selection. *Info*: Tel. (098) 25319. The Quay, Westport. Closed Mondays. During the off-season, they are closed Sundays and Mondays.

Connacht

The Malt House Restaurant €€
Great High Street restaurant. This small restaurant has a nice atmosphere and is known primarily for its fine fish dishes. Other offerings include duckling a l'orange and escalope of veal Normandy. *Info:* Tel. (091) 567866. High Street, Galway City. Closed Sundays.

McDonagh's Restaurant €€
Popular award-winning eatery at the end of High/Quay Street. Part of the building is a fresh fish store, part a fish-and-chips bar, and part an interesting restaurant. The tables and booths are themselves unremarkable, but there is interesting marine paraphernalia adorning the walls. At McDonagh's, you'll enjoy the best fish and chips around. *Info*: Tel. (091) 565001. 22 Quay Street, Galway City. Open daily.

O'Grady's Seafood Restaurant €€
Quiet restaurant on the main shopping street in Clifden. Known for their excellent seafood menu, you'll be pleased with the entrees you find here. Samples of their menu include fillet of cod, braised monkfish, or grilled fillet of turbot with a compote of rhubarb and champagne butter cream. There are a few non-seafood dishes, but the specialties here are from the depths of the deep blue. *Info*: Tel. (095) 21450. Lower Market Street, Clifden, County Galway. Closed Sundays.

The Quay Cottage €€
Great reputation for fresh, delicious fare. The fishing paraphernalia on the ceiling and walls tip you off that this is a seafood restaurant: lobster pots, fishing nets, glass floats. Fillet of lemon sole, fresh scallops, crab salad cocktail, and monkfish with tagliatelle are just a few of the seafood offerings available. There are other dishes, such as lamb and good Irish beef, but seafood is clearly the main focus. *Info*: Tel. (098) 26412. Westport House

Road, Westport, County Mayo. Open daily. (Closed from mid-January to mid-February.)

Bridge Mills Restaurant €

Overlooking the Corrib River in Galway. The restaurant is divided into a number of small rooms that gives the restaurant an intimate feel. The food is primarily snacks: scones, pastries, soups and salads, although dinner is also available in the evenings. Vegetarians in particular will like Bridge Mills Restaurant, as a number of vegetarian dishes are available. *Info*: Tel. (091) 566231. O'Brien's Bridge, Galway City. Open daily.

Destry's Restaurant €

Destry's is a small sandwich, salad and soup cafe in the center of Clifden on Main Street. A pleasant place, the furnishings are simple, the service great, and the food memorable. Destry's is owned by Paddy and Julia Foyle, and if you visit, you will assuredly meet one or the other (if not both) of them. *Info:* Tel. (095) 21722. Main Street, Clifden, County Galway. Open daily. Closed on Mondays during the off season, and are also closed from October through the March.

John J. O'Malley's €

"John J's" is a hot hangout for the younger set that lives in or visits Westport. Kind of a cross between a cafe and a pub, John J's specializes in burgers, pasta, and some seafood. *Info*: Tel. (098) 27307. Bridge Street, Westport. Closed Saturdays and Sundays.

ULSTER & NORTHERN IRELAND

BEST SLEEPS

Note: prices are given in British pounds sterling for hotels in Northern Ireland.

Castle Murray Hotel €€

Seaside hotel with exquisite views. Themed rooms – Honeymoon, Africa, Hunting, Sailing, etc. are intriguing. A family room is also available. Very comfortable, richly decorated hotel. An on-site award-winning restaurant is a nice amenity, as well as stunning seascape views from most of the rooms. One restaurant, one bar. *Info*: www.castlemurray.com. Tel. (074) 973-7022. St. John's Point, Dunkineely, County Donegal. 10 rooms.

Galgorm Manor £££
Converted Georgian "gentlemen's residence." Large and spacious rooms, many of which are endowed with antiques. Gillies Pub is a popular venue. Galgorm Manor sits amid 85 acres, and they have an equestrian center on-site that enables you to see the grounds via horseback if you wish. One restaurant, one bar, spa, hydrotherapy pool, hot tub. *Info*: www.galgorm.com. Tel. (028) 2588-1001. 136 Fenaghy Road, Ballymena, Northern Ireland. 23 rooms.

Ten Square Hotel £££
EurAsian hotel in the heart of Belfast. Talk about a mix of emotions – a European / Asian hotel in a Victorian building in the capital of Northern Ireland! But it works – understated elegance, superb rooms and appointments make Ten Square the place to stay in downtown Belfast. Right across from City Hall, within easy walking distance of theaters, restaurants and sights to see. One restaurant and one bar. *Info*: www.tensquare.co.uk. Tel. (028) 9024-1001. Donegall Square District, Belfast: 10 Donegall Square South. 23 rooms.

Ardnamona House €€
Beautiful house, lovely gardens. Radiant Rhododendrons and amazing Azaleas capture most of the attention, but the variety of other plants and trees is impressive. The house is pretty nice too. A former Victorian shooting lodge which features large and tastefully decorated bedrooms. The rooms in the front of the house offer an extra benefit: splendid views of the lake and surrounding woodlands and gardens. *Info*: www.ardnamona.com. Tel. (074) 972-2650. Lough Eske, Donegal Town. 6 rooms.

Bushmills Inn Hotel ££
Old-World feel in downtown Bushmills. Well-kept and clean, this 16th-century inn has a small reception area that is warmed by an open turf fire, warm dark wood, gas lights, and a grand

Ulster-
N. Ireland

staircase leading upstairs. The rooms are large, light, and airy. The rooms facing the main street are a bit noisy, so ask for a room off the street. *Info*: www.bushmillsinn.com, 25 Main Street, Bushmills, Northern Ireland. Tel. (028) 2073-3000. 11 rooms.

Ballygally Castle Hotel ££
Ballygally Castle Hotel (or at least parts of it) was once a genuine castle. Built in 1625, it was converted into a hotel in the 1970s. The rooms are large and comfortable. A few years ago they recently expanded the hotel, adding 30 new rooms. One restaurant, one pub and one ghost. *Info*: www.hastingshotels.com. Tel. (028) 2858-1066. Coast Road, Ballygally, Northern Ireland. 44 rooms

Best Haunted Hotel!

Ballygally Castle Hotel boasts their own friendly, albeit mischievous, ghost. Legend has it the Lady Isabel Shaw had been locked in one of the tower rooms by her cruel husband. To escape her confinement, she cast herself from the window. They say she still visits on occasion, moving softly through the halls, amusing herself by tapping on the doors of guests' rooms. Her room has not been converted to a guest room, and it is furnished much like it might have been during her confinement. You can see the room by ascending a narrow winding staircase up one of the turrets of the original castle.

Glassdrumman Lodge ££
Magnificent views, wonderful place. Seascapes or mountain scenes from your room. The rooms of this converted farmhouse are large and comfortable, with little additions such as mineral water, fresh flowers, and warm and friendly Irish hospitality. There is an excellent restaurant associated with this guesthouse also. Located in County Down in the village of Annalong. It is just north of the larger town of Kilkeel on the A2. One restaurant. *Info:* www.glassdrummanlodge.com. Tel. (028) 4376-8451. 85 Mill Road, Annalong, County Down, Northern Ireland. 10 rooms.

Templeton Hotel ££
One of the nicest hotels in the Belfast area. Warm wood and lots of crystal and bright lights

in the public areas are inviting. Furniture and furnishings range from Scandinavian to medieval, depending on which areas of the hotel you are in. The rooms are spacious, and decorated in soft colors, giving them a restful feeling. Several executive suites are available in a separate addition. The suites are spacious, and feature Jacuzzis and mini-bars. Two restaurants, bar, lounge. *Info*: www.templetonhotel.com. Tel. (028) 9443-2984. 882 Antrim Road, Templepatrick, Ballyclare, Northern Ireland. 24 rooms.

Whitepark House Country Home ££
One of the prettiest country home B&Bs in Northern Ireland. Over 250 years old, Whitepark House is richly and tastefully decorated. Whitepark House Country Home might be mistaken for a greenhouse with furniture. Siobhan and Bob Isles combine their domestic capabilities with green thumbs to provide you with a pleasant atmosphere to relax in. Each of the rooms is individually decorated, and each is large and roomy. The rooms either have garden or ocean views. *Info*: www.whiteparkhouse.com. Tel. (028) 2073-1482. 150 Whitepark Road (Coast Road), Ballintoy, Ballycastle. 3 rooms.

The Arches Country House €
The Arches earns my vote as the Best Irish Bed and Breakfast, and the main reason is its proprietor, Mrs. Noreen McGinty. She is a lovely and gracious hostess, and her B&B offers traditional Irish charm and elegance. Large, spacious rooms are tastefully decorated with lovely furnishings and light colors. Each room has large windows, which offer stunning views of peaceful Lough Eske. The bathrooms in each of the rooms have been recently refurbished with new tile and fixtures. The grounds surrounding The Arches include a lovely fountain, walking paths, and chairs and benches for sitting and enjoying the peaceful green Irish countryside. *Info*: homepage.eircom.net/~archescountryhse. Tel. (074) 972-2029. Lough Eske, Barnesmore, Donegal. 6 rooms.

Ardeevin Guest House €
Another pleasant B&B near Lough Eske. Each room is spacious and exquisitely furnished, and all have lovely views of Lough Eske. *Info*: ardeevin.tripod.com/index.htm. Tel. (074) 972-1790. Lough Eske, Barnesmore, Donegal. 6 rooms.

Caireal Manor £

Modern B&B on the A43 between Ballymena and Waterfoot at the edge of Martinstown. Pleasant and warm, the rooms are tastefully and comfortably furnished. The B&B features wheelchair access, one of the few in the country to do so. *Info*: Tel. (028) 2175-8221. 90 Glenravel Road, Glens of Antrim, Martinstown, Ballymena, Northern Ireland. 5 rooms.

BEST EATS

Note: because of the many fine restaurants in Belfast, I've listed it separately in its own subsection beginning on page 220. Prices are given in British pounds sterling for restaurants in Northern Ireland.

Castle Murray House Restaurant €€€

Overlooking McSweeney Bay, this light and airy restaurant offers stunning views of the bay to complement a varied menu. The menu is "French with an Irish flair." You can select a lobster and eat it within site of its home, McSweeney Bay. Or, if you prefer, try the *piece de veau du jour* (the veal of the day). The house special is prawns and monkfish in garlic butter. *Info*: Tel. (074) 9737022. St. John's Point, Dunkineely, County Donegal. Open daily.

Harvey's Point Country Restaurant €€€

Restaurant on the banks of lovely Lough Eske in County Donegal. The setting is marvelous, and parts of the dining room have views of the lake. Starched linens, crystal, and silver complement the excellent food, like the crepinette of tender farmhouse chicken or the grilled salmon fillet with leek and chive sauce. Or, if beef is your preference, you can't miss with the beef stroganoff and tagliatelle. *Info*: Tel. (074) 972-2208. Lough Eske, County Donegal. Open daily.

Kee's Restaurant €€€

A hidden gem that most will pass by unknowingly. Great restaurant on the main street of Stranorlar. Elegant, quiet and private atmosphere. The framed tapestries around the walls are the work of past owners of the hotel and restaurant. The menu is well represented by beef, lamb, seafood, and other wonderful concoctions. Try the roast rack of Donegal spring lamb or the grilled fillet steak with wild mushroom essence. Add one of the finest wine lists in the country, and you have a combination that's difficult to beat. *Info*: Tel. (074) 913-1018. Stranorlar, Ballybofey, County Donegal. Open daily.

Smuggler's Creek Inn €€
A seafood restaurant with splendid views of Donegal Bay and its long wide sandy beach. A number of tables on the veranda overlook the ocean, and it is a very popular — and busy — place during the summer months. Traditional Irish music is played in the bar on Friday and Saturday evenings from 10pm until midnight. The menu features a nice selection of seafood entrees with a smattering of beef and vegetarian dishes. Local sea beds yield oysters and mussels – a favorite. *Info*: Tel. (071) 985-2366. Waterville (near Rossknowlagh), County Donegal. Open daily.

Manor Lodge Restaurant ££
Wonderful restaurant at the foot of Glenariff Waterfall. Always busy, the restaurant offers excellent fare for a reasonable price. Try the fresh fillet of Red Bay plaice poached in white wine, or the tenderized Irish beef topped with prawns and sautéed in garlic butter. Plenty of patrons here are mid-hike on one of the numerous walking trails at Glenariff National Park. *Info:* Tel. (028) 2575-8221. 120 Glen Road, Glenariff, County Antrim. Open daily.

Bushmills Inn Restaurant ££
An open turf fire and warm welcome greet you at Bushmills Inn. The secret of their gastronomical success is in the freshness of the local produce, poultry, meat, and seafood they provide. Look for such main courses as roast rack of lamb or braised barony duckling, poached salmon, or smoked sea trout. The menu varies from time to time, and you're sure to find something you'll like. The restaurant itself is a series of booths; old white-washed stone walls and distressed pine gives kind of an old world ambiance. *Info*: Tel. (028) 2073-2339. 25 Main Street, Bushmills, County Antrim. Open daily.

Biddy O'Barnes €
Wonderful pub, complete with open turf fires, good food and

warm welcome. Pub grub, featuring snacks, soups, and sandwiches is available to accompany a pint of Guinness. *Info:* Tel. (074) 972-1402. Barnesmore Gap, County Donegal. Open daily.

The Blueberry Tea Room €

Just off the Diamond in Donegal and up a narrow staircase between the Olde Castle Bar and Restaurant and Melody Maker is The Blueberry Tea Room, a popular little sandwich shop. The fare is simple: sandwiches, soups and bread. *Info:* Tel. (074) 972-2933. Castle Street, Donegal Town, County Donegal. Closed Sundays during the off-season.

Valerie's Pantry £

In Bushmills, up the hill on Main Street. A delightful little cafe that offers snacks and sandwiches for a quick bite. From scones to roast beef sandwiches, Valerie's offers you good food at fair prices. The furnishings are simple and the food is good. *Info:* Tel. (028) 2073-1145. 125 Main Street, Bushmills, County Antrim. Open daily, closed Sundays during the winter.

BELFAST BEST EATS
Alden's £££

Bright and cheery, elegant, efficient service and excellent food. Try the breast of chicken with chunky ratatouille and basil jus or the breast of duck with roast fennel mash and star anise. For a treat, top it off with Pavlova with frozen yoghurt and tropical fruit salad. Just a few minutes out of downtown Belfast on the Newtownards Road. *Info:* Tel: (028) 9065-0079. Ballyhackamore, 229 Upper Newtownards Road, Belfast. Closed Sundays. Reservations required.

Cayenne £££

One of the top restaurants in Northern Ireland. All things considered – fare, service, facility – Cayenne provides one of the best Belfast dining experiences. Elegant but far from stuffy. Try the oyster mushrooms and peppercorn cream, the coconut-crusted cod or the breast of duck with wild rice pancakes. For dessert, you can't go wrong with the hot banana strudel. *Info:* Tel. (028) 9033-1532. Shaftesbury Square District: 7 Ascot House, Belfast. Open daily. Reservations required.

James Street South £££

One of the most popular upscale restaurants in Belfast. Starched linen, china and crystal greet you at this upscale restaurant, although it's not stuffy. Modern treatment of traditional Irish fare. Try the roast loin of lamb with celeriac and turnip gratin, or if seafood is on your mind, try the sautéed halibut with artichoke and foie gras. Several vegetarian dishes are also available, including bell peppers and Jerusalem artichokes. *Info:* Tel: (028) 9043-4310. Donegall Square District: 21 James Street, Belfast. Open daily. Reservations required.

N. Ireland
(Belfast)

Restaurant Michael Deane £££

Two restaurants in one: a Michelin-starred restaurant and a less formal brasserie. The rich décor in the restaurant is still elegant (though a bit dated) and the food is exceptional. Try the peppered venison with creamed artichokes, shiitake mushrooms and jus of lemon grass or the terrine of foie gras and pigeon, with salad of confit quail. *Info:* Tel. (028) 9033-1134. Donegall Square District: 38-40 Howard Street. Closed Sundays. Reservations required.

Tedford's Seafood and Steakhouse £££

As the name implies, your choices here will be primarily seafood and steak. Your dining experience can be plush or homey – your choice. The downstairs dining room has more of a tavern or bistro feel, while the upstairs dining room is much plusher, with thick carpet, starched tablecloths, etc. Try the prawns and mussels in light garlic butter, or the Barbary duck supreme. *Info:* Tel. (28) 9043-4000. Northeast of Donegall Square District: 5 Donegall Quay, Belfast. Open daily.

Cafe Society ££

This modern cafe near Belfast City Hall offers up excellent fare for sagging shoppers, tired tourists, and busy business people. The menus offer a nice selection, and presentation is an important aspect of the fare. Try their fillet of salmon in herb crust or roasted rack of pork. The dessert menu is great. *Info:* Tel. (028) 9043-9525. Donegall Square District: 3 Donegall Square East. Closed Sundays.

The Garden Restaurant at Belfast Castle ££
Located in the cellars of Belfast Castle, the atmosphere is decidedly cozy and the food is good. White-washed stone walls, antique lamps and wooden plank floors add to the atmosphere. Try the baked wild salmon with ratatouille or the char-grilled chicken fillet with cous cous and spiced tomato. *Info*: Tel. (028) 9077-6925. Belfast Castle, Antrim Road, Belfast. Open daily.

The Grill Room and Bar ££
Great grill food – hamburgers, steak, barbecue ribs, etc. While the menu offers other fare, the specialty here is beef. A chipper and friendly atmosphere is inviting also. Try the slow-cooked barbecue ribs or any of their steaks. For dessert, try the Chocolate Diane – it's superb. *Info*: Tel. (028) 9024-1001. Donegall Square District: Ten Square, 10 Donegall Square South, Belfast. Open daily.

Manor House Restaurant ££
Another of Belfast's excellent Chinese restaurants. Soft colors in the restaurant add a tranquil feeling to the dining experience, even though the place is filled with happy diners most of the time. The menu is extensive, offering over 200 choices. *Info*: Tel. (028) 9023-8755. University District: 47 Donegall Pass. Open daily.

Roscoff Cafe ££
Roscoff is a combo coffee bar, cafe, restaurant and deli counter. Chrome and cloth chairs and small two-person tables define the ambiance. In the cafe, the set menu changes on a regular basis, and you're never left with too few decisions: often you can choose from five to eight items per course. The main courses consist of such delicacies as confit duck, glazed monkfish, venison with roast shallots, and roast cod with a lobster and tarragon vinaigrette. Combine those offers with a wide variety of fresh appetizers, vegetables, and desserts, and you've got a feast on your hands. *Info*: Tel. (028) 9031-0108. Shaftesbury District: 12-14 Arthur Street. Closed Sundays.

The Tong Dynasty ££
Great Chinese restaurant. Basic décor but exceptional service and food. I always like to see members of the local Chinese community at a Chinese food restaurant. You'll find expected dishes

here: Szechwan chicken, dim sum, fried rice, etc., but if you're brave, ask for the Chinese menu, which lists Chinese favorites not usually found on western menus – things like stir-fried bitter melon and beef with black bean sauce or chicken feet with spare ribs in bean sauce. *Info*: Tel. 02890 439590. University District: 82 Botanic Avenue, Belfast.

N. Ireland
(Belfast)

Villa Italia ££
Great family Italian restaurant. Good pasta dishes are the fare here, although good meat dishes are also available. Although a popular and very busy place, the service is exceptional. Gingham tablecloths with floral centerpieces add to the homey, family feel of this restaurant. Try the Pollo al Basilico – chicken stuffed with mozzarella, or the pork fillet garnished with pine nuts, pineapple, cheese and sun-dried tomatoes. *Info*: Tel. (28) 9032-8356. University District: 37-41 University Road, Belfast. Open daily.

Bishop's Fish And Chips £
You'll find a little bit o' London at Bishop's Fish and Chips, located close to Shaftesbury Square. This establishment has a cafeteria atmosphere - noisy and chattery, booths lining the walls and down the center. They also have a variety of burgers available, but fish and chips is the main attraction. *Info:* Tel. (028) 9043-9070. Shaftesbury Square District: 34 Bradbury Place, Belfast. Open daily.

The Crown Liquor Saloon £
The Crown is worth stopping by just for a visit. It is like stepping back to Victorian times. Gaslights glisten, mosaics on the floor shine, *snugs* (small, semi-private booths with high walls) beckon patrons to share their most intimate secrets, brass fixtures shine brightly, and the ornate mirrors are a sight to behold. Located uptown across from the Europa Hotel. Pub grub is at its best here, with soups and sandwiches. The Irish stew is particularly good. *Info*: Tel. (028) 9024-9476. Donegall Square District: 46 Great Victoria Street. Open daily.

The Revelations Internet Cafe £
This small nondescript cafe gives new meaning to Surf and Turf - it is a combination coffee shop/computer lab. Guests can order

cappuccino and a sandwich while surfing the net on any of the half dozen computers they have set up for internet access. *Info*: Tel. (028) 9032-0337. Shaftesbury Square District: 27 Shaftesbury Square, Belfast. Open daily.

10. BEST ACTIVITIES

This chapter covers Ireland's best vacation activities: shopping, nightlife, and sports and recreation. You'll find **great stores** in Ireland offering everything from elegant to touristy, with everything in between. Looking for the latest in Dublin (and London!) fashion? Stop by Brown Thomas on Grafton Street. For a little of everything Irish, check out Blarney Woolen Mills, located throughout Ireland.

Ireland is famous for its pubs, and I'll point you to some of the best. Try the Stag's Head in Dublin, the Oyster Tavern in Cork or the Crown Liquor Saloon in Belfast. All are well over 200 years old. If you're looking for something a little more contemporary, don't miss POD in Dublin, or check out the local music or theater scene.

Ireland is justly famous for its **gorgeous golf courses.** Ireland offers some of the world's best courses, including Lahinch in County Clare, Portstewart in County Derry, Mt. Juliet near Thomastown and Adare Manor Golf Club in Adare – not to mention the championship course at the Kildare Country Club. If this isn't enough, I'll introduce you to **other sports popular in Ireland:** hurling, Gaelic football, biking, horseback riding and more!

DUBLIN

DUBLIN'S BEST SHOPPING

Dublin is a great place for shopping, with lots of interesting stores within easy walking distance of one another. A few deserve special mention here. **Grafton Street** is one of the liveliest shopping districts in Ireland, filled with promising stores and spiced by lots of happy shoppers, tourists and street entertainers.

Stop first at **Brown Thomas** (known affectionately as BT), an upscale department store about mid-way up Grafton Street. Such notables as Gucci, Armani, Versace, Hermes, Christian Dior and more are to be found here. If you've used the last of your Chanel #5, here is your chance to pick some up.

If you're looking for jewelry, slip into **Weirs & Sons** jewelers on Grafton Street – they claim to have more diamonds and gold than any other jeweler in Ireland. They also have a nice selection of Waterford crystal.

There are also top-notch stores off the streets that intersect and parallel Grafton Street: new and used book stores, craft shops, small boutiques, antiques and shoe stores. One of those intersecting streets is William Street; here you'll find a potpourri of stores in the **Powerscourt Townhouse Center** which boasts a bevy of cafés, antique shops, shoe stores and more in a converted Georgian Townhouse.

At the south end of Grafton Street you'll find the relatively new **St. Stephen's Green Centre**, a newish mall filled with a variety of clothing, jewelry, boutiques and dozens of other stores and restaurants. Once inside, it frankly has the feel of an American mall. Its nouveau Victorian design does make it a little more pleasant to the eye, however.

Not far from Grafton Street you'll find two stores that provide a variety of Irish products, including Waterford crystal, wool sweaters, tweed jackets, Claddagh rings and much, much more.

On Nassua Street, the **Kilkenny Shop** and **Blarney Woolen Mills** should fill all your tourist-shopping needs!

We can't leave a section on Dublin shopping without pointing out two other shopping opportunities: **Fleury Antiques** and the **Moore Street Market**. Fleury Antiques is located at 57 Francis Street, in the heart of Dublin's Antiques Row. Fleury's is one of the most recognizable names in Irish antiques, since they are one of the nation's largest dealers. It is more than worth a visit just to see the quantity and quality of furnishings and bric-a-brac they offer. The Moore Street Market, north of O'Connell Street just around the corner from the GPO, is an open-air market where vendors sell fruits, vegetables and flowers. You can hear the (mostly) women vendors shouting to call your attention to their produce. It's a fun place to go, and it's especially colorful and cheery on a sunny day.

DUBLIN'S BEST NIGHTLIFE

There are lots of things to do on an evening in Dublin. One of the most enjoyable is to participate in the **Dublin Literary Pub Crawl** – see the Dublin chapter for details. Also, the **National Concert Hall** just southeast of St. Stephens Green almost always has something worth seeing – a play, concert, comedian or magician. Check it out www.nch.ie.

Dublin is known for its plethora of pubs. Some of the best are **The Bailey** (Tel. (01) 677-5711), serving Dublin customers since 1837, **The Brazen Head** (Tel. (01) 660-5222), known for its excellent traditional Irish music, and **The Stag's Head** (Tel. (01) 679-3701), located at this site since prior to the American revolution.

For a delightful evening of friendship, traditional Irish music and Guinness, try the **Temple Bar Pub** (Tel. (01) 1 672-5287) on Dublin's "left bank" – Temple Bar. A special treat here is their Whiskey Whiskey café, which boasts one of

Ireland's largest whiskey collections. And don't forget the **Abbey Tavern** (www.abbeytavern.ie), a short DART ride away in Howth.

If you are looking for the less traditional Irish nightclub scene, then you should visit the **POD** (Place of Dance), which boasts Dublin's largest dance floor (www.pod.ie), or at **The Pink Elephant** (Tel. (01) 677-5876), a favorite hangout of Trinity students, you'll find a nice assortment of rising European rock groups.

If you are looking for plays, Dublin has a number of **theaters**, including **Abbey Theater** on lower Abbey Street (www.abbeytheatre.ie), the Gaiety Theater (Tel. (01) 677-1717) and the Olympia Theater on Dame Street (Tel. (01) 677-7744). Each features its own form of Irish theater.

DUBLIN'S BEST SPORTS & RECREATION
Gaelic Football
Gaelic football is a rough and tumble (literally) game that is a cross between rugby and soccer. Each team consists of 15 players who pass the ball to one another in an effort to move it down field and across an "end-zone." Kicking the ball into the net scores three points, and kicking it through the uprights scores one point.

Gaelic football is played in the spring and summer, and the All-Ireland finals are held in Dublin in September. If you find yourself in Dublin in September, treat yourself to a game - you'll love the fast action and excitement. Games are played at **Croke Park** (www.crokepark.ie).

Hurling
Another peculiarly Irish game is hurling. Hurling is a high-speed game of ancient (probably Celtic) origin that is extremely popular with the Irish. Fifteen players per team use a short (approximately 3') stick - called a caman or hurley - that is curved on the end to bat, catch, and hurl a small leather ball downfield and into the opponent's goal. The ball, called a sliotar, is slightly smaller than a tennis ball. Games are played throughout the summer at **Croke Park**, and the All-Ireland finals are held in Dublin in September. If you have the opportunity, stop and watch a game.

Rugby

Rugby is also a wildly exciting game played in Ireland, and its followers are as avid here as they are anyplace else. If you've never seen rugby, it's sort of a non-stop football game where husky men try and ram an over-inflated football through the defense of their opponent. One interesting aspect of rugby in Ireland is that their international team consists of players from both the Republic and Northern Ireland - the only team sport on the Emerald Isle that ignores political differences and has one Irish team made up of players from both countries. Games are played at **Lansdowne Road Stadium**, in the Ballsbridge area.

Dublin

Soccer

Soccer is played primarily in and around Dublin (attesting to centuries of strong English presence there) and Belfast. Having said that, let Ireland's team compete in the **World Cup**, and soccer is followed avidly on radio and TV. Unlike Gaelic football and hurling, soccer has gone the way of many pro sports in America. Players gravitate to whichever team pays the most, and many Irish players are on teams other than Ireland's team. In recent years, the English soccer team in Manchester has had significant Irish representation, and accordingly has a significant Irish following. You can go to a match at **Dalymount Park** in Phibsborough, **Richmond Park** in Inchicore and **Belfield Park** in the Ballsbridge district of Dublin.

Golf

Golf courses in Ireland are among some of the most beautiful and challenging in the world. Some are verdant, lush, and about everything you've ever dreamed of for a game of golf. Others are links courses, with their dunes and deep bunkers, and fairways that have cliff hazards along the edge of the fairway. Many of Ireland's golf courses are actually part of a golf club. But unlike America and other countries around the world, these courses welcome players who do not belong to their club. The only restriction is that weekends are sometimes reserved for club members (as are some other weekdays at some courses).

Some of the best Dublin-area golf courses are **Portmarnock** (www.portmarnockgolfclub.ie), and **Royal Dublin Golf Club** (www.theroyaldublingolfclub.com). Both have served as the venue for European and Irish Open championships through the years. Portmarnock is about ten miles from downtown Dublin, in northeast County Dublin, and the Royal Dublin Golf Club is located about three miles from Dublin's city center on an island in Dublin Bay. Both courses are also very expenive, ranging between €150 and €195 for 18 holes. For a more affordable golf outing, head to Howth, just outside of Dublin and you'll find pretty rolling **Deer Park Golf Course** (www.deerpark-hotel.ie).

LEINSTER

LEINSTER'S BEST SHOPPING

It is true that some of the best shopping in Leinster is actually in Dublin (see earlier in this chapter), but I have enjoyed several other places for practicing my shopping craft.

In central Leinster, take a few moments and stop in at the **Avoca Handweavers** in Avoca. The oldest weaving mill in Ireland (the mill dates to 1723), you'll find a nice selection of handwoven sweaters, scarves and other wool accessories. There are several shops in Ireland, but this is where their craft began.

Stroll the towns of Bray and Wexford south of Dublin, Howth and Skerries northeast of Dublin, and Drogheda north of Dublin. You'll find many shops, restaurants and interesting sights to capture your attention, time and perhaps a few of your euros. The experience of meeting the shopkeepers is as memorable as the purchases you may – or may not – make.

LEINSTER'S BEST NIGHTLIFE

A short DART or car ride northeast of Dulin is the **Abbey Tavern** (Tel. (01) 839-0307), which has gained international recognition for its traditional Irish music and entertainment.

Southwest of Dublin in the Wicklow Mountains, you'll find **Johnny Fox's Pub** (Tel. (01) 295-5647) for some great traditional Irish music, a heart- and soul-warming turf fire, wonderful atmosphere and a great time. Oh yes – the Guinness is good there too!

LEINSTER'S BEST SPORTS & RECREATION

In the Dublin section of this chapter, we discussed two traditional Irish spectator sports – Gaelic football and hurling. Both of these sports are avidly followed by the Irish – so keep an eye out, especially on a Saturday or Sunday – for crowds of people walking to or arriving at a field. Stop your car. Park and follow them and you're likely to experience the Irish equivalent of T-ball, Pop Warner or Babe Ruth League, etc., but for hurling and Gaelic football.

Horse Racing

Horse racing is followed as avidly as any other sport in the country. Results of races are broadcast hourly by many radio stations, and it is always part of the evening news sports section. At last count, races are held on 233 days of the year, at 27 different racetracks. (Remember - Ireland is about the size of Kentucky.)

Check the local newspapers or visit the local Bord Failte office for information on the location and times of the races closest to you. The **Jameson Irish Grand National** is run at **Punchestown Race Course** in County Kildare, a short ride into the countryside from Dublin. Another popular racetrack is at **Leopardstown** (near downtown Dublin).

Golf

Two of the of the most beautiful golf courses I have ever seen are in Leinster. **The Kildare Country Club** (K Club) (Tel. (01) 601-7200) is located in Kildare and has been the sight of several recent European Opens and the Ryder Cup. Two 18-hole courses offer you all you can hope for in an Irish golf experience.

Just down the road is another exquisite course at **Mt. Juliet** (Tel. (056) 24725). The velvety fairways and silky smooth greens are incredible, and the beauty is breathtaking. The course is renowned for their water hazards, so golfers beware!

Horseback Riding

If you're keen to see some of the Irish countryside astride a horse, then you might consider the **Mt. Juliet Equestrian Center** in Thomastown (Tel. (056) 24455). Or if you want to tour some of the

Wicklow Mountains on horseback, try **Devil's Glen Equestrian Center** in Ashford (Tel. (040) 440-013).

Sailing/Windsurfing

If you'd like to try a little sailing or windsurfing (plenty of water and wind in Ireland), head for Wexford in southeast Leinster and the **Rosslare Sailboard Center** (Tel. (053) 32101).

MUNSTER

MUNSTER'S BEST SHOPPING

One of the best shopping experiences you'll have in Ireland will be at the **Waterford Crystal Factory** in Waterford (Tel. (051) 875788). Beautiful crytal is everywhere, and you won't know where to begin your purchasing! Waterford Crystal practices national pricing, so don't expect this to be a factory outlet.

Munster is home to **Blarney Woolen Mills** – with stores in Blarney, Bunratty, Tipperary and Killarney. You'll find a little bit of Ireland in the Blarney Woolen Mills – not just woolen products, but you'll find crystal, china, gold and silver jewelry, etc.

Killarney's welcoming downtown streets are filled with shops of varying sizes and varieties. **Quill's Woolen Market** (Tel. (064) 32277) is a department store on High Street that offers a wide variety of touristy things (Claddagh rings, Aran sweaters, tweed coats and hats, etc.). If it's Celtic jewelry you're looking for, try **Brian de Staic** (Tel. (064) 33822), a fabulous place to find original designs as well as traditional Celtic jewelry.

You won't have to look far for shops that carry traditional tourist stuff, but two of the best are **Serendipity** (Tel. (064) 31056) and **Christy's Irish Stores** (Tel. (064) 33222). The latter is reminiscent of Blarney Woolen Mills, with its wide selection of sweaters, jewelry and most things Irish.

MUNSTER'S BEST NIGHTLIFE & ENTERTAINMENT

Several of Munster's cities offer a good variety of nightlife and entertainment. Cork, in particular, has more than it's fair share of pubs to try out. While you may not be able to correctly pronounce the name, **An Spailpin Fanach** (Tel. (021) 427-7949) is a place you'll want to visit. It is one of the most popular pubs in Cork City – it will probably be packed, especially on the weekends. Generally speaking, the clientele here will be more…mature…than you'll find in the other pubs in Cork. An Spailpin Fanach has become a popular watering hole for the business men and women as well as tourists in Cork. You'll enjoy a wide range of music from Sunday to Thursday evenings, ranging from traditional Irish to western to blues.

Not far from An Spailpin Fanach is **The Long Valley Bar** on Winthrop Street (Tel. (021) 427-2144). This ancient pub has been entertaining the citizens of Cork for over 150 years (and tourists for somewhat less time than that, I suppose). Another of Cork's landmark pubs is **The Oyster Tavern on** Market Lane (Tel. (021) 427-2716). It was nearly 10 years old when the 1798 Uprising was put down, and 130 years old when Ireland earned its independence.

If you're looking for a less traditional and more contemporary watering hole, try **Club FX** on Lynch's Street (Tel. 021) 427-1120). Live bands beckon the university crowd six nights a week, featuring music from the 70s through contemporary.

If you're in Cork and looking for contemporary drama, try the **Cork Arts Theater** (Tel. (021) 450-8398). **The Triskel Arts Theater** (www.triskelart.com), also in Cork, presents a wide range of performing arts, from poetry readings to dramatic productions to traditional Irish music.

As mentioned in the Munster Destination chapter, for an evening of mirth, frivolity and traditional Irish music, check out **Bunratty Castle** (www.shannonheritage.com/Bunratty_Ban.htm) or its sister castle, **Knappogue Castle** (www.shannonheritage.com/Knappogue_Ban.htm). Both offer evening entertainment of the medieval dining variety. Both castles are within just a few minutes of Limerick and the Shannon Airport.

If you find yourself in Killarney of an evening with nothing to do, never fear. Pubs abound, and one of the best is **O'Connors** on

High Street (Tel. (064) 30200). Depending on the evening you come, you may be serenaded by traditional Irish music, entertained by a local comedian or have a more contemplative evening of literary readings. Another pub worth stopping by is **The Laurels** on Main Street (Tel. 064/31149), where you'll enjoy a pint of Guinness while listening to traditional Irish music.

MUNSTER'S BEST SPORTS & RECREATION
Golf
Munster is home to some of Ireland's most legendary golf courses. **Ballybunnion** (Tel. (068) 27146) and the **Dooks Golf Club** are both located in County Kerry. Both have world-wide reputations for excellence – not to mention difficulty! Both these courses are links courses – stay in the fairway! And don't forget **Lahinch Golf Club** (www.lahinchgolf.com), located in Lahinch, County Clare. This seaside course features many tricky approaches and delicious idiosyncracies.

If you prefer the beauty and quiet of parkland courses, be sure and visit **Adare Manor Golf Club** (www.adaremanorgolfclub.com) in Adare, or **Dromoland Castle Golf Club** in Newmarket-on-Fergus. Both offer challenging and beautiful holes.

Horseback Riding
All of Ireland seems well suited for horseback riding, but Munster seems especially so. In County Cork, try **Ballmee Equestrian Center** (Tel. (022) 24135) or **Knocknamarra Stables** (Tel. (021) 887111). If it's County Kerry you wish to see astride a horse, try **Rocklands Riding Stables** (Tel. (064) 32592) or **Killarney Riding Stables** (Tel. (064) 31686).

Scuba Diving
Southwest Ireland provides some of the island's best diving. Try **Baltimore Diving and Watersports Center,** (Tel. (028) 20300), **Cork Sub-Aqua Club,** (Tel. (021) 271224) or **Derrynane Diving School** (Tel. (066) 977-5119). Diving out of Kinsale can be arranged through **Kinsale Dive Center** (Tel. (021) 772382).

Surfing/Windsurfing
Unbeknownst to many, western Ireland offers some fine surfing (at least by European standards). Try **Cork County Surf Beaches**

in Barley Cove, or **Jamie Knox Windsurfing and Surfing** (Tel. (066) 713-9411). In Kinsale, stop by the **Kinsale Outdoor Education Center** (Tel. (021) 772896) to try your luck.

CONNACHT

CONNACHT'S BEST SHOPPING

One of my favorite Irish cites to shop in is Galway. The shops are plenteous and interesting, and the shoppers on the pedestrianized streets seem to add an intriquing vibrance. While in Galway, check out **Faller's Jewellers** (Tel. (091) 561226) for that Claddagh ring or necklace that you haven't yet purchased. They offer a number of styles and sizes of Claddagh rings, necklaces and brooches. They also have a nice selection of Waterford crystal, Beleek china, and other upscale items.

Check out **Kenney's Books** (Tel. (091) 562739), which offers one of the largest selections in Ireland. They offer new and used books, and you could easily get lost in their store for a few hours.

If you're in Galway and looking for sweaters or other woolens, try the **Design Concourse of Ireland** (Tel. (091) 566016) or **O'Maille's** (Tel. (091) 562296). Both have a wide selection of Aran sweaters, hats and scarves.

Clifden is a small town in the Connemara district, but I found its shops, though limited in number, interesting places to visit. Try **O'Hehir's Woolen Shop** (Tel. (095) 21282) for woolens, tweeds and other fashions. If you're interested in art, stop in at either **Lavelle Art Gallery** (Tel. (095) 21882), or **Clifden Art Gallery** (Tel (095) 21788). Both offer marvelous works of art, much of it by local artists. Scenes of the Connemara landscape abound.

CONNACHT'S BEST NIGHTLIFE & ENTERTAINMENT

Galway offers a host of first-class, enjoyable pubs. Just follow your nose – or a crowd of people you think you'd like to get to know - and you'll be sure to find a pleasant pub. Try **McSwiggan's** (Tel. (091) 568917) if you're looking for good traditional music on the weekend. This is not your ordinary pub; it seems like three or four pubs in one building. There are no fewer than three levels and four bars. McSwiggan's tends to draw a younger crowd most nights, although most evenings seem to have their fair share of tourists. **The Snugs/Garravans** (Tel. (091) 562831) is a cavernous pub that was once a wine cellar in medieval times. Take notice of the alcove at the rear of The Snugs – it was once a very old and very large fireplace (what on earth did they cook here?). It has been determined that the beam above the hearth is over 700 years old! Upstairs you'll find a more traditional Irish pub in Garravan's. A turf fire, lots of dark wood and cozy atmosphere abound. Traditional, blues, or jazz music are part of the entertainment Thursday through Sunday evenings.

If you're looking for a dramatic performance, you might try the **Town Hall Theater** (Tel. (091) 569777). It plays host to the Galway thespian community, and has a very active schedule year-in and year-out. Events that have been staged here in the past include performances by the Royal Shakespeare Company, The Abbey Theater, and the Druid Theater.

CONNACHT'S BEST SPORTS & RECREATION
Golf

Along the shores of the Atlantic Ocean you'll find the **Connemara Golf Club**, (Tel. (095) 23502). The views are superlative, and the golf isn't too bad either. The fairways snake among small dunes and truly define links golf. You may find several of the holes unsettling, especially the tough 14th, which has its green set high on the hillside.

In County Mayo, you'll find the **Westport Golf Club** (Tel. (098) 25113). It meanders at the foot of Ireland's Holy Mountain, Croagh Patrick, and in addition to providing a challenging links-style course, it provides lovely views of island-studded Clew Bay. Some of the views of Clew Bay may be a little close for your tastes. Take for example the view you have of Clew Bay from the 15th tee. Yes, the view of the inlet is lovely, until you realize that it lies between you and the green.

The **Galway Golf Course** (Tel. (091) 522033) offers fabulous views of the ocean, Aran Islands, and the Burren.

Horseback Riding

The Connemara district of Connacht offers many opportunities for horseback riding its wind-swept vistas. Try **Broadfield Stables** (Tel. (091) 797075) or **Errislannan Manor** (Tel. (095) 21134) for two of the more enjoyable rides in the area. Close to Sligo, try **Munsboro Riding Holidays** (Tel. (0903) 26449) or the **Sligo Equestrian Center** (Tel. (071) 61353).

Scuba is not as popular in Connacht as in Munster, but there are several dive centers that take divers out. Try the **Atlantic Dive Center** (Tel. (096) 32797) or **Scubadive West**, (Tel. (095) 43922).

Sailing/Windsurfing

While scuba isn't as popular in Connacht as it is in Munster, there seems to be no lessening of popularity for sailing and windsurfing in Connacht. In County Sligo, try the **Sligo Yacht Club** (Tel. (071) 77168) or **Sunset Sails and Windsurfing** (Tel. (071) 62792), or in County Galway, try **Galway Sailing Center** (Tel. (091) 794527) or **Little Killary Adventure Center**, (Tel. (095) 43411).

ULSTER-NORTHERN IRELAND

ULSTER-NORTHERN IRELAND'S BEST SHOPPING

Donegal is one of the most interesting shopping places in Ulster. Its shops line the small town square (called **The Diamond**) and provide ample opportunity to sample Irish goods. For that Aran sweater you've been craving, try **McGinty's Sweater Shop**, just off the square. Or for more of a tweedy adventure, try **Magee's** (Tel. (074) 972-2660) for a wide variety of beautiful hand-woven tweed suits, jackets, hats, ties, scarves, etc. Take a few minutes and slip into **Melody Maker Music** (Tel. (074) 972-2326) just off The Diamond on Castle Street to make a selection of music CDs to take home.

About one mile south of Donegal on the N15, watch for the signs directing you to the **Donegal Craft Shops**, where you'll find a number of craft-type stores offering woolens and tweeds, paintings and pottery created by local artists and a number of other interesting stores.

In Belfast, there are two large shopping areas: Shaftsbury Square and the area around city hall. One of my favorite stores is along Belfast's Antique Row (Donegall Pass) and is **Oakland Antiques** (Tel. (028) 9023-0176), which features a wide array of furniture and brick-a-brac. For a different shopping experience, try **St. George's Market**, near Belfast's Central Station. It is a large indoor market, and features everything from food to clothing to antiques and books. The market is open Tuesday through Saturdays from 6:00am to mid-afternoon. If you're looking for a wide selection of books, try **No Alibis** (Tel. (028) 9020-1261).

ULSTER-NORTHERN IRELAND'S BEST NIGHTLIFE & ENTERTAINMENT

For a traditonal Irish pub experience, stop in at **Biddy O'Barnes** (Tel. (073) 21402) about six miles outside Donegal. Two centuries of County Donegal's residents have made the journey to Biddy O'Barnes, and you should make the trip there too.

Closer to town, stop in at **Eas Dun Pub** (Tel. (073) 21014) on The Diamond. The bar at the Abbey Hotel is an enjoyable gathering place for a few of the locals as well as many tourists. Weekday evenings you'll find traditional Irish music going strong, and on the weekends you can join in the dancing.

In Belfast, be sure and stop by the **Crown Liquor Saloon** (Tel. (028) 9024-9476), a Victorian-era pub. Gaslights glisten, mosaics on the floor shine, snugs (small, semi-private booths with high walls) beckon patrons to share their most intimate secrets, brass fixtures shine brightly, and the ornate mirrors are a sight to behold. It is truly an experience. If you're looking for more of a contemporay pub experience, try **Auntie Annie's Porterhouse** (Tel. (028) 9050 1660) — currently one of the hottest pubs in Belfast. Several clubs and different contemporary musical experiences can be found here.

If you're looking for a theatrical experience while in Belfast, try the **Grand Opera House** (Tel. (028) 9024 1919). Local and touring thespian troupes perform at the Victorian-era Grand Opera House. Local artists can be found on the smaller stage and more intimate setting of the **Lyric Theater** (Tel. (028) 9038 1088).

ULSTER-NORTHERN IRELAND'S BEST SPORTS & RECREATION

Golf

Lots of golfing opportunities in the northern end of the island. In Donegal, try the **Donegal Golf Club** (Tel. (073) 34054), a pretty links golf course that is popular with the locals as well as the occasional tourist.

Northern Ireland boasts three world-class golf courses: **Royal County Down** (Tel. (028) 4472-2419), **Royal Portrush Golf Course** (Tel. (028) 7082-2311) and **Portstewart Golf Club** (Tel. (028) 7083-2015). Each offers several courses, and several of the holes overlook the ocean. All are spectacular venues for your golf holiday.

Horseback Riding

There are many places to arrange for horseback riding in this northern-most province of Ireland. Some of the better ones include **Ashleigh Riding School** (Tel. (073) 22386) and **Carrigart Riding Stables** (Tel. (074) 55114) in County Donegal. In County Antrim in Northern Ireland, you can try **Cairnview** (Tel. (028) 2858-3269), **Dan Campbell's** (Tel. (028) 2827-7222) or **Te An Teasa** (Tel. (028) 2858-3591).

Sailing/Windsurfing

County Donegal has earned the reputation for great sailing and windsurfing. To get outfitted, stop in at **Marble Hill Windsurfing** (Tel. (074) 36231) in Dunfanaghy, County Donegal.

Scuba Diving

If you want to try your hand at scuba diving off the northern coasts, try the **Donegal Surf Center** (Tel. (073) 21179) in Donegal, or the **Atlantic Dive and Surf**, (Tel. (028) 7082-3272) in Portrush, County Antrim.

11. PRACTICAL MATTERS

GETTING AROUND

Flights from the United States and Canada arrive at either Shannon Airport or Dublin Airport.

Car Rental
For some reason, rental car pricing for Ireland seems to fluctuate rapidly and from agency to agency, so be sure to check the major rental agencies - Avis, Budget, Hertz, National – you're likely to find a surprisingly wide range of prices. For a two-week rental, I was quoted prices from $425 to over $975 for the same class of car and the same coverages!

You'll need a valid US or Canadian driver's license and a major credit card to drive in Ireland, but you do not need an International Drivers license unless you are staying for more than one year. Most car rental agencies in Ireland will only rent to drivers who are at least 23 years old and younger than 75 years old. Some rental agencies require you to be at least 25.

If you are accustomed to renting cars in the United States, you know your own car insurance usually covers you while you are driving a rental car in the US. Such is not the case in Ireland. Your domestic car insurance will not cover you while you are driving a rental car in Ireland.

Trains
The railways in Ireland literally criss-cross the country and you'll be able to get within striking distance of just about any place in Ireland you'd like to go. If you choose to travel in Ireland by train, you should purchase a **Train Timetable** at any train terminal, or

at the many Newsagents scattered across the country (typically in small grocery stores). There are several types of passes available:

- **Irish Explorer Rail** - Valid for any eight days of travel within a 15-day window - ideal if you want to stay a day or two and explore the surrounding areas before moving on to explore other cities or regions.
- **Irish Rover Rail** - Valid for any eight days of travel within a 15-day window. Similar to the Irish Explorer Rail listed above, except this pass allows you to go to Northern Ireland.

Taxis
Taxis are available in most of the large cities, but hailing them successfully is another issue. Most taxis prefer to line up in taxi stands (ranks) outside hotels, at the airport and some tourist information centers.

Bus
Bus Eireann (www.buseireann.ie) is the state-run organization that runs the bus (and train) lines. They run all the long-distance buses, as well as most of the local and sightseeing buses. If you choose to travel in Ireland by bus, you should purchase a **Provincial Bus Schedule** at any bus terminal, or at the many Newsagents scattered across the country (typically in small grocery stores). There are several types of passes available:

- **Irish Explorer Rail/Bus** - Valid for any eight days of travel within a 15-day window. For travel in the Republic of Ireland only.
- **Emerald Card Bus/Rail** - Valid for any eight days of travel within a 15-day window. Similar to the Irish Explorer Bus/Rail pass listed above, except this allows you to go to Belfast and elsewhere in Northern Ireland. There is also a pass for travel on any 15 days out of a 30-day window.

BASIC INFORMATION

BANKING & CHANGING MONEY
Ireland uses the **Euro**, along with other members of the European Union. To find out what the current conversion rate is, go to

242 OPEN ROAD'S BEST OF IRELAND

www.xe.com/ucc/convert.cgi. There are other currency converters on the web, but I find this one the easiest to use.

The euro uses the same numbering schemes as US and Canadian dollars. But instead of dollars and cents, you'll find euros and cents. Euro coins come in the following denominations: €2 and €1 euro coins, and 50-, 20-, 10-, 5-, 2- and 1-cent coins. All euro coins have a common European face, while the obverse side (tails!) of each coin contains a motif chosen by and specific to each EU country. Regardless of the motif on the obverse side, the coins can be used in any country of the European Union.

If you forget or can't get to a bank or currency exchange office to exchange your money before you leave, don't worry. There are currency exchange kiosks in most gateway city airports (Chicago, Boston, New York, and Atlanta), as well as at the Shannon and Dublin airports. You'll have to pay a minimal service charge, usually around $5.

In the Republic, businesses accept euros; however, **in Northern Ireland, most businesses only accept British pounds**.

Banks in Ireland are open…well…they're open banker's hours. Traditionally, banks in the Republic are open Monday through Wednesday and Friday from 10am to 12:30pm, and from 1:30pm to 3pm. On Thursdays their extended hours are from 10am to 12:30pm and 1:30pm to 5pm. Banks in Northern Ireland are open from 9:30am to 4:30pm and closed from 12:30pm to 1:30pm. In the larger cities (Belfast and Derry), they don't close for lunch. The banks in the Shannon, Dublin, and Belfast airports, however, are open every day to service incoming international flights.

Automatic Teller Machines (ATMs) are nowhere near as ubiquitous as in America, but they can usually be found on the outside wall of banks. **Cirrus** and **Plus** are the international networks most of these ATMs are part of. Most of the banks that provide ATMs charge a small transaction fee for withdrawals (about $1.50). Check with the bank that issued your ATM card to see if your current Personal Identification Number (PIN) will work overseas. Many of the ATMs overseas only accept four-digit PINs.

Business Hours
Businesses are generally open from 9am to 5pm, although in practice most stores open at 9:30am or 10am. In some of the larger cities, stores will stay open later one night of the week. In Dublin, that day is Thursday.

Climate & Weather
Ireland enjoys a temperate climate year-round, thanks to the warm waters of the Gulf Stream. Most tourists find the weather pleasant and more than acceptable for vacationing from April through October, although I have been there in the winter months and found it to be delightful as well, although a wee bit chilly. During April and May, the temperatures are generally in the mid-50s during the days. During the summer months, you can expect the temperatures to be in the 60s, with even an occasional day or two in the 70s. Fall temperatures generally emulate those of the springtime, with daytime temperatures ranging from the high 40s to mid-50s most of the time. For the most part, winters on the Emerald Isle are also mild, with average temperatures in the mid-30s to low 40s.

But beware! There is a reason Ireland is known as the Emerald Isle. There are more shades of green than you can count, and they remain that way due to the frequency of rain, all year. (The average annual rainfall in Ireland is 43 inches.) However, despite frequent rain showers, it seldom rains hard enough to dampen the enjoyment of the many sights there are to see. I've found that a sweater (purchased in Ireland, of course), a lightweight rain-coat, and (perhaps) an umbrella will make your touring pleasant.

Consulates & Embassies
- **American Embassy**, 42 Elgin Road, Dublin 4, Tel. (01) 668-8777. Open Monday through Friday from 8:30am to 5pm.
- **Canadian Embassy**, 65 St. Stephen's Green, Tel. (01) 478-1988. Open Monday through Wednesday from 8:30am to 12:30pm, and from 2pm to 4pm, and Thursday and Friday from 8:30am to 12:30pm.
- **American Consulate in Northern Ireland**, 14 Queen Street, Belfast, Tel. (028) 9032-8239. They are open Monday through Friday from 9am to 5pm.

244 OPEN ROAD'S BEST OF IRELAND

- **Canadian Embassy for Northern Ireland**, Lesley House, Shaftesbury Square, Belfast 2, Tel. (028) 9033-1532. They are open Monday through Wednesday from 8:30am to 12:30pm, and from 2pm to 4pm, and Thursday and Friday from 8:30am to 12:30pm.

Electricity

Electricity in Ireland is **220 volts** (50 cycles) and **an adapter is required**. Most discount stores like Target, K-Mart, and Wal-Mart, as well as Sears and J.C. Penny's carry inexpensive adapters that will do the job nicely. Remember, if you expect to use your hair dryer, curling iron, or electric razor, you'll need an adapter. Oh yes - and unless you're going to bring lots of very expensive (and heavy) batteries, you'll want that adapter to recharge the batteries for your camcorder (common oversight).

Emergencies & Safety

Before you leave for your holiday in Ireland, check with your health insurance company to see if you will be covered in the event of an emergency, illness, or injury during your travels in Ireland. If you are covered, find out the procedure they require you to follow before seeking treatment. As you may know, both Ireland and Northern Ireland have national health care systems, and unless you have insurance, you will only be treated in the event of an emergency. As of this writing, Medicare doesn't cover overseas medical expenses, but some of their supplemental plans do. Check before going.

Safety? If you use common sense in your travels you should be fine. Ireland is far from crime-free, although it is still one of the safest countries in which to travel.

I think the biggest concern I have in the area of safety is **driving**. Driving on the "wrong" side, narrow roads, fast speeds, and there are a lot of Americans on the roads! Don't try to keep up with the locals until you have logged a few miles on these narrow roads. And on the exceptionally narrow roads of Counties Cork, Connemara, and Donegal, give way to those who are driving faster than you, and enjoy the scenery.

Festivals & Holidays

Most offices and stores are closed on the following public holidays in Dublin:

- January 1 — New Year's Day
- March 17 — St. Patrick's Day (what did you expect!?)
- Monday following Easter Sunday – Easter Monday
- First Monday in May – May Holiday (most commonly called Bank Holiday)
- First Monday in June — June Holiday (most commonly called Bank Holiday)
- First Monday in August – August Holiday (most commonly called Bank Holiday)
- First Monday in October — October Holiday (most commonly called Bank Holiday)
- December 25 – Christmas Day
- December 26 – St. Stephen's Day

Internet Access

Internet cafés located in the larger cities in Ireland (Dublin, Cork, Killarney, Belfast, etc.) offer the opportunity to log on, as do many youth hostels and hotels.

Language

Irish is the official language of the Republic of Ireland, with English recognized as a second language under the Constitution. **Gaelic** and **Irish** are generally interchangeable terms, although today the language is almost always referred to as Irish. Gaelic is most often used to refer to the language of the ancient inhabitants of Ireland, the Celts.

By the way, *Celtic* is pronounced differently than the way we pronounce the name of the NBA team from Boston. The Celtic you see in Ireland is pronounced Keltic, with a hard K, and it was spoken by Kelts. (Not Seltic spoken by Selts!)

Passport Regulations

Ireland requires only a passport for entry into their country. No visa is necessary if you are a citizen of the United States, Canada, Australia, or New Zealand and if your stay is less than 90 days

(180 days in Northern Ireland). If you plan an extended stay that lasts longer than that, you must demonstrate that you have adequate funds to stay and already possess a return airline ticket.

The US government has provided a very informative website covering about any question you might have on US passports. It can be found at travel.state.gov/passport/passport_1738.html.

Postal Services
Letters sent from the Republic of Ireland to the US and Canada cost 75 eurocents and postcards cost 75 cents as well. If you have occasion to send them to Europe, letters and postcards also cost 75 cents. Stamps are available from the post office, or from most Newsagents. Postcards from the North to the US cost 40p (British Sterling, not euros!) and letters cost 45p.

Most post offices in the country are open Monday through Saturday from 9am to 6pm. In the larger cities some of the post offices may have extended hours. For example, the General Post Office (GPO) in Dublin is open Monday - Saturday from 8am to 8pm.

Telephones
Be warned: you will not find the same consistent, user-friendly interface you are accustomed to in North America. Without a doubt you will experience uncooperative phones, occasional poor reception, and just plain frustration. It may take you two or three times dialing exactly the same numbers to get a call through, or you may need to deposit your coins two or three times before they'll register. But, with a little patience, you will be able to get your calls placed.

Most of your calls within Ireland will be made from one of two types of public telephones: coin phones or phonecard phones.

Coin phones in the Republic have been updated and will accept only €.20 and €.50 coins; coin phones in the North only accept 20 and 50 pence and £1 coins. All calls are metered. A digital screen on the phone registers the amount of money you enter, and counts down to 0 as you talk.

Phonecard phones are very popular in Ireland. Post Offices and Newsagents sell phonecards of varying denominations: €2, €5, €10, €15 and €25. Like the coin phones, once the card is inserted, a digital readout on the phone displays remaining units. On local calls, one unit is roughly equal to three minutes; slightly less for long distance calls, depending on the distance involved.

Cell phones are ubiquitous in the United States. Some carriers have coverage plans that reach Ireland – on a recent trip to Ireland, we were able to call home using our cell phone with Cingular service from virtually the entire country. Check with your carrier before you leave for Ireland to see if you will be able to call from there.

If you're going to call Ireland from the United States to make hotel reservations, you must dial the country code (353 for Ireland; 44 for Northern Ireland), and the city code, then the telephone number. Sort of. In the case of Dublin telephone numbers, the city code is 01, but you drop the 0 when dialing from the United States. Therefore, if you were calling the Berkeley Court Hotel from the United States, you should dial 011-353-1-497-8275. Any time you see a lead zero in a city code, drop that 0 when calling from the United States. Alternately, when calling within Ireland, include the lead 0, but do not dial the country code.

In both the North and the Republic, **911 = 999**. If you have an emergency requiring police, an ambulance, or a fireman, dial 999.

Time
Ireland is on Greenwich Mean Time, and that means they are five hours ahead of New York and Montreal, and eight hours ahead of Los Angeles and Vancouver.

Tipping
Tipping is acceptable and expected in Ireland. But be warned that if you give your customary 15% to 20% tip for outstanding service, you may in reality be giving over 35%. Many hotels and restaurants automatically tack on a service charge of 10% to 15% to your room or meal.

It's customary to tip cab drivers around 10% (they don't auto-matically add it to the fare), more if the driver acts as a tour guide, filling you in on interesting tidbits of trivia about the sites you're passing. Porters should be tipped €1 per bag.

Tourist Information
Watch for the green TI signs located outside Tourist Information centers throughout Ireland. There are always maps and brochures and most important, helpful people to assist you with your questions. Most Tourist Information centers have B&B / hotel booking services to assist you in that area if you wish.

Water
There is no problem drinking the water in Ireland. But if you have become accustomed to drinking bottled water, that is available at News Agents and grocery stores.

Websites
These are the best websites for planning your trip:

AA Roadwatch: www.aaroadwatch.ie. Summary reports, traffic alerts, upcoming events and trip-planning assistance all make this a great website to bookmark.

Bus Eireann: www.buseireann.ie. Planning on using the bus and/or train to get around Ireland? This is the website for the organization that runs the buses and trains in Ireland. Up-to-date schedule and fare information available here.

Dublin Tourist Office: www.visitdublin.com. A good overview of what to see and do in Dublin, along with listings of hotels, pubs, etc. Includes links to golf courses, hotels, sights, car rental agencies, etc.

Entertainment Ireland: www.entertainment.ie. Everything you always wanted to know about entertainment in Ireland: TV schedules, which bands are playing at what pubs, where to see your favorite Irish comedian, movie theater features, etc.

Ireland Hotels.com: www.irelandhotels.com. Search for hotels by county or by town, with links to various other Irish hotel websites.

Irish Genealogy: www.irishroots.net. A great place to start or continue searching for your Irish ancestors. Message boards, county-by-county information, research assistance.

Irish Tourist Board: www.ireland.ie. A good summary of what to see and do in Ireland. Includes upcoming events across the country, accommodation search, featured locations and links to golf courses, car rental agencies, ferries, etc.

US Passport Agency: travel.state.gov/passport/passport_1738.html. Great place to learn US passport requirements is this US State Department website.

Yahoo Weather: weather.yahoo.com. Should you bring a sweater or sunscreen? An umbrella or sunglasses? There are many websites that can tell you what the weather will be in Ireland. I like this one because I can get an extended 10-day forecast. Handy information to know.

INDEX

Things Change!

Phone numbers, prices, addresses, quality of service – all change. If you come across any new information, let us know. No item is too small! Contact us at :

jopenroad@aol.com
or
www.openroadguides.com